Russia's New Ground Forces

Capabilities, Limitations and Implications for International Security

Igor Sutyagin with Justin Bronk

www.rusi.org

Royal United Services Institute for Defence and Security Studies

Russia's New Ground Forces: Capabilities, Limitations and Implications for International Security
Igor Sutyagin with Justin Bronk

First published 2017

Whitehall Papers series

Series Editor: Professor Malcolm Chalmers
Editor: Dr Emma De Angelis

RUSI is a Registered Charity (No. 210639)
ISBN 978-1-138-56370-4

Published on behalf of the Royal United Services Institute for Defence
and Security Studies
by
Routledge Journals, an imprint of Taylor & Francis, 4 Park Square,
Milton Park, Abingdon OX14 4RN

Cover Image: Russian T-72 tank. *Courtesy of Alamy/Alexsey Suvorov*

SUBSCRIPTIONS
Please send subscription orders to:

USA/Canada: Taylor & Francis Inc., Journals Department, 530 Walnut Street, Suite 850, Philadelphia, PA 19106, USA

UK/Rest of World: Routledge Journals, T&F Customer Services, T&F Informa UK Ltd, Sheepen Place, Colchester, Essex CO3 3LP, UK

MIX
Paper from
responsible sources
FSC
www.fsc.org   FSC™ C013985

Printed in the United Kingdom
by Henry Ling Limited

Contents

About the Authors

Igor Sutyagin is Senior Research Fellow for Russian studies at RUSI. His research is concerned with US–Russian relations, strategic armaments developments and broader nuclear arms control, and anti-ballistic missile defence systems.

Igor has a PhD in the History of Foreign Policy and International Relations (1995) from the Institute for US and Canadian Studies in Moscow and a Master's in Radiophysics and Electronics from Moscow State University (1988).

He has written extensively on nuclear and conventional arms control, including naval arms control, the safety and security of nuclear weapons, the modernisation and development of modern armaments as well as issues associated with anti-ballistic missile systems and their stabilising influence on US–Russian relations. He has authored more than 100 articles and booklets published in the Soviet Union/Russia, the US, UK, Germany and Switzerland. He is also the co-author of the book *Russian Strategic Nuclear Forces* (MIT Press, 2001).

Igor worked at the Institute for US and Canadian Studies for twelve years in the Political-Military Studies Department, where he held the position of the head of section for US military-technical and military-economy policy.

Justin Bronk is Research Fellow for airpower and military technology at RUSI. Alongside a primary focus on airpower, his research also includes weapons system and munitions analysis in conflict zones, in particular Ukraine and Syria. Justin is also Editor of *RUSI Defence Systems*.

Justin has written on military issues for the *RUSI Journal*, *RUSI Defence Systems*, *RUSI Newsbrief*, the *Journal of Strategic Studies* and the *RAF Airpower Journal*, as well as contributing regularly to the international media.

He holds an MSc in the History of International Relations from the London School of Economics and Political Science, and a BA (Hons) in History from York University.

Acknowledgements

Igor Sutyagin would like to thank the Canadian government for its financial support for a research project on the Russian armed forces in 2015, on which this Whitehall Paper is based. Furthermore, this paper would never have appeared without the great assistance provided by Justin Bronk, Emma De Angelis and Charlie de Rivaz – to whom he is greatly thankful.

Justin Bronk would like to thank Igor for the great privilege of being able to work with him on this project, and the RUSI publications team and Pete Quentin for all their hard work and support.

List of Tables and Figures

List of Acronyms and Abbreviations

ACV	Airborne combat vehicle
APC	Armoured personnel carriers
AShM	Anti-ship missile
ATGM	Anti-tank guided missile
BCT	US brigade combat team
BKhiRVT	Storage and maintenance bases for vehicle fleets and equipment
BREMs	Armoured repair and recovery vehicles
BTGr	Battalion tactical groups
CBRN	Chemical, biological, radiological and nuclear
DNR	Donetsk People's Republic
DTO	Rear-area guard battalion/division
ELINT	Electronic intelligence
EW	Electronic warfare
FLOT	Forward line of troops
GRU	Main Intelligence Directorate; Russia's primary military foreign-intelligence service
IFV	Infantry fighting vehicle
ISR	Intelligence, surveillance and reconnaissance
KOOR	Kaliningrad Special Defence Region
KSSO	Special operations forces command
LNR	Luhansk People's Republic
LRS	Long-range surveillance
MBT	Main battletank
MD	Military district
MPC	Military provider company
MGMs	Precision-guided missiles
MRSI	Multiple rounds, simultaneous impact
OA	Russian combined arms army
OR	Other ranks
OSC	Operational strategic command
PLK	Transhipment and logistics centre
PMC	Private military company
RMG	Rocket multipurpose grenade
SMP	Northeast Passage, Arctic
SV	Russian Ground Troops
TA	Russian tank army
TUGP	Armata heavy universal tracked platform
VDV	Russia's Airborne Troops

Reader's Companion

This companion is intended to assist readers who have knowledge of Western military structures and terminology by highlighting some important structural and linguistical differences between the systems used by NATO and Russia.

The Russian army, officially called the Russian Ground Troops, has a manpower target of 300,000 men.[1] However, at the end of 2016, the authors' best estimate of its actual strength was around 243,500, including 26,000 officers, 109,000 professional other ranks and 108,500 conscripts (see Appendix I for a breakdown of how these numbers were calculated). In the interests of keeping the length of this paper manageable, the Russian Air-Space Forces and Navy are not discussed with the exception of the Navy's marines, which are included because they comprise an important element of Russia's ability to fight on land. The airborne troops and special operations forces which sit outside the main Ground Troops' command structure and report directly to Russia's central military command are also discussed. 'Land forces' is used throughout this paper as a term encompassing these airborne, marines and special operations forces as well as those of the regular Russian Ground Troops.

There are substantial differences in the organisational structures of the Russian land forces compared with their Western counterparts despite surface commonality in terms. The most important to raise in the context of this paper is how divisions, brigades, regiments and battalions fit into the overall Russian force structure. '*Soedinenie*' (formations) – either army corps, divisions or brigades – have their own responsibilities and generate units capable of acting independently on the battlefield. '*Chast*' (units) – either regiments or (independent) battalions – are self-contained entities with organic support enablers assigned from their parent division or brigade, respectively and are able to exercise mission command over their sub-units at the operational level. '*Podrazdelenie*' (sub-units/elements) – (non-independent) battalions, companies, platoons – are completely dependent upon their parent units for direction on the battlefield.

---

[1] *TASS*, 'Den' Sukhoputnykh voysk Rossii. Dosje [Russia's Ground Troops' Day. Dossier]', 1 September 2015, <http://tass.ru/info/2303642>, accessed 9 December 2016.

In terms of formation types, divisions are made up of regiments which themselves contain non-independent battalions. These non-independent battalions within regiments are considered to be sub-units and do not have their own legal status as entities or command responsibilities. By contrast, Russian brigades are formations composed of unit-level (independent) battalions which are larger than those (sub-unit) battalions found within divisions and are capable of independent operations with organic support enablers. Russian brigades contain their own 'divisional' support enablers and are, therefore, larger and more independent than their Western equivalents which exist within overarching divisional structures. Russian brigades, even if combined to form part of a larger formation, do not form divisions, but instead become part of army corps or armies.

This distinction is important given that since 2008, Russia's land forces reforms have attempted to move away from chronically undermanned and cumbersome divisional scale formations to a force structure based around fully manned brigades, which generate independently deployable, high-readiness battalion units. However, as will be discussed, political concessions to the army top brass and a desire for strategic messaging towards the West since 2014 have led to the founding of some new divisions in addition to the brigades around which the rest of the Ground Troops are now organised. In contrast to the regular Ground Troops, the airborne forces have retained their divisional structure throughout.

Divisions and brigades are subordinated in terms of overall command structure to armies or army corps within Russia's five military districts. These armies are classified in Russian terminology according to the composition of divisions/brigades that they command as Tank Armies or Combined Arms Armies.

In terms of the overarching timeline of Russian land forces reforms that will be discussed in this paper, while there are many nuances that will be explored, three key milestones should be taken as a guideline. First, the main internal trigger for urgent land forces reforms was the poor Russian performance in Georgia in 2008. Second, the Western-enabled removal of Colonel Muammar Qadhafi in 2011 in the aftermath of the Arab uprising solidified the Kremlin's perception of a coordinated regime-change strategy by the West, which constituted a serious threat to Russia. Finally, the Ukrainian revolution and subsequent annexation of Crimea in 2014 was seen in Russia as the 'start of the show' for active political-military confrontation with the West.

Figure 1: Military District/Operational Strategic Command

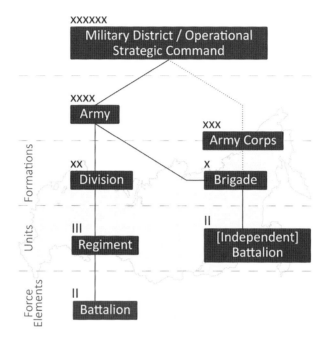

INTRODUCTION

Russia is widely seen by NATO as one of its primary military threats following President Vladimir Putin's annexation of Crimea and the destabilisation and invasion of Eastern Ukraine. This paper provides an in-depth analysis of the Russian army's current conventional capabilities and deployments in those geographic areas of interest to Western Europe. While Russian cyber and information warfare capabilities play an important role in and are interlinked with conventional forces within Russia's operational doctrine, in the interests of brevity and clarity they are not addressed in this paper. Discussion of these important Russian capabilities can be found in other authors' very useful publications.[1]

This paper also looks at the Russian army's post-2008 reform process. Russia's operations in Crimea and Eastern Ukraine will be examined through case studies as these involved the first large-scale use of land forces since the start of the current round of military reform. These operations shed light on the strengths and weaknesses of Russia's military, and analysis could help to inform Western understanding of the nature and scope of changes within the Russian armed forces. As land forces are playing the subordinate role in Russia's operations in Syria, officially designated 'the Air-Space Force's operation' by Moscow, analysis of the Syrian operation is not discussed at length.

This paper is also intended to contribute to an understanding of the dangers posed by the evolving Russian military posture, and how they are perceived by the established and newer NATO member states. A better understanding of the Russian armed forces – and how different NATO members perceive the threat – will contribute to more cohesive security policy decision-making.

The current Russian political leadership objectively acts from a position of military and economic inferiority relative to NATO. This complicates the achievement of Russia's aspiration to be an indispensable

---

[1] See, for example, Keir Giles, *Handbook of Russian Information Warfare*, Fellowship Monograph No. 9 (Italy: NATO Defence College, November 2016).

major international player that must be consulted on all important international issues.[2] The Russian leadership uses the military as one of a number of tools to shape its 'near abroad' (a term universally applied to describe the former Soviet Union republics) and global positions. It does so in a way that will not provoke full-scale, prolonged and conventional conflict with NATO, since this would almost inevitably end in heavy defeat for Russia, given the Alliance's significant numerical and economic advantage.

However, as this paper will argue, Russia's pursuit of the ability to concentrate forces for short, sharp operations and achieve operational goals before large-scale opposing forces can respond has involved revitalising the army's capability to conduct specifically offensive operations. Offensive capabilities, if credible enough, could make a substantial contribution to Russia's claim to what it sees as its place on the international stage and to deter Western military reaction.

Since Russia has been more assertive,[3] Putin has been able to challenge the US leadership of what he describes as a US-led unipolar world. He underlined this view in a February 2007 speech at the Munich Security Conference, in which he claimed a much larger share of influence in world politics for Russia.[4] Until the price of oil crashed in 2014, Russia could count on a certain level of influence based on the comparative strength of its economy. However, Russia was among the countries hit hardest when oil prices plummeted, leading to an even greater reliance on military means to achieve what Putin sees as Russia's rightful place in the world.

One early military intervention demonstrated to Moscow the potential use of armed force in securing international geopolitical advantage. In August 2008, furious at Georgia's intention to join NATO, Russia launched a 'five-day war' to prevent the move. Despite the seemingly poor performance of the Russian military, the West 'swallowed' Russia's

---

[2]   According to Russia's 2015 National Security Strategy, its ability to stand out as 'one of the world's leading powers' in the international arena is a key strategic priority. 'Strategiya natsionalnoy bezopasnosti Rossiyskoy Fedcratsii [National Security Strategy of the Russian Federation]', approved by the Presidential Decree of the Russian Federation No. 683 of 31 December 2015, Articles 6 and 30, <http://www.kremlin.ru/acts/news/51129>, accessed 17 October 2016.

[3]   *Nezavisimaya Gazeta*, [*Independent Gazette*]. 'Myunkhenskaya rech [Munich Speech]', 28 December 2007, <http://www.ng.ru/politics/2007-12-28/1_munhen.html>, accessed 17 October 2016.

[4]   Vladimir Putin, 'Vystuplenie i discussiya na Myunkhenskoy konferentsii po voprosam politiki bezopasnosti [Presentation and Discussion at the Munich Conference on Security Policy]', 10 February 2007, <http://kremlin.ru/events/president/transcripts/24034>, accessed 17 October 2016.

strategy without a significant punitive reaction, suggesting to the Kremlin that such an aggressive strategy could be feasible in the future.

As a result of this poor performance, Putin ordered a comprehensive reform programme for the military, announced by Minister of Defence Anatoly Serdyukov on 14 October 2008,[5] and to be concluded by 2020. The war in Georgia also forced Russian military officials to admit that the armed forces had nearly exhausted the reserves of modern armaments and military equipment inherited from the Soviet Union.[6] It was therefore crucial to speed up rearmament with qualitatively new weapons (as opposed to sporadic upgrades to existing assets), originally planned to start in 2011–12.[7]

In 2008, the outline of the reform seemed clear. The Russian armed forces needed to be streamlined to avoid duplication of functions. This would release manpower that had been otherwise locked in duplicating and performing secondary tasks to fill ranks in combat units, making them permanently combat ready, with troops rearmed with modern weapons. The structure of forces – from the strategic and operational to the tactical level – needed adjusting to take into account existing and foreseeable challenges rather than hypothetical ones. Force planning, generation and fielding needed to be executed in a manner that would guarantee Russia the most effective use of limited resources. This would put more emphasis on sophisticated operational planning, the mobility and agility of troops and their rear support, as well as a combination of the most advanced military tactics and technologies to achieve force multiplication.

The progress of reform was not smooth, however. Changes were authorised without thorough preliminary analysis of their influence on Russia's military posture. Furthermore, potential opposition to changes from within the military and defence industry was not properly considered and 'neutralised'. This led to ad hoc reforms rather than the development and introduction of a well-thought-out plan. This meant there were inevitable, sometimes radical, readjustments throughout the reform process. For instance, the optimal structure for ground troop

---

[5] Yuri Gavrilov, 'Generalskoe sokraschenie [Generals Reduction]', *Rossiyskaya Gazeta* [*Russian Gazette*], 15 October 2008, <https://rg.ru/2008/10/15/vooruzh-sily.html>, accessed 15 October 2016.

[6] *Newsru*, 'Voyna pokazala: rossiyskaya armiya vetshaet, zapas sovetskogo vooruzheniya vyrabotan polnostjyu [War Has Shown: The Russian Armed Forces are Decaying and the Stock of Soviet Weapons is Fully Exhausted]', 2 October 2008, <http://www.newsru.com/russia/02oct2008/old_weapon.html>, accessed 16 October 2016.

[7] *Ibid.*

formations has been changed dramatically three times,[8] resulting in the 'new' (authorised after studies in 2009), 'newest' (early 2011), 'corrected newest' (late 2011) and 'super-new shape of Ground Troops' (2013). This has been the source of endless bitter jokes in the Russian military. The Russian air force suffered similar changes. Serdyukov and the Chief of the General Staff,[9] Army General Nikolay Makarov, the main drivers of the first stage of reform, fell victim to the process: Serdyukov was reluctantly dismissed by Putin on 6 November 2012;[10] Makarov was fired by Sergey Shoigu, the new defence minister, three days later.[11]

Alongside Russia's growing assertiveness and increasing use of military tools for foreign policy purposes, the Kremlin is concerned about the possibility of Russia being unintentionally dragged into an unplanned military conflict with Western-sponsored forces or even with the West itself.[12] It would be a mistake to underestimate the influence of the Marxist-Leninist indoctrination that the current crop of Russian leaders experienced under the Soviet Union. According to this worldview, imperialist (that is, Western) countries invariably choose war as the universal way to resolve their economic troubles. Since the West is still struggling to recover from the 2007–08 economic crisis,[13] a Marxist would inevitably see war as the West's natural choice to deal with such circumstances. From this perspective, the Kremlinites see the Arab

---

[8] Alex Ramm, 'Sverkhnoviy oblik Sukhoputnykh voysk [Ground Troops' Super-New Shape]', *Novosti VPK* [*Military-Industrial Complex News*], 11 September 2013, <http://vpk-news.ru/articles/17376>, accessed 20 October 2016.

[9] The General Staff of the Russian armed forces is the direct equivalent of the British Defence Staff; the Russian Main Command of Ground Troops is the equivalent of the British Army's General Staff.

[10] Surprisingly, both pro-Kremlin and strongly anti-Kremlin commentators agree that Putin was forced to sack Serdyukov. See, for instance, Mikhail Delyagin in Aleksander Sargin, 'Putin kategoricheski ne khotel uvolnyat Serdyukova [Putin Categorically Did Not Want to Dismiss Serdyukov]', *Gorod Novostey* [*City of News*], 9 November 2012, <http://www.city-n.ru/view/314984.html>, accessed 16 October 2016; Andrey Piontkovskiy, 'Putin ne khotel snimat Serdyukova, ego zastavili [Putin Did Not Want to Dismiss Serdyukov, He was Forced to]', *Stringer*, 19 November 2012, <http://stringer-news.com/publication.mhtml?Part=50&PubID=23396>, accessed 16 October 2016.

[11] *Gorod Novostey* [*City of News*], 'Nachalnik Genshtaba podal v otstavku [Chief of the General Staff Resigns]', 9 November 2012, <http://www.city-n.ru/view/314972.html>, accessed 16 October 2016.

[12] The term 'the West' is used here and at various points throughout this paper to refer to the Kremlin-perceived and ill-defined hostile block comprising NATO plus partners. The authors recognise that 'the West' is a highly oversimplified term from a Western perspective but is used here to reflect Russian thinking.

[13] Larry Elliott, 'Global Financial Crisis: Five Key Stages 2007-2011', *The Guardian*, 7 August 2011.

uprising that began in December 2010, followed by the Libyan uprising in late February 2011 and the events in Syria since mid-March 2011, as Western-inspired.

As instability erupted in the regions where Moscow had security cooperation agreements, the Russian leadership, from its Marxist theory-shaped, Russo-centric viewpoint, evidently feared the spread of Western-inspired instability and revolt. This would run contrary to its own strategic plans, and that alone meant Moscow could not sit by and watch Western policy unfold.

These fundamental suspicions towards the West are deeply ingrained in the psyche of the Russian political class, and the brief period of *entente cordiale* between Russia and the West following the fall of the Soviet Union did not fundamentally change this perspective. Even the 'pro-Western' former president Boris Yeltsin used the threat of nuclear weapons to warn the US against meddling in Kremlin policy in 1999.[14]

The origins of this political culture were described in the '1946 Long Telegram' sent to the State Department by then-US chargé d'affaires in Moscow George Kennan. It rings true to this day. Kennan wrote:

> At bottom of Kremlin's neurotic view of world affairs is traditional and instinctive Russian sense of insecurity. Originally, this was insecurity of a peaceful agricultural people trying to live on vast exposed plain in neighborhood of fierce nomadic peoples. To this was added, as Russia came into contact with economically advanced west, fear of more competent more powerful, more highly organized societies in that area. But this latter type of insecurity was one which afflicted rather Russian rulers than Russian people; for Russian rulers have invariably sensed that their rule was relatively archaic in form, fragile and artificial in its psychological foundation, unable to stand comparison or contact with political systems of western countries. For this reason they have always feared foreign penetration, feared direct contact between western world and their own, feared what would happen if Russians learned truth about world without or if foreigners learned truth about the world within. And they have learned to seek security only in patient but deadly struggle for total destruction of rival power, never in compacts and compromises with it.[15]

---

[14]   Dmitriy Gornostaev, 'Eltsin Napomnil Klintonu i miru: Rossiya ostaetsya yadernoy derzhavoy [Yeltsin Has Reminded Clinton and the World: Russia Remains a Nuclear Power]', *Nezavisimaya Gazeta* [*Independent Gazette*], 10 December 1999, <http://www.ng.ru/world/1999-12-10/1_pekin.html>, accessed 16 October 2016.

[15]   George Kennan to George Marshall, 'Long Telegram', Harry S Truman Administration File, Elsey Papers, 22 February 1946, pp. 5–6, <https://www.trumanlibrary.org/whistlestop/study_collections/coldwar/documents/pdf/6-6.pdf>, accessed 16 October 2016.

It is hardly necessary to explain that these fears – and the strategic worldview associated with them – are near universal for the current Russian rulers. They seek a de facto restoration of the 'relatively archaic' and 'artificial' Soviet model of domestic and foreign policy. They also believe they are witnessing Western encirclement and penetration into Russia's traditional spheres of influence – the Middle East and Ukraine.

Alarm bells have been ringing loudly in the Kremlin since the unfolding of the 2011 Arab uprising and especially since the West's intervention in Colonel Muammar Qadhafi's military crackdown against opponents in Libya. For Moscow, Qadhafi's bombing of Benghazi in 2011 was not much different from Yeltsin and Putin's crackdown on and siege of Grozny, the Chechen capital, in 1995 and 2000 respectively. However, it was the association agreement under discussion between the EU and Ukraine in 2013 that was the real turning point.

Moscow has always seen Ukraine as indisputably and legitimately being in its own backyard and has at times even rejected the idea of Ukraine as an independent state, with Putin claiming it as part of Russian territory.[16] As far as Moscow was concerned, it was not up to the Ukrainian people to determine their own future, and Kiev's drift away from Moscow towards a closer association with the West (specifically, in this instance, the EU) has been perceived as a poorly disguised attack on Russia's vital interests.[17]

---

[16] Vladimir Putin made the comment in 2015, revealing the Kremlin's mood regarding Ukraine's independence, de facto stating that the former republics of the Soviet Union that had gained independence after its dissolution were 'Russia's own territory': 'after the collapse of the Soviet Union and after Russia voluntarily – I emphasise – voluntarily and deliberately self-imposed absolutely historic self-restrictions, related to *abandonment of its own territory*' (emphasis added). See 'President', *Rossiya 1* TV documentary, 26 April 2015, <https://russia.tv/video/show/brand_id/59329/episode_id/1193264/video_id/1165983/>, accessed 17 October 2016. See also Kseniya Kirilova, 'Putin fakticheski nazval Ukrainu territoriey Rossii [Putin Actually Called Ukraine Russian Territory]', *Noviy Region* [*New Region*], 28 April 2015, <http://nr2.ru/blogs/Ksenija_Kirillova/Putin-fakticheski-nazval-Ukrainu-territoriey-Rossii-95566.html>, accessed 10 January 2016.

[17] See Vladimir Putin at the press conference after the EU–Russia Summit, Brussels, 28 January 2014, <https://www.youtube.com/watch?v=xGE6KS56pw4>, accessed 15 October 2016; The Kremlin, 'Obraschenie Prezidenta Rossiyskoy Federatsii k Federalnomu Sobraniyu Rossiyskoy Federatsii [Address of the President of the Russian Federation]', Vladimir Putin's address to the Federal Assembly of the Russian Federation, 18 March 2014, <http://www.kremlin.ru/news/20603>, accessed 15 October 2016. The same position was repeatedly expressed by Putin's spokesman, Dmitriy Peskov, see Alexander Gamow, 'Dmitriy Peskov: Rossiya nikogda ne budet vmeshivat'sya vo vnutrennie dela Ukrainy [Dmitriy Peskov: "Russia Will Never Interfere in Ukraine's Internal Affairs"]', *Komsomolskaya Pravda* [*Komsomol Truth*], 22 January 2014, <http://www.kp.ru/daily/26184/3073444/>,

A credible military posture and suite of capabilities is vitally important for the Kremlin under such circumstances to secure Russia's interests, as well as its ability to carry out policy and to maintain its sovereignty. Despite the flaws, the 2008 military reforms have led to significant improvements in the capabilities and equipment quality of the Russian armed forces. However, manpower shortages, morale problems and a lack of standardised equipment continue to limit overall effectiveness.

In order to cover these issues fully, this Whitehall Paper is divided into three sections. The first examines the use of armed force by the Russian government, with the emphasis on forces tasked with land-based operations, thereafter referred to as land forces, to differentiate them from the Russian Ground Troops (*Sukhoputnye Voyska*, or SV). These include ground and airborne troops, as well as the marines of the Russian Navy and the special operations forces.[18] The Russian Air-Space Force (*Voenno-Kosmicheskie Sily*)[19] and Navy (*Voenno-Morskoy Flot*) are not discussed as these require papers in their own right. Interior forces are discussed in the isolated regions of Kaliningrad and Crimea only where they represent a substantial contribution to the overall potential of deployed Russian forces. This section analyses the leadership's employment of the army as a tool to advance Russia's foreign policy interests. It discusses the implications of the various trends in the reforms to date and those still under way. Finally, it addresses the current capability in the Russian land forces.

---

accessed 15 October 2016. The upper chamber of the Russian parliament, the Federation Council, expressed the same position – see Sovet Federatsii Federalnogo Sobraniya [The Federation Council of the Federal Assembly], 'Zayavlenie Soveta Federatsii Federalnogo Sobraniya Rossiyskoy Federatsii o situatsii na Ukraine [Statement of the Federation Council of the Federal Assembly on the Situation in Ukraine]', 29 January 2014, <http://www.council.gov.ru/press-center/news/38854/>, accessed 15 October 2016.

[18] The direct equivalent in Russia of the British (or US) Army are the Ground Troops (*Sukhoputnye Voyska*). The Airborne Troops (including airborne, air-assault and mountain air-assault formations) are a separate branch of the armed forces directly subordinated, along with the Strategic Rocket Forces, to the General Staff. Special operations forces include two branches – Spetsnaz brigades and naval reconnaissance units, and Special Operations Command – subordinated to the General Staff of the Russian armed forces and the minister of defence, respectively.

[19] The English-language version of the Russian Ministry of Defence's official website uses term 'Aerospace Forces'. However, the authors consider this term slightly misleading here since the Russian 'Aerospace Forces' or VKS (*Vozdushno-Kosmicheskie Sily* – 'Air-Space Force') consist of the 'Air Force', 'Space Forces' and 'Aerospace Defence Forces' – while the latter is called 'Air Defence – [Ballistic] Missile Defence Troops' (*Voyska PVO-PRO*) in the Russian version of the MoD's website. Therefore, for the purposes of this study, the literal translation of VKS – 'Air-Space Force' – is used.

The second section examines the equipment, tactical deployment concepts and envisaged roles of Russia's land forces. These include: combined arms manoeuvre forces; airborne and air-assault formations; reconnaissance units; missile and artillery units; CBRN (chemical, biological, radiological and nuclear) forces; engineer units; and electronic warfare elements. It argues that the ongoing, ambitious equipment modernisation efforts will significantly increase the combat power and operational flexibility of each of these components if they can be completed as planned.

The third section provides a detailed analysis of the geographical distribution of Russian land forces in the Western, Southern and Central military districts, including Crimea, Kaliningrad and the Russian-controlled rebel territories of Donetsk and Luhansk in Eastern Ukraine, and in the Arctic. The analysis concludes with an examination of what Russia perceives as threats and its possible plans, with troop deployment revealing what the national military command envisages as their tasks. This paper describes only the areas with direct implications for European security, including the Arctic. (This paper will not cover the Russian military posture against threats originating from the Asian and Asia-Pacific regions.)

This Whitehall Paper argues that Russian land forces are being geared towards fighting in aggressive, short, sharp and complex offensive operations in enemy territory, as well as being streamlined to increase readiness levels and deployability at short notice. However, operations against Ukraine have shown that Russia's ability to sustain even a moderate tempo of operations in the medium term is limited and has required force generation efforts from almost every Russian military formation, including those in the Far East. Furthermore, the Russian Ground Troops continue to be plagued by chronic undermanning and morale issues, which will be exacerbated by the political – rather than operationally driven – decision to re-establish division-scale units, in spite of a successful doctrinal shift to battalion tactical groups since 2007. Western sanctions and Russia's increasingly desperate economic situation are severely hampering efforts to extend equipment reforms across the whole force, in spite of the highest political priority attached to them.

The paper also argues that the land forces deployment patterns reveal Moscow's perceived insecurity, as they are focused first on Kaliningrad, occupied Crimea and the Arctic. At the same time, Russian armed forces deployments reflect Moscow's sophisticated planning culture, with moves skilfully tailored to stay below thresholds that would initiate unwanted reactions from Russia's peer opponents, while letting Russia achieve its multifaceted political goals with minimal friction. The deployment of forces in a manner designed to maintain pressure on Ukraine in the most cost-effective way while at the same time influencing NATO decision-making at no additional cost is one example of such sophistication. Countering NATO's enhanced forward presence in Eastern Europe with Russian forces' actions in the Arctic is another illustrative example of the Russian *modus vivendi*.

This paper's sources are mainly printed and online Russian- and Ukrainian-language publications, specialist internet forums and blogs. This includes social media in Russia and the former Soviet Republics, including the Baltic States. On several occasions, data was obtained from private conversations with members (active and retired) of the Soviet, Russian, Ukrainian and Belorussian armed forces. The lead author's many years of experience working with the Soviet and Russian Ministry of Defence was also useful in analysing the information gathered. Only material in the public domain has been used.

The authors have endeavoured to present the most up-to-date and complete references possible in this work, including translation of Russian publication titles into English and transliteration of Russian phrases where judged helpful. However, some sources – especially print media from the 1990s and early 2000s – do not exist in accessible online form and were drawn from hard copies in the authors' possession. Furthermore, certain sources drawn upon during the research process that led to this publication have subsequently been removed from the internet and so are cited without functional hyperlinks. In such cases, readers wishing to discuss the primary source material in question should contact the authors, especially Igor Sutyagin in the case of Russian-language sources.

I. MILITARY FORCE AS A TOOL OF RUSSIAN FOREIGN POLICY

The Russian leadership understands that military tools alone cannot bring Moscow decisive success in its pursuit of international influence. And although this is true of every state, it is especially true of Russia. The dramatic mismatch between Russia's aggressive foreign policy ambitions and the resources needed to achieve them is the single most compelling contradiction in the Kremlin's policy. Russia's economy is increasingly uncompetitive in the modern international market and its soft power almost non-existent for a mainstream actor in a global arena. Fully aware of the limitations of their military tools, Russian politicians use a wide variety of other means, from diplomacy to psychology, in pursuit of their goals.[1] However, armed force remains the most valued tool for Russia's political-military elite. As such, the capabilities and posture of the military tends to define certain limits of the country's foreign policy. The Kremlin understands well that an international perception of Russia's capabilities *and* intent is a prerequisite for success in its aggressive foreign policies.

Since 2008, Russian land forces have been undergoing an active modernisation programme. This fact alone is significant, given the large size of Russia's army in comparison to those of most of its neighbours, with the exception of China.[2] But the most significant change is not to the army's size but to its posture and composition. From a force primarily

---

[1] Igor Sutyagin, 'Driving Forces in Russia's Strategic Thinking', in Janne Haaland Matlary and Tormod Heier (eds), *Ukraine and Beyond: Russia's Strategic Security Challenge to Europe* (London: Palgrave Macmillan, 2016).

[2] See Appendix I for the authors' estimate of the size of Russian Ground Troops in 2016. A direct comparison of forces has not been included here given the subjective nature of determining which of NATO's members count as Russia's 'neighbours', considering the structure of the Alliance and rotational deployments. Furthermore, paramilitary forces in, for example, France and Italy, as well as Russia, are mostly irrelevant to such a comparison, Russian paramilitary forces in its exclaves would need to be accounted for, rendering any simplistic numerical comparison misleading.

structured for territorial defence operations on Russian soil in a large-scale military conflict against peer opponents (while retaining the capability to carry out operations in low-intensity conflicts), the Russian army is being moulded into a force optimised mainly, but not exclusively, for offensive operations in Russia's 'near abroad', with capabilities tailored for high-end warfare against peer opponents armed to modern Western standards. Russia's current warfighting model visibly abandons the Soviet model of an extremely large army of moderate quality in favour of a compact (by Russian standards), high-tech version, optimised for comparatively small-scale, short, intense conflicts. The strategy is to achieve operational goals in a short period of time, then to de-escalate and secure the gains made, via the threat of nuclear weapons use if necessary.

This task is made easier because, despite the painful military reforms undertaken after the dissolution of the Soviet Union, the General Staff has preserved a core of expertise related to planning large-scale offensive, conventional – that is, general non-nuclear – military operations. Russia's military involvement in Ukraine (and more recently in Syria) demonstrated the General Staff's ability to prepare and conduct complex military operations abroad involving the use of integrated conventional and sub-conventional capabilities and tactics. The emphasis on Russia's medium- to high-intensity warfighting command capabilities contrasts with the counterinsurgency, peacekeeping and humanitarian operations that have dominated Western military operations over the past fifteen years. Large-scale conventional operations against comparable powers, including major NATO Allies (for which Russia is currently restoring its capability), are a planning contingency to which Western militaries are only recently starting to readjust, while they have remained the focus for the Russian military since the dissolution of the Soviet Union.

Against this backdrop, mutual trust between the West and Russia has greatly eroded since Russia's annexation of Crimea in March 2014,[3] and the confidence-building measures designed to maintain a stable and predictable security environment from the Atlantic to the Urals have largely been rendered void due to Russia's actions and policies. Russia has withdrawn from the 1990 Treaty on Conventional Armed Forces in Europe and emasculated the NATO–Russia Founding Act of 1997.[4] One important

---

[3] Andrey Vasilyev, 'Churkin nazval otnosheniya mezhdu Rossiey i SShA khudshimi s 1973 goda [Churkin Says Russian–US Relations at their Lowest since 1973]', *Rossiyskaya Gazeta* [*Russian Gazette*], 16 October 2016, <https://rg.ru/2016/10/16/churkin-nazval-otnosheniia-rossii-i-ssha-hudshimi-s-1973-goda.html>, accessed 16 October 2016.

[4] Igor Sutyagin, 'How Putin Killed NATO's Agreement with Russia', *Newsweek*, 3 June 2016.

result is a steady decline in the information about Russia's military activities available to Western military planners, which affects their ability to reassure their political leaders about Russia's intentions. At the same time, Russia's political-military leadership regularly conducts exercises that demonstrate its ability to conduct large-scale offensive operations,[5] including numerous snap exercises near the borders of NATO member states in recent years,[6] and surge deployments of air-defence, army, logistical support, special forces and artillery assets to Syria. In Syria specifically, the US-led anti-Daesh (also known as the Islamic State of Iraq and Syria, or ISIS) coalition has been repeatedly presented with new Russian capabilities in theatre as a fait accompli, many of which are then swiftly employed on combat operations, or in the case of air defences, used to compel coalition forces to deconflict with Russian forces in Syria.[7]

The current state of Russian–Western military relations means that Russia's continuing military reforms should alert the West to the need to take Russia seriously as a primary security threat for the foreseeable future. Russia's political leadership displayed willingness to use its military capabilities in an aggressive manner outside its frontiers during the annexation of Crimea and subsequent destabilising actions in Eastern Ukraine, as well as in its military intervention in Syria. The Kremlin is demonstrating both capability and intent. Moreover, it has shown great skill in managing deployments and combat operations in a way that minimises the potential justification for a military response from the West. Russia perfectly understands where the West's 'red lines' lie and skilfully tailors its actions to stay just below the threshold that would trigger a reaction from the West. This combination of skill, intent and capability – while not an indicator of a direct and imminent prospect of a Russian invasion – is nevertheless a threat that it would be irresponsible of NATO to ignore.

Sophisticated Military Planning in Crimea and Ukraine

The crucial early stages of Moscow's military operation against Ukraine from March to June 2014 can inform analysis of current Russian military capabilities as it was the first time Russian forces had been employed on a large scale in real conflict since the war with Georgia in August 2008. The operation revealed both the achievements and direction of Russian

---

[5] Stephen Blank, 'What Do the Zapad 2013 Exercises Reveal? (Part One)', *Eurasia Daily Monitor* (Vol. 10, No. 177, 4 October 2013).

[6] *Associated Press*, 'NATO: Russia Increasingly Stages Snap Military Drills', 29 August 2016.

[7] Mark Hosenball, Phil Stewart and Matt Spetalnick (*Reuters*), 'US Spy Agencies were "Caught Off-Guard" by Putin's Sudden Dramatic Escalation in Syria', *Business Insider UK*, 8 October 2015.

military reforms since 2008 and provided ample evidence that the General Staff is capable of sophisticated and high-level strategic planning in offensive operations.

During the annexation of Crimea, the deployment of Russian troops along the mainland border with Ukraine in spring 2014 was intended to deter Kiev from using military means to challenge Russian annexation. After the annexation, deployments continued in order to dissuade Ukrainian attempts to suppress Russian-backed rebels in eastern Ukraine. The deployment began as Russia had gradually been taking control of Crimea and preparing political measures – a referendum – to legitimise annexation. It continued as Kiev scrambled to regain military control of Ukraine's eastern regions, which had been subjected to sub-conventional destabilisation operations by Russian forces, with widespread use of Russia-inspired insurgents.[8] When Ukrainian forces showed signs from July to early August 2014 that they might defeat the rebellion by force,[9] Russian troops invaded the country to save the Russian-held rebel territories and defeat the Ukrainian forces.[10] The aim of Moscow's military deployment was to support its sub-conventional actions, which sought to undermine Ukraine's territorial integrity, although the operation as a whole was offensive in nature.

Officially, Russia portrayed the deployment of regular military units as a sequence of snap exercises. In some instances, exercises transitioned from one to another, but usually they built to a crescendo: up to 40,000–50,000 combat troops (or 90,000–95,000 troops including combat support and combat service support units and elements) participated.[11]

Ordinarily, such 'exercises' would be subject to the notification requirements stipulated by the OSCE's 'Vienna Document 2011 on Confidence- and Security-Building Measures', which states that all participating states must be notified of any military activity involving more than 9,000 Ground Troops at least 42 days in advance of the exercise.[12]

---

[8] Ewen MacAskill, 'Putin's Military Exercises are More than a Game', *The Guardian*, 23 April 2014; Igor Sutyagin and Michael Clarke, 'Ukraine Military Dispositions: The Military Ticks Up while the Clock Ticks Down', RUSI Briefing Paper, April 2014.

[9] *Newsru.ua*, 'Ukrainskaya armiya blizka k pobede na Donbasse, uveren Geletey [Ukrainian Army Close to Victory in Donbass, Geletey Said]', 4 August 2014, <http://rus.newsru.ua/ukraine/04aug2014/geletey.html>, accessed 13 October 2016.

[10] Joinfo.ua, 'ATO na Donbasse: khronika i karta sobytiy ot nachala i do segodnyashnego dnya [Anti-terrorist Operations in Donbass: Chronicle and Map of Events from the Beginning to the Present Day]', 18 October 2014, <http://joinfo.ua/politic/1032314_ATO-Donbasse-hronika-karta-dinamiki-sobitiy.html>, accessed 13 October 2016.

[11] Sutyagin and Clarke, 'Ukraine Military Dispositions'.

[12] OSCE, 'Vienna Document 2011 on Confidence- and Security-building Measures', FSC.DOC/1/11, 30 November 2011, p. 20, paras 38 and 40.1.1.

To avoid these notification requirements, the General Staff carefully tailored troop deployments to stay under this threshold, making it possible for Russia to seize and retain operational surprise while violating the spirit but not the letter of the Vienna Document.

Russia's efforts in this area took two main forms. First, the troops were organised as battalion tactical groups (*Bataljonnye Takticheskie Gruppy* – BTGr), which are similar to US brigade combat teams in doctrinal terms, but are of battalion size and have a flexible structure. These appeared to operate independently of each other, but were covertly controlled by central command of the General Staff and/or the headquarters of the Southern Military District (MD).[13] This arrangement allowed Russia to bypass the provision contained in Paragraph 40.1.1 of the Vienna Document, which requires parties to provide notification of military activities if the troops involved are 'organized into a divisional structure or at least two brigades/regiments'.[14] Russia has refused to publicly admit that the troops deployed for these 'exercises' were under central command and in so doing prevented the application of the terms of the Vienna Document to the situation near the Russian–Ukrainian border.[15]

Second, the deployment was tailored so that Russian troop concentrations – with one notable exception – did not exceed the Vienna Document notification threshold of 9,000 troops in any single zone. The exception was the concentration of reserve troops in '*Tavriya*' Group (Figure 2), where there were around 11,700 troops stationed on high alert for possible rapid reinforcement. But again Russia avoided the Vienna Document provisions as these reserves did not leave their permanent camps and were therefore not formal participants in any exercises.

These two factors allowed Russia to concentrate a substantial number of troops near its border with Ukraine while avoiding the international confidence-building measures that were designed to provide notice of such movements. The Kremlin's practice of exploiting loopholes in international law, as in this instance, is likely to feature in any future interventions. The care taken in the intimidation of Ukraine with large troop deployments shows how Russian military muscle-flexing is often significantly more sophisticated than it appears at first glance. It also shows that Russia is keen to avoid being held directly in violation of the

---

[13] Igor Sutyagin, 'Russia Confronts NATO: Confidence-destruction Measures', RUSI Briefing Paper, 6 July 2016.
[14] OSCE, 'Vienna Document 2011 on Confidence- and Security-building Measures', para. 40.1.1.
[15] Igor Sutyagin, 'Venskiy dokument [Vienna Document]', *Radio Liberty*, 5 September 2014, <http://www.svoboda.org/a/26563418.html>, accessed 17 June 2016.

Figure 2: Groupings of Russian Troops Deployed for the Operation against Ukraine

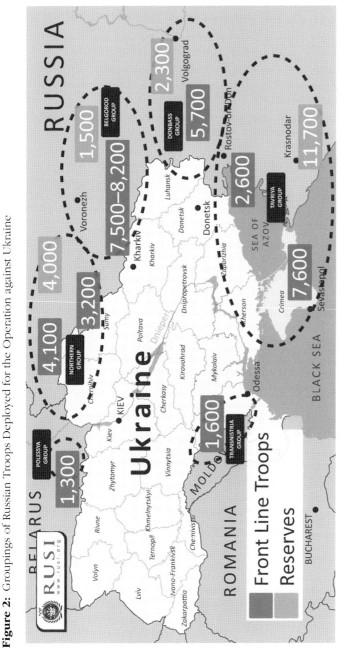

Source: Sutyagin and Clarke, 'Ukraine Military Dispositions'.

letter of the law on confidence-building agreements such as the Vienna Document, since their existence remains useful for Russia in complicating NATO force deployments.

Western political and military planners should not overlook the key lessons from these Russian deployments. Moscow's military machine has demonstrated that it can prepare and employ conventional military forces abroad on a significant scale while deliberately avoiding the international notification and monitoring frameworks put in place to provide military stability between Russia and NATO. Russia's confrontational attitude towards its neighbours, the West and international agreements and frameworks, alongside its proven skills in planning military activities and its pronounced offensive-oriented structures, are rightly sounding alarm bells for NATO's military planners.

Building the Logistics Required for Strategic Mobility

The flexible nature of Russian troop deployments as part of elaborate strategic plans, as demonstrated in Ukraine and more recently in Syria, is possible thanks in large measure to determined efforts by Russian military reformers. Military reforms since 2008 have notably included a combination of measures aimed at dramatically improving the strategic mobility of Russian land forces. For example, the modernisation programme for the ammunition storage infrastructure involves reconfiguring the Russian system to create thirteen large modern ammunition/missile/explosives storage sites ('arsenals' in Russian military parlance) with numerous storage bunkers at each centralised location, making a total of around 580 separate storage bunkers.[16] Each arsenal will contain a wide variety of military munitions and will serve as the main ammunition supply centre for those Russian military units and formations deployed in an entire region of Russia.

There are two primary motivations behind this logistical reform programme. The first is to eliminate the outdoor storage of ammunition and missiles,[17] which was common practice until recently. Moving ammunition inside enables faster preparation of munitions for combat use.

---

[16] *RIA Novosti*, 'Shoigu: bolee 450 khranilisch dlya boepripasov budet postroeno v 2015 godu [Shoigu: More Than 450 Ammunition Storage Facilities will be Built in 2015]', 3 February 2015, <http://ria.ru/defense_safety/20150203/1045644039.html>, accessed 8 June 2016.

[17] *Voennoe obozrenie* [*Military Review*], 'V Tverskoy oblasti poyavitsya sovremenniy arsenal [A Modern Arsenal will be Built in the Tver Region]', 7 December 2015, <http://topwar.ru/87467-v-tverskoy-oblasti-poyavitsya-sovremennyy-arsenal.html>, accessed 8 June 2016.

Once the programme is complete, this will be carried out in purpose-built storage bunkers.

The second motivation is to achive a ten-fold reduction in the number of individual storage facilities,[18] from 140 to thirteen central arsenals,[19] which should ease the flow of ammunition and supplies to forces in the field. The larger universal supply installations will reduce the need to coordinate the logistical support of units from previously separate and dispersed storage facilities. If achieved, and assuming that the arsenals have adequate transhipment potential, this should result in faster delivery of ammunition supplies and increase the speed at which formations can be brought to high readiness in a crisis – a key element of strategic mobility in the broadest sense. Arsenals are being constructed in heavily defended areas and thus have a reasonable chance of survival, at least in the early stages of a conflict, even with peer opponents. However, consolidation remains a trade-off between the need for agile logistical support and the vulnerability of large arsenals in an all-out war. It is worth noting that the arsenal construction programme was initiated in 2012, well before the post-2014 'active' phase of Russia's confrontation with the West.

As with many of Russia's military modernisation plans, this programme continues to be negatively affected by Russia's economic situation. It was originally meant to be completed by January 2015.[20] The deadline was moved to the end of 2015 after only 126 storage bunkers out of 580 had been built. The revised plan envisaged construction of 454 storage bunkers in 2015 alone, which would complete the modernisation of all thirteen arsenals.[21] However, by the end of 2015, the Russian Ministry of Defence reported the construction of just 390 storage bunkers 'in 2014 and 2015',[22] indicating that at least 160 bunkers (and probably

---

[18] *Lenta.ru [Tape.ru]*, 'Minoborony v 10 raz sokratit kolichestvo khranilisch boepripasov ['Ministry of Defence Will Reduce the Number of Storage Facilities Ten-fold]', 23 October 2012, <https://lenta.ru/news/2012/10/23/cuts/>, accessed 8 June 2016.

[19] *Lenta.ru [Tape.ru]*, 'Minoborony potratit 90 milliardov rubley na voennye arsenaly [Ministry of Defence Will Spend 90 Billion Roubles on Military Arsenals]', 1 February 2012, <https://lenta.ru/news/2012/02/01/arsenal/>, accessed 8 June 2016.

[20] *Voenno-promyshlenniy kurjer [Military-Industrial Courier]*, 'Dlya khraneniya boepripasov – sovremennye arsenaly [Modern Arsenals to Store Ammunition]' (No. 48 (516), 11 December 2013), <http://vpk-news.ru/articles/18507>, accessed 8 June 2016.

[21] *RIA Novosti*, 'Shoigu: bolee 450 khranilisch dlya boepripasov budet postroeno v 2015 godu [Shoigu: More Than 450 Ammunition Storage Facilities will be Built in 2015]'.

[22] *RIA Novosti*, 'Shoigu: Rossiya zavershaet obnovlenie khranilisch raket i boepripasov [Shoigu: Russia Completes the Updating of Missiles and Ammunition

more) were incomplete. Nevertheless, the programme is representative of a trend towards a military infrastructure capable of more rapid and large-scale support to operations, and demonstrates the considerable efforts being made in pursuit of that aim.

Similar measures are being undertaken for land forces. Working to the same basic principle, the Ministry of Defence is consolidating the general logistics infrastructure from 330 storage sites to 24 large transhipment and logistics centres also known as PLKs (*Perevalochno-Logisticheskie Kompleksy*) (Figure 3).[23] These are separate from the central ammunition storage sites. In addition to streamlining supply procedures for units, it is hoped that the 24 PLKs, along with consolidation of ammunition storage, will allow the Ministry of Defence to halve the costs associated with the storage of military materiel, armaments and equipment from RUB 29.4 billion a year to RUB 14.8 billion[24] (approximately $452 million and $228 million at the June 2016 exchange rate). Perhaps even more significant is the target to cut more than 50,000 Ministry of Defence personnel from the units running the current storage system.[25] These efficiency gains are crucial as a potential source of desperately needed manpower for other parts of the military system, and billets freed from the ammunition and equipment storage system can be redirected to other parts of the military machine, including to the Ground Troops, which are undermanned, without exceeding the total number of uniformed servicemen – 1 million – stated by presidential decree.[26]

Storage]', 11 December 2015, <http://ria.ru/defense_safety/20151211/1340185174. html#ixzz41ib3mAiO>, accessed 21 March 2017.

[23] Ivan Safronov, 'Minoborony menyaet sklady na kompleksy [Ministry of Defence Swaps Storage for Centres]', *Kommersant*, 29 February 2016, <http://www.kommersant.ru/doc/2926598>, accessed 8 June 2016.

[24] *Ibid.*

[25] *Ibid.*

[26] 'Ukaz Prezidenta Rossiyskoy Federatsii ot 08.07.2016 No 329 'O shtatnoy chislennosti Vooruzhennykh Sil Rossiyskoy Federatsii [Presidential Decree of 8 July 2016 No. 329 "On the Regular Number of Staff of the Armed Forces of the Russian Federation"]', President of Russia, <http://www.kremlin.ru/acts/bank/41115>, accessed 21 March 2017. The decree states that there are 885,371 civilian billets in the armed forces in addition to 1,000,000 uniformed billets. The number of staff of the Russian armed forces has been changed by the Presidential Decree of 28 March 2017 No. 127 to 1,013,628 uniformed billets since, backdated to 1 January 2017; the number of civilian billets was reduced to 884,066 from 1 January 2017, increasing to 889,432 billets by 1 July 2017. 'Ukaz Prezidenta Rosiyskoy Federatsii ot 28 marta 2017 No. 127 'O vnesenii izmeneniya v Ukaz Prezidenta Rossiyskoy Federatsii ot 08.07.2016 No 329 'O shtatnoy chislennosti Vooruzhennykh Sil Rossiyskoy Federatsii' [Presidential Decree of 28 March 2017 No. 127 On Making Changes to the Presidential Decree of 8 July 2016 No. 329 "On the Regular Number of Staff of the Armed Forces of the Russian Federation"]', Ofitsialniy internet-portal pravovoy

Figure 3: Transhipment and Logistics Centres to be Established by the Russian Ministry of Defence

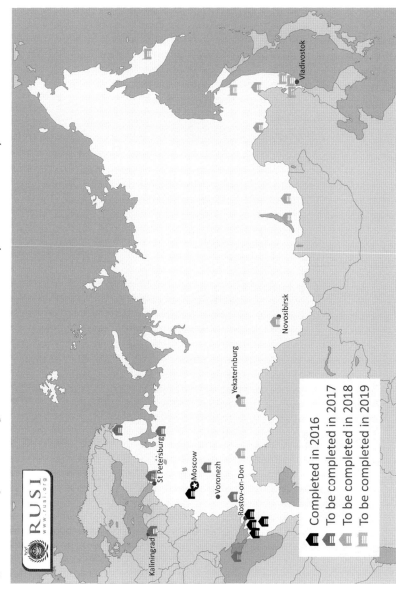

Completed in 2016

To be completed in 2017

To be completed in 2018

To be completed in 2019

Vladivostok

Novosibirsk

Yekaterinburg

St Petersburg

Moscow

Voronezh

Rostov-on-Don

Kaliningrad

Source: Ivan Safronov, 'Minoborony menyaet sklady na kompleksy [Ministry of Defence Swaps Storage for Centres]', *Kommersant*, 29 February 2016, <https://www.kommersant.ru/doc/2926598>, accessed 18 May 2017.

Another element of the Russian logistical support system is also being reformed with the aim of improving the strategic mobility of Russia's land forces. This has parallels with the US military strategy of 'pre-positioning' critical assets. Dedicated storage and maintenance bases (*Bazy Khraneniya i Remonta Vooruzheniy i Tekhniki*, or BKhiRVT) have been located in areas considered by the General Staff to be potential sources of military threat. These bases contain pre-positioned, brigade-level assets, including heavy weapons, armoured vehicles and other equipment, as well as two-and-a-half times the brigade's full combat load of ammunitions of all types, maintained by a limited detachment (111 men and women) of the MoD's civilian personnel under the command of a uniformed officer. The level of vehicle fleet and other equipment readiness maintained at each BKhiRVT is an improvement on previous arrangements due to this manning provision, which allows regular turning over of vehicles (which are kept fuelled) and testing of equipment. In this way, it is intended that vehicle fleets and equipment are kept at such high readiness that they can be used rapidly by incoming troops in an emergency.

In the event of an emergency – and the need for rapid reinforcement – troops from regular brigades deployed elsewhere in Russia would leave their 'organic' vehicles, equipment and heavy weapons and be transported by the fastest means, usually by air with light arms only, to BKhiRVTs near the anticipated combat zone in order to access the heavy equipment stored there before deploying. The airlifting of Russian Ground Troops personnel is exercised on a comparatively regular basis, and Russia's Military Transport Aviation can transport up to five motor-rifle brigades with light arms in one flight. To accomplish this, the five transport air regiments of the 12th Transport Air Division (117th, 334th, 196th, 566th and 708th Guards regiments) are equipped with six An-124 Condor (Ruslan), five An-22 Cock (Antey), and 82 Il-76 Candid transport aircraft, which together have the capacity to airlift between 25,200 and 26,800 troops in one wave. Despite such capacity for swift redeployment of forces, the Ministry of Defence plans to further expand its airlift capacity to guarantee mobility for troops and effective rear support for forward-operating troops,[27] which is partly in response to the experience gained during Russia's operation in Syria.

---

informatsii [Official Legal Information Internet-portal], 29 March 2017, <http://publication.pravo.gov.ru/Document/View/0001201703290001>, accessed 29 March 2017.
[27] Artem Grachev, "'Ermak' pridet na smenu 'Anteyam' i 'Ruslanam' ['Ermak' Will Replace the 'Antey' and 'Ruslan']', *Utro.ru* [*Morning.ru*], 20 April 2016, <http://utro.ru/articles/2016/04/20/1279286.shtml?utm_medium=referral&utm_source=

Table 1: Distribution of BKhiRVT by Military Districts (MDs)

Type of BKhiRVT	Western MD	Southern MD	Central MD	Eastern MD	Total
Motor-rifle	2	0	3	9	14
Tank	1	0	0	0	1
Artillery	2	1	1	2	6
Total by MD	5	1	4	11	21

Source: www.rpg7.ru. This site has now been closed by the Russian government.

The use of pre-positioned equipment enables brigades to be redeployed to threatened areas without needing to transport their own vehicles and heavy weapons, which enables local forces to be strengthened in a matter of days. Although this core principle remains sound as a means to increase the strategic mobility of land forces in the geographic expanse of Russia, it does not always work as planned. The Russian armed forces lack standardised equipment – a feature inherited from the Soviet era, when preserving equipment of all generations was the only way to maintain stocks large enough for a mass mobilisation in the event of general war. This problem continues to plague the armed forces, and means that units might arrive at a BKhiRVT to discover types of hardware which they have not been trained to use.[28]

Equipment pre-positioning also has another function: the BKhiRVTs provide a reserve of additional weaponry and equipment for units that do not exist during peacetime. Should a mass mobilisation be required due to escalation towards an existential war, the strategically located BKhiRVTs can act as bases from which to set up additional brigades, manned by new troops conscripted from the general population, and with equipment readily available. (In fact, every numbered BKhiRVT has a parallel designator as 'the XXth wartime brigade', which denotes the unit it would generate *in extremis*.) There are currently 21 BKhiRVTs for motor-rifle, tank and artillery brigades deployed within Russian territory (see Table 1), with six and fifteen in the European and Asian parts of Russia, respectively. There are additional BKhiRVTs for combat support and service support formations. Of course, the use of heavy equipment in BKhiRVTs in generating wartime reserve formations would have a significant impact on the capacity of those facilities to supply regular units being swiftly brought in from elsewhere in the country.

---

lentainform&utm_campaign=utro.ru&utm_term=1257940s5249&utm_content=
4297774>, accessed 8 August 2016.
[28] Igor Sutyagin, 'Russia's Overestimated Military Might', RUSI *Newsbrief* (Vol. 34, No. 2, March 2014).

In terms of military logistics – a key enabler of strategic mobility – Moscow has already achieved impressive results in the current round of reforms. The reforms were triggered by the army's unimpressive performance during the Russia–Georgia war of August 2008. However, they are now close to enabling the General Staff to swiftly deploy heavily equipped forces for defensive or offensive purposes after their arrival from thousands of kilometres away, providing the problem of armament standardisation is resolved.[29] The doctrinal requirement is that this process of equipping for action be completed within 24 hours (although according to recent exercises, this can take up to 72 hours in practice).

Of course, an efficient and well-structured supply and logistics capability is of little value without military units capable of taking advantage of it. This paper now examines the ability of Russia's land forces to generate and sustain effective combat units in a crisis.

High-readiness Forces: The Battalion Tactical Groups Concept

Russia's need for high-readiness forces has long been clear given the vast geographic expanse of the country and its limited military resources. The maintenance of high-readiness forces is achieved through the proven concept of battalion tactical groups, similar in concept to the US brigade combat team (BCT), but on a smaller scale – around 700–800 men per BTGr for manoeuvre troops, with some as large as 900 men,[30] compared with around 4,000 for a BCT. Like the BCT, the BTGr consists of one full combined arms manoeuvre battalion, and its assigned support and fire elements. These support elements usually include a tank company (motor-rifle company for tank BTGr), artillery battery or battalion and air-defence battery, as well as reconnaissance, communications, combat engineer, chemical, biological, radiological and nuclear and rear support elements.[31]

---

[29] This paper does not cover the development of Russia's mobilisation reserves. This subject is discussed in detail in Julian Cooper, 'If War Comes Tomorrow: How Russia Prepares for Possible Armed Aggression', *Whitehall Report*, 4-16 (August 2016).

[30] *Novosti VPK* [*News of the Military-Industrial Complex*], 'Kolichestvo bataljonnyih takticheskikh grupp v rossiiskoi armii vozrastet pochti vdvoe [Number of Battalion Tactical Groups in the Russian Army Will Nearly Double]', 15 September 2016, <http://vpk.name/news/163581_kolichestvo_batalonnyih_takticheskih_grupp_v_rossiiskoi_armii_vozrastet_pochti_vdvoe.html?new>, accessed 19 October 2016.

[31] Vladimir Shurygin, 'Voyna 08.08.08. Vpervye o ney rasskazyvaet general Khrulev [War on 08.08.08. General Khrulev Speaks about it for the First Time]', interview with Lieutenant General Anatoliy Khrulev, commander of the 58th Combined Arms Army in 2006–10. *Livejournal*, 25 April 2012, <http://shurigin.livejournal.com/347559.html>, accessed 1 August 2016.

One BTGr – fully manned with professionals, according to the Commander-in-Chief of the Russian Ground Troops[32] – is formed in every manoeuvre brigade (including marines), every manoeuvre/airborne/air-assault regiment, and every air-assault brigade. The BTGr in each formation is usually organised around one battalion, which is maintained in a permanent state of high readiness. To maintain this readiness, any gaps in this battalion due to personnel being on leave or weapons and equipment needing repair or maintenance are immediately filled by temporary supply from the brigade's other battalions. The model allows two-hour combat readiness to be maintained indefinitely,[33] and for one BTGr to be on high alert in each of Russia's manoeuvre formations at any given time. Senior Russian military officials claim that some formations have two BTGrs.[34] While two-hour readiness seems too optimistic for BTGrs, their readiness for combat well inside 24 hours is likely a reality.

The same model is used in Spetsnaz (special forces) and reconnaissance brigades. These elite formations have a higher average readiness level, meaning that those brigades that have more than three Spetsnaz battalions (3rd, 22nd, 24th Guards brigades and the 14th brigade) are able to generate two battalions each. However, due to their different operational roles, these lack the supporting assets normally attached to a BTGr. The number of BTGrs in the Russian land forces is steadily increasing.

General Valery Gerasimov, Chief of the General Staff, claimed in September 2016 that the number of BTGrs would be increased from 65 in September 2016 to 96 by the end of 2016, to 115 in 2017 and 125 in 2018.[35] However, these figures include the number of battalions fully manned by professionals rather than the actual number of formations permanently on high alert. Nevertheless, it is realistic to expect that every brigade/regiment is able to generate a single BTGr in 2–24 hours – which gives Russia at least 47,000 troops in a permanent state of high readiness.

Using BTGrs as the framework for Russia's rapid reaction forces, Russia's Military Transport Aviation is in theory capable of moving 35–38 BTGrs (20,000–25,000 troops), with light weapons only, in one airlift to join pre-positioned equipment at BKhiRVTs near a combat zone. The

---

[32] Viktor Khudoleev, 'Voyska s velikoy istoriey [Troops with a Great History]', interview with Commander-in-Chief, Russian Ground Troops, Colonel General Oleg Salyukov, *Krasnaya zvezda* [*Red Star*], 29 September 2015, <http://www.redstar.ru/index.php/component/k2/item/25942-vojska-s-velikoj-istoriej>, accessed 13 October 2016.

[33] Shurygin, 'Voyna 08.08.08 [War on 08.08.08]'.

[34] Khudoleev, 'Voyska s velikoy istoriey [Troops with a Great History]'.

[35] *Novosti VPK* [*News of the Military-Industrial Complex*], 'Kolichestvo bataljonnyih takticheskikh grupp v rossiiskoi armii vozrastet pochti vdvoe [Number of Battalion Tactical Groups in the Russian Army Will Nearly Double]'.

worrying aspect of this capability for the West is that, as former Airborne Troops Commandant General Vladimir Shamanov announced in August 2016, the high-readiness airborne and air-assault battalions ('more than ten', according to the general; twelve in practice) are intended and ready for combat actions abroad.[36] In other words, Russian officials have openly stated that around 4,800–5,400 airborne/air-assault troops are maintained at two-hour readiness for operations abroad[37] – that is to say, for offensive operations. In addition, the approximately 1,000-strong, highly professional (manned exclusively by officers and warrant officers, without sergeants and/or privates) Special Operations Forces Command (*Komandovanie Sil Spetsialnykh Operatsiy*, or KSSO) are also specifically intended for operations deep inside enemy territory. Indeed, there is some evidence that the KSSO has been employed in Ukraine and Syria.

New Divisions for Russia's Ground Troops

As effective as the BTGr construct can be for quickly generating self-contained combat formations, the rapid deterioration of Russia's relations with the West after the annexation of Crimea and military intervention in eastern Ukraine has convinced Moscow of the need for much larger division-level formations.[38] Since implied and explicit military threats play an important role in Russian foreign policy towards NATO, new divisions are being established to try to generate a demonstrable capability to fight a high-intensity, albeit comparatively short, ground war with NATO.

---

[36] Janelle Kuandykova, 'Komanduyuschiy VDV rasskazal o 10 gotovykh k operatsiyam za rubezhom bataljonakh [Airborne Troops Commandant Announces that 10 Battalions are Ready for Overseas Operations]', *RBK News Agency*, 18 June 2015, <http://top.rbc.ru/politics/18/06/2015/5582b25d9a7947e83903e826>, accessed 8 August 2016.

[37] Airborne/air-assault battalions are smaller than their ground troops counterparts in the Russian armed forces. As such, the airborne/air-assault BTGrs' manpower is under 700 men.

[38] As Moscow's predictions regarding foreign policy are usually made on the established pattern of other states' behaviour, it was hard to predict the bitter crisis in its relations with the West over its annexation of Crimea. The West accepted the de facto Russian intervention – although peaceful – in Kosovo at Pristina airport in 1999, and also accepted Russia's attack on Georgia in August 2008, which led to the ceding of approximately 20 per cent of Georgian territory to the Kremlin-controlled separatist 'republics' of Abkhazia and South Ossetia. The Kremlin therefore did not have reason to expect a fundamentally different reaction to Russia's intervention in Ukraine, which has led to the ceding of approximately 5 per cent of Ukraine's territory (although this is 'safe guarded', from Moscow's viewpoint, by 'legal' procedures of 'referenda' in both Crimea and eastern Ukraine), thus equating them, as far as Moscow is concerned, to the Kosovo independence referendum and the Western recognition of Kosovo independence.

Putin uses military intimidation to try 'to subdue the enemy without fighting', Sun Tzu-style – counting on European democracies, in particular, to lack the political will to call his bluff. For instance, aggressive nuclear rhetoric, unprecedented brinkmanship and large-scale military exercises near the borders of NATO member states are designed to divert the attention of Western politicians from what is happening in Ukraine. The autocratic nature of the current Russian governing system makes such tactics more feasible for Moscow than for Western democracies. At the same time, the Kremlin has demonstrated substantial will and skill in using 'divide and conquer' tactics of tailored intimidation and 'charm offensives' against the weaker links of the West. It is hard to avoid the conclusion that the Kremlin has been spectacularly successful in this, as demonstrated by the continued resistance of Europe and the US to supplying Ukraine with lethal weapons to help Kiev counter Russian and Russian-backed forces. The intensity of the debates on whether to lift EU sanctions on Russia is another example of the political strength and divisive abilities Moscow has displayed in its current confrontation with the West. However, to mitigate the danger that the West might call Moscow's bluff, the military force behind these tactics of intimidation must appear credible.

These were among the considerations that, in mid-2014, persuaded Russian political-military planners to revisit the force structure that had been pursued in a longstanding military reform programme. The mix of brigades and divisions in Russia's land forces was first considered as early as 1992.[39] The plan then considered the retention of one or two combined arms divisions in each of Russia's military districts, with the remaining forces reorganised into a brigade structure. Brigades would bear the burden of operations in low-intensity conflicts, while divisions would provide a reserve force to be sent into combat if a heavy, concentrated blow were needed. In other words, divisions would have represented a moderate 'hedging' force in the event of a conflict with a modern military adversary such as NATO or China. Divisions were retained in the structure of Russia's land forces until 2008, when – given that a conflict with NATO in particular was then considered extremely remote – they were abolished. The Ground Troops have since been reorganised around a brigade structure, while Russia's Airborne Troops successfully lobbied to retain a divisional structure. It may be that their operational concept assumed that airborne operations behind enemy lines, without support from friendly forces, required heavier forces at divisional rather than brigade level.

---

[39] Pavel Grachev, 'Pri formirovanii armii Rossii nuzhen chetkiy raschet i zdraviy smysl [Clear Calculation and Common Sense are Needed in the Process of the Russian Army's Formation]', *Krasnaya zvezda* [*Red Star*] (No. 162, 21 July 1992).

Russia's demographic and economic situation was among major factors behind the 2008 decision to abolish division-level formations in the main land force. Even with the manpower target reduced in December 2008 to 1 million uniformed personnel (plus 884,829 civilian personnel) for the armed forces as a whole, the government struggled to attract enough professional recruits, due in large part to poor contract terms.[40] There are currently around 930,000 uniformed personnel.[41] At the same time, demographic changes and better enforcement of medical standards made it difficult to recruit conscripts. The army was therefore unable to recruit enough combat-ready troops even for a comparatively small-scale operation such as the suppression of the Chechen rebellion in 1999–2000. In order to carry out the 'counterterrorist operation' against separatists in Chechnya in 1999,[42] the General Staff had to create ad hoc units, gathering personnel from numerous nominally mighty, but in reality impotent, divisions from across Russia. This was the main driving force behind the 2000–04 military reform. It was also a major issue for Putin, who realised the humiliatingly poor readiness of his armed forces as soon as he became prime minister in 1999, and then president in 2000, and was faced with the task of defeating the Chechen rebellion by force.

The August 2008 conflict with Georgia demonstrated that efforts undertaken in 2000–04 were insufficient, due to the low mobility of the division-based force structure. A leaner force structure was adopted in 2008, using smaller but (in theory) fully manned brigades. The 'heavy blow' requirement was met via pre-positioning brigade sets of hardware at BKhiRVTs and increasing the strategic mobility of troops to allow the rapid concentration of forces where needed. The retention of a handful of divisions was considered an unnecessary waste of resources due to the

---

[40] *Garant.ru*, 'Ukaz Presidenta RF ot 29 dekabrya 2008 No 1878ss "O nekotorykh voprosakh Vooruzhennykh Sil Rossiyskoy Federatsii" [Presidential Decree of 29 December 2008 No. 1878ss "On Some Issues of the Armed Forces"]', <http://www.garant.ru/products/ipo/prime/doc/94685/>, accessed 14 October 2016. The number of civilian billets has since been increased to 885,371 by the Presidential Decree of 8 July 2016, No. 329.

[41] President of Russia, 'Rasshirennoe zasedanie kollegii Ministerstva oborony Rossiyskoy Federatsii [Extended Meeting of the Russian Federation Ministry of Defence's Collegium]', 22 December 2016, <http://www.kremlin.ru/events/president/news/53571>, accessed 21 March 2017.

[42] *RIA Novosti*, 'Kontrterroristicheskaya operatsiya v Chechne 1999–2009 gg. Spravka [Counterterrorist Operation in Chechnya, 1999–2009. Factsheet]', 26 March 2009, <https://ria.ru/defense_safety/20090326/166106234.html>, accessed 21 March 2017.

low probability of operational scenarios requiring division-size formations in concentrated strikes.

This brigade-based structure remained a central part of Russian military reform from 2008 to 2012 under Serdyukov, the minister of defence appointed by Putin in the role played by Robert McNamara for the US armed forces in the 1960s: to rebuild the Russian military in the most cost-effective shape possible. Even the restoration of two 'palace' divisions in suburban Moscow in 2013 – the 2nd Guards Tamanskaya Motor-Rifle and the 4th Guards Kantemirovskaya Tank divisions – by incoming Minister of Defence Sergey Shoigu was not really a departure from Serdyukov's plan, as a brigade-based structure of the armed forces remained. These two divisions were restored in reduced form, with four regiments instead of six, and were not much larger than brigades. It was a symbolic gesture aimed at regaining the support of the military, which was dissatisfied with the dismantling of the armed forces' traditional structure. These two divisions had been downrated to the 5th Guards Motor-Rifle Brigade and the 4th Guards Tank Brigade respectively in 2009. Their restoration by Shoigu symbolised a reversal of Serdyukov's reform, which was considered disastrous by the majority of the senior Russian officer corps, and granted the new defence minister badly needed support to carry out his modified version of the policy.[43]

The brigade-based structure of the Ground Troops as the backbone of Russia's land forces was considered sufficient for the country's defence in the period before the annexation of Crimea, Russia's operation in eastern Ukraine and the subsequent – unanticipated – crisis in Russian–Western relations. The collapse of relations with the West after Crimea changed this trajectory and led to the re-establishment of full-strength (six-regiment) divisions.[44] In January 2016, Shoigu announced that three new combined arms divisional headquarters would be established in western Russia in 2016.[45] The Commander-in-Chief of Russia's Ground Troops, Colonel General Oleg Salyukov, specified four days after Shoigu's

---

[43] *Komsomolskaya Pravda* [*Komsomol Truth*], 'Sergey Shoigu: Reforme armii nuzhen zdraviy smysl [Sergey Shoigu: Common Sense is Needed for the Army's Reform]', 12 February 2013, <http://www.kp.ru/daily/26030/2947853/>, accessed 19 October 2016.

[44] *Vzglyad* [*Look*], 'Istochnik: Divizii 1-y tankovoy i 20-y armiy budut imet po shest polkov [Source: Divisions of the 1st Tank and 20th Armies Will Have Six Regiments in Their Structure]', 1 April 2016, <http://vz.ru/news/2016/4/1/802954.html>, accessed 9 August 2016.

[45] *TASS*, 'Shoigu: Minoborony RF v 2016 godu sformiruet tri novye divizii na zapadnom napravlenii [Shoigu: The Russian Federation Ministry of Defence Will Establish Three New Divisions in the Western Direction in 2016]', 12 January 2016, <http://tass.ru/armiya-i-opk/2579480>, accessed 15 January 2016.

announcement that the plan actually called for four divisions, three of them in the Western MD and one in the Central MD.[46] In practice, the Western MD has received two divisions, with a third established in the Southern MD, also in western Russia.

The move did not come as a complete surprise to observers. As early as June 2015, high-ranking Russian military officials had been making statements about the need to establish new divisions to counter what Moscow termed 'provocative' developments by NATO.[47] Moscow was specifically concerned about NATO plans to deploy several battalions to the territory of the Alliance's eastern member states. The three new divisions in western Russia can partly be seen as a response to these plans by ensuring that Russia's conventional deterrent in Europe has credibility. However, maintaining military pressure on Ukraine is probably the new divisions' primary task for the foreseeable future. This is discussed in greater detail in Chapter II of this paper.

The re-establishment of divisions in the Ground Troops' structure may help to alleviate an unexpected deficiency in implementing the brigade structure. One of the problems experienced by brigade headquarters is that they are expected to control too many subordinate elements, an issue that was overlooked in the transition from divisions to brigades. Brigade headquarters control eighteen elements on the battlefield, fifteen of which will be directly involved in combat. Received wisdom suggests that control of any structure with more than seven to eight elements cannot be effective.

By comparison, the more 'modular' brigades within the 3rd (UK) Division of the British Army have only five organic combat units from the infantry or Royal Armoured Corps, with a further five to seven combat support (artillery, intelligence, signals, engineers) and combat service support (logistics, medical, electrical and mechanical engineers) units organised as required, routinely bringing deployed brigades to a total of between ten and twelve force elements. (It is worth noting that during Operation *Herrick* in Afghanistan, brigades were formed of up to eight combat units and a further dozen or more support elements, which was considered to have overburdened brigade headquarters and justified a re-emphasis on divisions in the 2015 Strategic Defence and Security Review.)

---

[46] *Rossiyskaya Gazeta* [*Russian Gazette*], 'Glavkom: v Krymu seychas net soedineniy i chastey Sukhoputnykh voysk [Commander-in-Chief: There are No Ground Troops Formations and Units in Crimea Now]', 22 January 2016, <http://www.rg.ru/2016/01/22/salukov-site-anons.html>, accessed 22 January 2016.

[47] *Lenta.ru* [*Tape.ru*], 'Rossiya otvetit na ucheniya NATO chetyrjmya novymi diviziyami [Russia Will Respond to NATO Exercises with Four New Divisions]', 22 January 2016, <http://lenta.ru/news/2016/01/22/division/>, accessed 22 January 2016.

Similarly, the US Army's 32 Brigade Combat Teams are typically established on the basis of four combat units, plus two combat support (engineers and artillery) units and one logistics unit. However, UK/US brigades sit within divisional structures rather than the Russian approach of self-sufficient brigade formations.

The new Russian division headquarters will have twelve to fourteen elements to control, of which seven or eight will be directly involved in combat. This promises to significantly improve the combat effectiveness of Russian forces under divisional command structures.

The following formations are currently being re-established in western Russia:

- 3rd Guards Motor-Rifle Division in Boguchar (near Voronezh, Western MD).[48]
- 90th Guards Tank Division in Chebarkul (near Chelyabinsk, South Urals, Central MD).[49]
- 144th Guards Motor-Rifle Division in Elnya (Smolensk, Western MD).
- 150th Motor-Rifle Division in Novocherkassk (near Rostov-on-Don, Southern MD).[50]

Russian officials have already announced further divisions to be established, including:

- 42nd Guards Motor-Rifle Division, in Chechnya (Southern MD).[51]
- A 'coastal defence' division – presumed to be the 99th Motor-Rifle Division renamed the Coastal Defence Division – on Chukotka Peninsula (Eastern MD).[52]

---

[48] Ivan Petrov, 'Shoigu rasskazal o postuplenii novoy tekhniki v voyska [Shoigu Told about the Arrival of New Equipment to the Troops]', *Russkoe oruzhie/Rossiyskaya Gazeta [Russian Weapons/Russian Gazette]*, 21 October 2016, <https://rg.ru/2016/10/21/shojgu-rasskazal-o-postuplenii-novoj-tehniki-i-vooruzhenij-v-vojska.html>, accessed 11 December 2016.

[49] *TASS*, 'Tankovaya diviziya na Urale budet sformirovana do 1 dekabrya etogo goda [Tank Division Will be Established in the Urals by 1 December This Year]', 11 September 2016, <http://tass.ru/armiya-i-opk/3612149>, accessed 19 October 2016.

[50] *TASS*, 'Istochnik: novoe soedinenie na yuge RF poluchit imya divizii, bravshey rejkhstag [Source: The New Formation in the South of Russia Will Receive the Name of the Division That Stormed the Reichstag]', 24 April 2016, <http://tass.ru/armiya-i-opk/3233691>, accessed 15 October 2016.

[51] *Izvestiya*, 'Minoborony vozrozhdaet legendarnuyu "chechenskuyu diviziyu" [Ministry of Defence Will Re-establish the Legendary "Chechen Division"]', 27 September 2016, <http://izvestia.ru/news/634572#ixzz4LRXMGoNj>, accessed 15 October 2016.

Table 2: Estimate of the Size of Full-strength Divisions and Brigades

	Divisions		Brigades	
	Motor-rifle	**Tank**	**Motor-rifle**	**Tank**
Manoeuvre battalions	16	16	4	4
Tanks	214	322	40	94
Total artillery batteries/artillery pieces[a]	32/192–222	27/162–180	12/72–81	8/48–51
Air-defence batteries	12	12	5	5
Air targets that can be engaged simultaneously[b]	80–112	80–112	36–60	36–60

Source: Authors' estimate based on the standard structure of current Russian brigades and divisions.

Notes:

[a]Alongside regular artillery guns, MLRS and mortars are included in these figures, anti-tank missile launchers are not. Fluctuations in total pieces are due to variations in the composition of battalion-level mortar batteries which can include 6, 8 or 9 mortars.

[b]Figures in this row do not include MANPADS. Targets which can be engaged simultaneously depend on whether the formations in question are still operating the Tor M1 or more modern and capable Tor M2 air-defence system.

Table 2 gives an estimate of the size of full-strength divisions and brigades and shows that the four new divisions announced will, in theory, add a great deal of combat power to Russia's land forces.

However, establishing even four new divisions will place a huge additional manpower burden on Russia's Ground Troops, which are already undermanned by approximately 19 per cent, currently numbering roughly 243,500.[53] The demographic trend created by the low birth rate in Russia during the difficult post-Soviet period of the 1990s is currently hitting military recruitment. There seems to be no clear solution to this manpower problem, with the four new divisions alone requiring at least 37,000 men altogether. The new divisions are being created alongside new tactical ballistic missile, air-defence, and other support brigades (the Ministry of Defence announced plans in September 2013 to establish 40 new brigades by 2020, without increasing the total number of personnel),[54] as well as the new Ground Troops brigades already

---

[52] Russian Ministry of Defence, 'V Moskve sostoyalos zasedaniye Kollegii Ministerstva oborony [Board of the Ministry of Defence Meet in Moscow]', 23 August 2016, <http://function.mil.ru/news_page/country/more.htm?id=12093516@egNews>, accessed 16 October 2016.; Sergey Ishchenko, 'Krepost Chukotka protiv bazy "Elmendorf" [Fortress Chukchi vs Fort "Elmendorf"]', *Svobodnaya Pressa* [*Free Press*], 26 August 2016, <http://svpressa.ru/war21/article/155298/>, accessed 16 October 2016.

[53] See Appendix I for the authors' estimate of the size of Russian ground forces in 2016.

established, and much-needed personnel uplifts for the Air-Space Force and Navy. It is unlikely that even the manpower savings being made in the logistics apparatus, discussed earlier in this chapter, will be sufficient to prevent further undermanning difficulties in the land forces. This, in turn, is likely to lead to the hollowing out of existing formations or of new divisions, or both.

Paradoxically, therefore, while on paper the new divisions add significantly to the combat potential of Russia's land forces, there may be a reduction in their overall readiness and effectiveness. Indeed, the Russian military learned the hard way in the 2000s that trying to spread limited resources too thinly risks leading to a hollow force. This problem dogged the Russian armed forces until the 2008 military reforms, and it was precisely to address this problem that Putin and Serdyukov launched the reforms. The solution decided upon – to ensure that units were fully manned and well trained – is now being partially reversed, as new formations are being established without a corresponding increase in manpower.

Serdyukov was ousted as minister of defence by Putin in November 2012 under pressure from generals and the heads of Russia's military industries, who were angry that Serdyukov's ruthless pursuit of effectiveness was endangering the privileges they had enjoyed under the old system.[55] However, it was Serdyukov's battle to create a lean and efficient army that gave Putin the capabilities that he is currently using to conduct operations in Ukraine and Syria. Instead of the humiliating experience of gathering troops to provide individual augmentees for operations against Chechen rebels and partially in Georgia, in 2014–15 Putin was able to send troops to the 'near' or 'far abroad' whenever he considered it necessary. However, in apparently abandoning the pursuit of leaner but more capable armed forces in favour of expansion without the required manpower, Putin is ultimately

---

[54] Yuri Gavrilov, 'Armiya v rezhime ozhidaniya [Army on Standby]', *Rossiyskaya Gazeta* [*Russian Gazette*] (No. 6196 (220), 10 January 2013), <https://rg.ru/2013/10/01/voiska-site.html>, accessed 19 October 2016.

[55] Aleksandr Sargin, 'Putin kategoricheski ne khotel uvolnyat Serdyukova [Putin Categorically Did Not Want to Dismiss Serdyukov]', *Argumenty-Live* [*Arguments-Live*], 8 November 2012, <http://argumenti.ru/live/2012/11/212831>, accessed 17 March 2017; Andrey Piontkovskiy, 'Putin ne khotel snimat Serdyukova, ego zastavili [Putin Did Not Want to Dismiss Serdyukov, He was Forced to]', *Stringer News Agency*, 19 November 2012, <http://stringer-news.com/publication.mhtml? Part=50&PubID=23396>, accessed 17 March 2017; *Komsomolskaya Pravda* [*Komsomol Truth*], 'Sergey Shoigu: Reforme armii nuzhen zdraviy smysl [Sergey Shoigu: Common Sense is Needed for the Army's Reform]'.

endangering his prospects for success in the use of military force to achieve his political goals.[56]

The Reality: Overstretch and Morale Problems

On paper, the new Russian logistical support, command and response BTGr structures delivered by the current round of reforms should allow Russia to effectively deploy and sustain military forces in offensive and defensive operations in pursuit of Moscow's geopolitical goals. However, Russia's operations in and around Ukraine from early 2014 provide an excellent case study of the capabilities and limitations of the revitalised land forces. While Russia's ability to move units from various parts of the country to the Ukrainian theatre was impressive, there are many indications that the pre-positioning of equipment did not always function as intended, manpower shortages were a serious issue and morale problems were endemic. This gives some clues as to the general problems encountered by Russia's land forces (and armed forces in general) now and in the near future.

The Russian military operation against Ukraine has been conducted in accordance with the revised operational doctrine, popularly (but not absolutely correctly, as some analysts show) referred to as 'hybrid warfare' or 'ambiguous warfare' doctrine in the West.[57] Key elements of this doctrine have been integrated into the new Russian Military Doctrine approved in December 2014.[58] Operations in Ukraine have also been used to test established and experimental tactics, such as the tactical tricks of combat employment, as well as to train personnel. The capabilities and equipment being widely tested in eastern Ukraine include electronic warfare (EW) tactics and equipment, such as tactical- and operational-level communications jamming stations, UAVs with mobile phone network-jamming equipment, EW stations to defend troops against artillery fire (shells using radio proximity fuses), as well as

---

[56] Aleksandr Golts, 'Novye divizii ponizyat boegotovnost [New Divisions Will Decrease Combat Readiness]', *Ezhednevniy zhurnal* [*Daily Journal*], 13 January 2016, <http://www.ej.ru/?a=note&id=29191>, accessed 9 August 2016.

[57] For a detailed discussion of Russia's doctrine see, for instance, Keir Giles, *Russia's 'New' Tools for Confronting the West: Continuity and Innovation in Moscow's Exercise of Power*, Chatham House Research Paper (London: Royal Institute of International Affairs, March 2016); Charles K Bartles, 'Getting Gerasimov Right', *Military Review*, January–February 2016, pp. 30–38.

[58] President of Russia, Voennaya doktrina Rossiayskoy Federatsii [The Russian Federation's Military Doctrine], *Rossiyskaya Gazeta* [*Russian Gazette*], 30 December 2014, <http://www.rg.ru/2014/12/30/doktrina-dok.html>, accessed 17 March 2017.

a wide range of electronic intelligence (ELINT) equipment.[59] Artillery troops from many units, as well as personnel from reconnaissance and special operations forces (Spetsnaz) and formations, are also gaining combat experience.[60]

At the same time, the intervention has revealed the limited capacity of Russia's land forces to sustain an operational commitment on the scale of the Ukrainian conflict. The number of formations required to contribute forces from all over Russia in order to maintain the operational tempo suggests that Moscow would find it difficult to support more than one operation of a similar or greater scale simultaneously.

During the early stages of Russia's intervention, 28 military units were required to generate approximately 40,000–50,000 combat troops (90,000 including support and rear units) to be stationed on the Russia–Ukraine border and in Crimea in spring 2014 (Table 3).[61] According to the authors' estimate, that number was approximately 31–32 per cent of the total manpower of Russian land forces available at that time.

The 28 units that participated in the initial deployment from spring to early summer 2014 – before the first direct Russian incursions into Ukraine – were drawn from a relatively limited geographical area of Russia (Figure 4).

With Russia's increasingly large-scale involvement in direct combat operations against Ukrainian troops during the second half of August 2014,[62] the number of Russian troops on Ukrainian soil was estimated by different sources at between 3,500 and 6,500.[63] To support these

---

[59] Maxim Yatsenko, 'Marchuk: Rossiya ne sobiraetsya ukhodit s vostoka Ukrainy [Marchuk: Russia is Not Going to Leave Eastern Ukraine]', *Novostimira.ua*, 18 July 2016, <http://www.novostimira.com.ua/news_171394.html>, accessed 8 August 2016.

[60] Very large groups of artillery school cadets, rather than single officers/cadets were sent to practise artillery fire control in combat in eastern Ukraine, with the region becoming a proving ground for Russian artillery military schools. See, for instance, *Donbass.ua*, 'V Donetsk na praktiku pribyli kursanty-artilleristy iz Kazani [Artillery Cadets from Kazan Arrive in Donetsk for Exercises]', 4 August 2016, <http://donbass.ua/news/region/2016/08/04/v-doneck-na-praktiku-pribyli-kursanty-artilleristy-iz-kazani.html>, accessed 8 August 2016.

[61] For additional details, see Sutyagin and Clarke, 'Ukraine Military Dispositions'; Igor Sutyagin, 'Russian Forces in Ukraine', RUSI Briefing Paper, 9 March 2015.

[62] Special operations forces (Spetsnaz) and reconnaissance parties operated on Ukrainian soil much earlier; for example, the 45th Detached Guards Special Operations (reconnaissance) regiment of the Russian Airborne Troops was involved in the separatists' attempt to capture Donetsk airport in May 2014.

[63] Serhiy Leshchenko, 'Ukraina: mizh vyboramy ta voennym stanom [Ukraine: Between Elections and the State of War]', *Ukrayinsjka Pravda [Ukrainian Truth]*, 5 September 2014, <www.pravda.com.ua/articles/2014/09/5/7036848>, accessed 12 January 2016; author's interview with the senior officer of the Operations Directorate, Ukrainian General Staff, 9 February 2015.

Table 3: Units Involved in Generating Troops for the Spring and Summer/Winter Stages of the Russian Operation against Ukraine

Unit type	Spring (28 units)	Summer/Autumn (116 units)	
		Units involved in combat actions in Ukraine (101 units)	Other units (15 units)
Motorised infantry	2 Guards Motor Rifle Division; 15, 18, 205 Motor Rifle Brigades; 20, 23, 27 Guards Motor Rifle Brigades; 33, 34 Mountain Brigades	2 Guards Motor Rifle Division; 9, 15, 17, 18, 19, 21, 28, 32, 35, 36, 37, 200, 205 Motor Rifle Brigades; 20, 23, 25, 27, 74, 136, 138 Guards Motor Rifle Brigade, 8 Guards Mountain Brigade; 33, 34 Mountain Brigades; 7 Military base	4 Guards Military base; 201 Military base
		Special Purpose Operational Division; 107 Operational Brigade; Chechen Battalion (Ministry of Interior)	
Armour	4 Guards Tank Division; 6 Tank Brigade	4 Guards Tank Division; 467 Guards Training Centre (formerly 26 Guards Training Tank Division); 5 Guards Tank Brigade; 6 Tank Brigade; Kazan Tank School	7 Guards Tank Brigade
Airborne	98, 106 Guards Airborne Divisions; 7, 76 Guards Air-Assault Division; 31, 56 Guards Air-Assault Brigades; 45 Guards Airborne Intelligence Regiment	98, 106 Guards Airborne Divisions; 7, 76 Guards Air-Assault Divisions; 11 Guards, 31 Guards, 56 Guards Air-Assault Brigades; 83 Air-Assault Brigade; 45 Guards Airborne Reconnaissance Regiment	
Marines and coastal defence	810 Marines Brigade	61, 810 Marines Brigades; 336 Guards Marines Brigade; 536 Anti-Ship Missile Brigade	155 Marines Brigade
Special operations forces	2, 3, 10, 16, 346 Spetsnaz Brigades; 22 Guards Spetsnaz Brigade; 25 Spetsnaz Regiment	2, 3, 10, 14, 16, 24, 346 Spetsnaz Brigades; 22 Guards Spetsnaz Brigade; 25 Spetsnaz Regiment; 100 Reconnaissance Brigade; 54 Reconnaissance Training Centre; 561 Naval Reconnaissance Point	15 Special Purpose Detachment (Ministry of Interior)
		'Vympel' (FSB); 7, 17, 34 Special Purpose Detachment (Ministry of Interior)	

(Continued)

Table 3: Continued

Unit type	Spring (28 units)	Summer/Autumn (116 units)	
		Units involved in combat actions in Ukraine (101 units)	Other units (15 units)
Field artillery	943 MLR Regiment	1 Guards Missile Brigade; 9, 120, 200, 268, 288, 291, 385 Artillery Brigades; 8 Artillery Regiment; 79, 439 Guards MLR Brigades; 232 MLR Brigade; 943 MLR Regiment; 18 Self-Propelled Mortar Battalion (formerly 45 Artillery Brigade); 860 Flamethrower Battalion; 212, 631 Artillery Training Centre; 573 Artillery Reconnaissance Battalion	18 Machinegun-Artillery Division; 305 Artillery Brigade
Missile air defence		53 Guards Zenith-Rocket Brigade; 67 Zenith- Rocket Brigade; 531, 1721 Zenith-Rocket Regiments	
Electronic warfare	82 SIGINT Brigade	154 SIGINT Brigade; 74 SIGINT Regiment; 1020 SIGINT Centre; 15 Electronic Warfare Brigade; 35, 59, 95 C3 Brigade	18 Electronic Warfare Brigade; 34, 66, 175, 176 C3 Brigades
Combat service support		78 Combat Service Support Brigade; 31 Engineer-Sapper Regiment; 656 Engineer- Sapper Battalion; 147, 474 Auto (HGV) Battalions; 7015, 7016 Artillery Storage and Maintenance bases; 282 Artillery Repair base; 29 Railway Brigade; 36 Field Hospital	99 Combat Service Support Brigade; two unidentified Field Hospitals

Source: Authors' estimate.

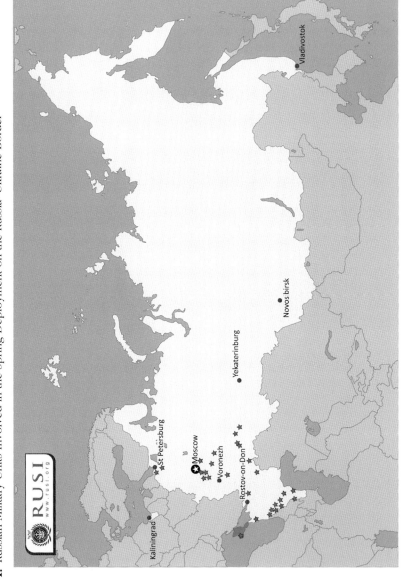

Figure 4: Russian Military Units Involved in the Spring Deployment on the Russia–Ukraine Border

Source: Compilation of information from Igor Sutyagin, 'Russian Forces in Ukraine', RUSI Briefing Paper, March 2015.

incursions, the Ministry of Defence and other official agencies (Ministry of Interior and the Federal Security Service) had to draw on 116 combat and combat-support units to generate approximately 42,000 combat troops (plus an as yet unspecified number of combat service support troops) on three- to six-month rotational deployments to the Russia–Ukraine border. These units were either stationed on the Russian side of the border, delivering artillery fire against Ukrainian targets, or contributed personnel for direct combat operations on Ukrainian sovereign territory. It is noteworthy that 101 out of 116 units were involved in combat operations in at least one of these two forms during this period – almost four times more than the number involved in Operation *Russian Spring* in Crimea and in and around southeastern Ukraine in spring/early summer 2014. The normal peacetime locations of the units involved in the late summer/ winter stage of the operation against Ukraine are presented in Figure 5.

It is important to note that military units from as far as Pechenga, Buryatia, Vladivostok and the Kuril Islands have been identified as participating in operations against Ukraine. It is noteworthy that seven out of ten Russian combined arms armies existing at the time – the 2nd, 6th and 20th Guards, and the 49th, 41st, 36th and 29th Armies – had *all* the manoeuvre units under their command mobilised in order to generate sufficient troops for the spring/early summer and late summer/winter stages of the operation. Given that Ukraine has greatly inferior military strength, and that Russian proxy forces also made a sizeable contribution during combat operations, the scale of participation is striking.

Significantly, the 58th Combined Arms Army mobilised all but one – based at the 102nd Military base in Armenia – of its manoeuvre units to support the operation. The 102nd Military base is the Russian 'beach head' in Armenia, which has been involved in a conflict with neighbouring Azerbaijan over the disputed Nagorno-Karabakh area since September 1988 (open hostility with military-scale operations erupted between Armenian and Azeri forces in August 1990).[64] Since that conflict has shown signs of heating up in recent months, Russia was probably interested in maintaining its level of military presence in Armenia as Russian military transit over Georgian territory is not guaranteed due to the current state of Russia–Georgia relations, and Azerbaijan has intermittently banned Russian military transit to Armenia.[65] It is illustrative

---

[64] While conflict between Armenia and Azerbajan started as early as in 1987, the large-scale hostility, where the Soviet Army was involved, erupted with the attack of Armenian forces on the Kazakh District of Azerbaijan in August 1990. *Istoriya Armenbii i Karabakha* [*History of Armenia and Karabakh*], '1990. Avgust. Arkhiv pressy [1990, August, Archive of Publications]', <http://karabah.h18.ru/press/1990/august1.html>, accessed 21 March 2017.

Figure 5: Russian Military Units Involved in the Late Summer/Winter Stage of the Operation against Ukraine

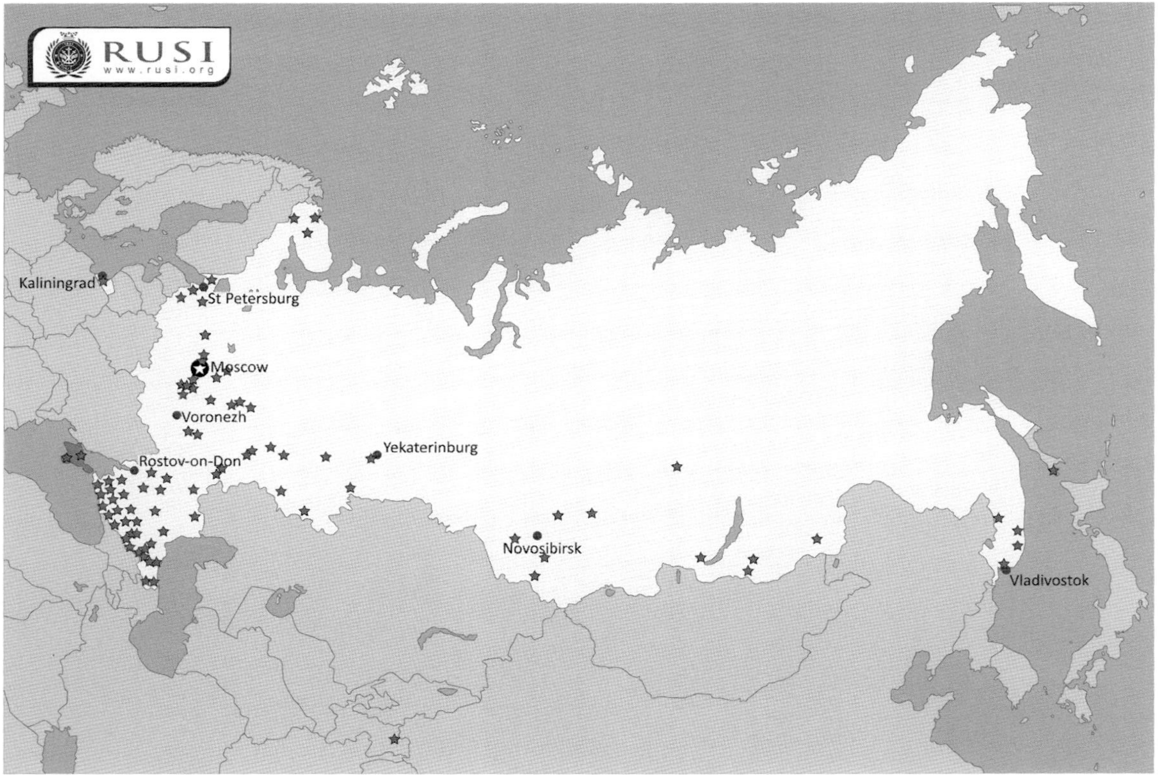

Source: Compilation of information from Igor Sutyagin, 'Russian Forces in Ukraine', RUSI Briefing Paper, March 2015.

that the other Russian military base without direct access to Russian territory – the 201st Military base in Tajikistan – was reported to be sending troops to the Russia–Ukraine border in late January 2015.

Only two out of the ten contemporary field armies – the 35th and 5th, which were tasked to directly oppose China – did not generate troops for the late summer/winter stage of the Ukraine operation. Military units were redeployed from Ussuriysk and Vladivostok, but they were drawn from the Eastern MD subordination, not from the 5th Red Banner Combined Arms Army.

The depletion of personnel in units involved in operations against Ukraine forced Russian commanders to establish ad hoc formations combining detachments from different units into combined tactical groups,[66] thereby repeating the experience during the conflict in Chechnya, instead of using BTGrs originating from one brigade/division, as envisaged by the reforms. This led some observers to identify a lack of regular, pre-formed Russian military units in the combat zone – with individual 'volunteer' servicemen, organised under a single command, fighting instead. Using ad hoc units is contrary to the Russian armed forces' regulations as it degrades units' combat readiness and effectiveness. The cohesion of an ad hoc unit is almost always reduced compared with regular units, because its personnel have not undergone the collective training required to mould standard operating procedures, tactics, techniques and procedures, build personal familiarity and develop a durable *esprit de corps*.[67]

It could be argued that the distant locations of units involved in generating troops for operations against Ukraine was simply a result of the military planners' desire to 'train' troops in combat environments at

---

[65] *EurAsia Daily*, 'Azerbaydzhan zapretil rossiyskomu "Ruslanu" prolet cherez svoe vozdushnoe prostranstvo [Azerbaijan Bans Russian "Ruslan" Flight via its Airspace]', 18 November 2015, <https://eadaily.com/ru/news/2015/11/18/azerbaydzhan-zapretil-rossiyskomu-ruslanu-prolet-cherez-svoe-vozdushnoe-prostranstvo>, accessed 8 August 2016.

[66] For instance, a company-size detachment of professionals – missile specialists of the 536th Coastal Defence Missile Brigade were ordered in late January 2015 to the 61st Marine Brigade to serve as marines with the 61st's battalion tactical group heading for Ukraine; on another occasion, in summer 2014, a similar detachment of the 536th brigade was dispatched to the 61st with the same purpose. Vladimir Dergachev, Denis Telmanov and Andrey Vinokurov, '"Tam russkie gibnut, vy dolzhny ikh zaschischat" ["Russians are Dying There, You must Protect Them"]', *Gazeta.ru* [*Gazette.ru*], 13 February 2015, <https://www.gazeta.ru/politics/2015/02/11_a_6408545.shtml>, accessed 21 March 2017.

[67] See, for instance, Evgeniy Alekseev, 'Voprosy optimizatsii organizatsionno-shtatnoy struktury obshevoyskovykh podrazdeleniy [Questions about the Organisational Structure of the Optimisation of Combined Arms Military Units]', *Voennoe obozrenie* [*Military Review*], 21 May 2014, <https://topwar.ru/index.php?newsid=48266>, accessed 19 October 2016.

every opportunity. That motivation was certainly a factor, as confirmed by the use of Ukraine as a proving ground for EW and artillery units. However, observed changes in units' deployment patterns, as well as reported difficulties with manning units dispatched for deployment in or near Ukraine, suggest that this was not the only reason for the involvement of such distant units.

During the early stages of the operation against Ukraine in spring 2014, the units permanently located in the Southern and Western MDs generated BTGrs.[68] However, they were able to supply smaller company tactical groups only during autumn and especially winter.[69] At the same time as the Southern and Western MDs were reaching a point where they could no longer generate battalion-level forces, Siberian units were ordered to generate larger formations than BTGrs for service in the operation against Ukraine. For example, the 5th Tank Brigade's contribution was of nearly regimental size, with tank, motorised infantry and artillery battalions, plus additional smaller combat support units.[70] The timing suggests that large demands were placed on distant units due to a shortage of manpower in the Western and Southern MDs after several months of operations.

Furthermore, the Siberian units were transported to the Ukrainian theatre with their own organic weapon systems and heavy equipment, rather than relying on pre-positioned hardware as the reformed strategic mobility doctrine would normally dictate. This is likely to have been the result of a shortage of military hardware stocks in the BKhiRVTs and armament storage sites near Ukraine due to the existing distribution of strategic reserves on Russian territory, which forced the Ministry of Defence to depart from its planned logistics framework to maintain a supply of fresh units for combat operations. It could also be evidence of another limitation of the new logistics construct, which does not include the assumption that distant units were incorporated into an operation simply to provide them with combat experience. In addition, although doctrinally the concept of pre-positioning equipment at BKhiRVTs should

---

[68] *Podrobnosti.ua [Details.ua]*, 'Podgotovka k proryvu: chem opasny udarnye bataljony Rossii [Preparation for Breakthrough: What is the Russian Shock Battalions' Danger]', 21 January 2015, <http://podrobnosti.ua/1012254-batalonno-takticheskie-gruppy-rossii.html>, accessed 21 March 2017.
[69] Igor Sutyagin, 'Russian Forces in Ukraine'.
[70] *Tsenzor.net [Censor.net]*, 'Podrobnosti perebroski iz Buryatii 5-y tankovoy brigady rostovskoy gruppirovki sil vtorzheniya. Fotoreportazh [Details of Movement of the Rostov Invasion Force Grouping's 5th Tank Brigade from Buryatiya. Picture Story]', 25 November 2014, <http://censor.net.ua/photo_news/313485/podrobnosti_perebroski_iz_buryatii_5yi_tankovoyi_brigady_rostovskoyi_gruppirovki_sil_vtorjeniya_fotoreportaj>, accessed 21 March 2017.

have allowed units from distant bases to use hardware stored in Western Russia, the lack of standardised equipment across the Russian land forces means that units based in Siberia, for example, are mostly untrained in the types of equipment stockpiled in the Western and Southern MDs. Since distant units' organic equipment often differs substantially from the variants stockpiled at BKhiRVTs in other parts of Russia, the pre-positioning logistics concept is often of only limited practical value in the Russian land forces' current circumstances. Using unfamiliar equipment in a combat zone would put troops at greater risk, reduce their combat effectiveness and limit the training benefits in relation to their regular deployment location and role.[71]

The reportedly widespread practice of generating new 'professional troops' from unwitting conscripts is another key indicator of the capacity of Russia's land forces to sustain an operational commitment on the scale of the Ukrainian conflict.[72] Since Russian law prohibits conscripts from participating in combat during peacetime, but professional soldiers cannot refuse orders to do so, many conscripts were forced to sign professional contracts so that they could be sent to Ukraine.[73] On several occasions, conscripts have been fraudulently converted to professional status, sometimes after being recorded as 'expressing a desire to become professionals'.[74] It has even been reported that commanders forged contracts, signing them without conscripts' knowledge.[75] There have also been reports of the intimidation of Russian military personnel to pressure them into 'volunteering' for covert combat in eastern Ukraine, alongside rebel forces.[76] Such oppressive activities undoubtedly have a deleterious

---

[71] For a discussion of problems related to the practical implementation of 'pre-positioning', see, for instance, Sutyagin, 'Russia's Overestimated Military Might'.
[72] Reports on conscripts being forced to sign contracts for professional service came from the provinces (*Oblast*) of Kostroma, Kursk, Leningrad, Murmansk, Nizhniy-Novgorod, Tula, and from several locations in Siberia. See Lyudmila Vakhnina, 'Prinuditelniy kontrakt vernulsya [Forced Sign-up for Professional Service is Back]', *Ezhednevniy zhurnal* [*Daily Journal*], 11 February 2015, <ej.ru/?a=note&id=27066>, accessed 8 August 2016.
[73] *Ibid.*
[74] *Voennoe.rf* [*Military.rf*], 'V odnoy iz chastey ZVO izobreli nou-khau po sozdaniyu lipovykh kontraktnikov [Know-how on How to Generate Fake Professionals is Invented at One of the Western Military District's Units]', 11 March 2015, <http://военное.рф/2015/СлужбаПоКонтракту15/>, accessed 8 August 2016.
[75] *Boshsoz.com*, 'Trebuyutsya kontraktniki. Srochno [Urgent: Professionals Wanted]', 4 February 2015, <http://boshsoz.com/novosti/33377-soldat-srochnikov-zastavlyayut-podpisy-vat-kontrakty>, accessed 8 August 2016; Vakhnina, 'Prinuditelniy kontrakt vernulsya [Forced Sign-up for Professional Service is Back]'.
[76] Maksim Solopov, 'Sluzhba ponevole: kak srochnikam navyazyvayut kontrakt i poezdku pod Rostov [Forced Service: How Conscripts are Forced to Sign Contracts

effect on the morale of Russian troops, as well as being a strong indicator that shortage of manpower, rather than the interests of troops' combat training, was a key driver of such measures.

The reported deployment of the Russian Guards' Detached Division (special purpose; known as the Dzerzhinskiy division), and other Russian Guards' units as 'barrier squads' in Ukraine is further evidence of serious morale problems.[77] These 'punitive action' or 'anti-retreat' troops operated behind the lines of rebel forces and Russian regular troops, and were reportedly deployed in the northern part of rebel-controlled territory near Debaltsevo and near Mariupol in the south. On numerous occasions, detachments of the Dzerzhinskiy division were reported to have undertaken punitive action against retreating rebels and regular Russian troops.[78]

The need for drastic measures, including converting conscripts to professional contracts against their will and using punitive action forces to deal with retreating troops, highlights the serious problems experienced by Russia during the operation against Ukraine, with manpower shortages and poor morale among Russian troops and Russia-controlled rebel forces. Combined, these factors are compelling evidence that despite deep and ongoing reforms, Russia's land forces did not find it easy to sustain the operation on the scale required in Ukraine during the heaviest phases of operations from 2014 to late 2015.

---

and Go to Rostov]', *RBC.ru*, 3 February 2015, <http://top.rbc.ru/politics/03/02/2015/ 54cfa2519a79477e6df87cc4>, accessed 21 March 2017.

[77] *Crime: Archive*, 'Kapkan zakhlopnulsya. Za spinoy okkupantov i terroristov vystroilis putinskie zagradotryady [The Trap Snapped Shut: Putin's Barrier Squads Lined Up Behind Occupants and Terrorists]', 31 January 2015, <http://crime.in.ua/ node/8250>, accessed 9 December 2016; *Crime*, 'Okkupanty demoralizovany. Iz Rossii na Donbass perebrasyvayut zagradotryady [Occupants Demoralised: Barrier Squads Relocated from Russia to Donbass]', 13 March 2016, <http://crime-ua.com/ node/14455>, accessed 9 December 2016.

[78] See, for instance, *Glavred*, 'Begstvo boevikov i 'kazachkov' iz-pod Uglegorska ostanavlivali zagradotryady rossiyskikh 'politsaev' [Russian Police Barrier Squads Stopping Flight of Rebels and "Cossacks" from Uglegorsk]', 3 February 2016, <http://glavred.info/politika/begstvo-boevikov-i-kazachkov-iz-pod-uglegorska- ostanavlivali-zagradotryady-mvd-rossii-301919.html>, accessed 11 December 2016.

II. EQUIPMENT, ORGANISATIONAL AND DOCTRINAL REFORMS OF LAND FORCES

Reinforcing the combat potential of Russia's land forces is a central component of Moscow's military reform programme. The equipment, organisational structures and doctrine of the various unit types that make up Russia's land forces are being upgraded to better meet the requirements of modern warfare and to provide the muscle behind Russian foreign policy. The restoration and expansion of combat, combat support and support units are seen as a critical element that can provide a force multiplier effect for Russian forces' combat potential as a whole. This chapter provides an overview of these efforts and their progress.

Combined Arms Manoeuvre Forces

The rapid establishment of new formations to fill gaps in the structure of combined arms armies is the most striking organisational development in the Russian land forces since 2013. The discrepancy between the standard structure required to allow armies to achieve full combat efficiency and the formations actually available has been the central difficulty confronting the Russian military since the current reform programme began in 2008. It is generally accepted in the Russian military that each of its armies must have the *armeyskiy komplekt* ('army set') of organic fires, combat support and support formations to fulfil its operational tasks. The army set is meant to include command and control, reconnaissance, artillery, rocket artillery, missile, air-defence and logistics brigades, as well as engineer-sapper, pontoon-bridge, chemical, biological, radiological and nuclear (CBRN) and helicopter regiments.[1] However, none but the 58th

---

[1] Alexey Ramm, 'Reformy i rezultaty [Reforms and Results]', *Novosti VPK* [*News of the Military-Industrial Complex*], 23 December 2015, <http://vpk.name/news/146871_reformyi_i_rezultatyi.html>, accessed 20 October 2016; see also *Livejournal*,

Army in the Russian land forces has a full standard set of these brigades and regiments yet.

This problem is not critical if a large-scale conflict is not expected for the foreseeable future. After all, army-level deployments are only militarily required in the event of high-end, state-on-state warfare. It is, therefore, significant that the Russian political-military leadership continues to dedicate substantial financial and material resources to the goal of equipping all Russian armies with the necessary brigades and regiments to meet the army set requirements in full. This effort is aimed at strengthening the much-needed military muscle of foreign policy to compensate for Russia's weaknesses in other areas, and it is also a salve for the self-fulfilling paranoia of the Russian leadership. While a desire to have a fully fledged military structure in place before a critical shortage of financial resources strikes Russia in the near future is probably the main driving force behind the rush to establish new army set formations, it is an unavoidable conclusion that this activity also bears all the hallmarks of hurried preparations for a full-scale war. Other characteristics of Russian land forces' organisational and doctrinal changes do nothing to diminish that perception.

In terms of the core armoured firepower and manoeuvre units, the Russian military envisages substantial doctrinal changes in terms of combined arms tactics with the large-scale introduction into service of the Armata family of armoured combat and support vehicles. Despite popular perceptions, Armata is not just Russia's new main battle tank (MBT), but a heavily armoured chassis with an integrated combat information management and control system that can be equipped with different mission-fit modules to fill a variety of roles. Armata is the family name for a series of modular, tracked, heavy-armoured vehicles, of which the T-14 next-generation MBT (which also carries the Armata name as its specific designator) is the leading member. All vehicles in the Armata family are based on the TUGP (*Tyazhyolaya Universalnaya Gusenichnaya Platforma*) Armata heavy universal tracked platform. Various unmanned combat and service modules installed on to the TUGP chassis result in different types of combat, combat support and support vehicles. Personnel are always contained within the body of the TUGP, and are thus provided with protection equal to that of the world's best MBTs. This in itself will greatly increase the survivability of Russian military personnel on the modern battlefield.

'Brigada razvedki v Korenovske [Reconnaissance Brigade in Korenovsk]', 10 March 2016, <http://twower.livejournal.com/1921611.html>, accessed 20 October 2016.

Flexibility is the basis of the 28 combat and support vehicle variants that make up the Armata family. The philosophy behind the design is to equip units with highly survivable standardised vehicles of all necessary types, ranging from combat vehicles, such as the MBT (T-14 Armata) and the infantry fighting vehicle (IFV; T-15 Bagulnik), combat support vehicles – such as self-propelled guns, multiple-launch rocket systems, and heavy flamethrowers – to support vehicles, such as combat repair and recovery vehicles (T-16), ammunition transporter and minelaying variants, among others. The standardisation of the chassis means units can operate with a mix of vehicles relevant to the situation without operational effectiveness being impeded by differences in mobility and protection. If vehicles used different chassis, it would be difficult to maintain a unit's formation and cohesion in battle because of the vehicles' differing ability to negotiate terrain and hostile fire, thus diluting the punch of an armoured formation.

Armata is the conceptual equivalent of the US Stryker family of modular armoured vehicles. Discussions are already under way in Russian military circles about standardising the hardware of Armata-equipped units to form a single Armata-only structure, thus eliminating vehicle diversity. The fundamental difference between Stryker and Armata, however, is that the former is a family of light-armoured vehicles, while the latter are heavy-armoured vehicles. Due to the high battlefield survivability of Armata vehicles, Armata units would be more difficult to counter and, therefore, more suitable for offensive operations than their Western equivalents. But they would suffer the same drawbacks in terms of logistical requirements and deployability over long distances as heavy-armoured formations in any army. If a conflict occurs close to Russian territory, the BKhiRVT network could significantly alleviate these difficulties by making large stocks of spare vehicles, parts and other pre-positioned equipment available relatively close to the combat zone. This would work providing that the opponent is not NATO in a full-scale war, which could target the BKhiRVTs behind the main lines of engagement. Recognition of this fact by the Russian political-military leadership explains Moscow's nervous reaction to NATO's gradual military build-up in the Baltic States, and its aggressive opposition to the prospect of NATO enlargement closer to Russian soil – as in Georgia and Finland.

Studies into the optimal structures for battalion- and lower-level tactical groups, as well as concepts for their combat employment and resupply, have been under way in the Russian military since 2014. This work is motivated by the widespread conclusion that the existing tactical structures of Russian tank and motor-rifle elements are inadequate to meet the requirements of modern warfare or to make the best use of modern weaponry's combat potential. The need to develop new tactical structures is, therefore, widely recognised.[2]

The idea is that future units will be composed of 'combat modules' integrated at the lowest possible level. These will allow a combination of fighting, fire support and support vehicles in a single fighting formation, rather than relying on standard motor-rifle and/or tank companies and platoons. The composition of these modules would differ depending on the tactical environment – the tactical requirements of fighting in urban areas differ greatly from those in open steppes, for example. However, one variant of a typical unit composition currently being considered includes one or two T-14 MBTs, two or three T-15 heavy IFVs, one fire-support vehicle with the AU-220M Baikal 57-mm automatic cannon module for both battlefield fire support and air defence, one heavy assault fire support vehicle with a low-velocity 152-mm gun, one command-and-control vehicle, and one combat supply vehicle. All these vehicles will be designed around the common Armata chassis.[3] It is also planned to equip the T-15 IFVs and/or Armata command-and-control vehicles with miniature, short-range UAVs as a core element of their standard weapons/equipment to give units an integrated combined arms, distributed sensor-shooter combat capability.

The transition from current tactical structures to that outlined above should allow a reduction in manpower at unit level – not an insignificant benefit for the Russian military. It is estimated that the number of personnel in a generic combat module would be around 70–110 men, with combat potential advertised as equivalent to a full modern motor-rifle battalion (which currently requires up to 600 personnel). In other words, the manpower needed for motor-rifle battalion level capabilities would be less than that currently required for a company tactical group of around 150 men.[4]

Experimenting with combat modules has been common practice on an ad hoc basis in the Soviet and Russian military for a long time. For example, in Chechnya between 1994 and the early 2000s, tactical groups consisting of one or two MBTs, up to three IFVs, one or two ZSU-23-4

[2] Timur Alimov, 'Stalo izvestno o skrytykh vozmozhnostyakh Armaty [Armata's Hidden Capabilities become Known]', *Russkoey Oruzhie/Rossiyskaya Gazeta* [*Russian Weapons/Russian Gazette*], 28 March 2016, <http://rg.ru/2016/03/28/stalo-izvestno-o-skrytyh-vozmozhnostiah-armaty.html>, accessed 20 October 2016.
[3] Vyacheslav Khalitov and Mikhail Khodarenok, 'Ideologiya boevoy systemy buduschego [Ideology of the Combat System of the Future]', *Novosti VPK* [*News of the Military-Industrial Complex*], 22 July 2016, <http://vpk.name/news/159847_ideologiya_boevoi_sistemyi_budushego.html?new#new>, accessed 20 October 2016.
[4] Alimov, 'Stalo izvestno o skrytykh vozmozhnostyakh Armaty [Armata's Hidden Capabilities become Known]'.

Shilka air-defence vehicles (whose four 23-mm automatic cannons can engage with targets on the upper floors of buildings), and sapper and flamethrower elements, were a common tactic.[5] However, the new combat module tactical structure is different. First, incorporation of the various elements will be more formalised, which should lead to higher unit cohesion in combat. Second, the new units will have a higher and homogenous level of armour protection for all sub-elements due to the common Armata chassis, as well as a higher readiness level associated with greater equipment commonality.

Another interesting new idea under discussion is the establishment of additional rotational tank crews for the new-generation MBTs.[6] While breakdowns, availability of spare parts and fuels, for example, all affect MBT availability, crew endurance is the primary limiting factor. A combination of these factors means that combat-ready MBTs are sitting idle between 40 and 60 per cent of the time. Having additional crews to rotate in shifts around the clock could significantly improve every tank's combat output – and the overall efficiency of investments in land forces.[7] However, the current chronic undermanning issues affecting the Russian military make this policy an aspiration at best.

Measures are also being undertaken to improve the combat effectiveness of existing tactical structures. For example, analysis by Russian armour specialists revealed that training for current Russian tank crews was inadequate; the standard 1,600–1,800-metre engagement range that gunners were trained to achieve was too short for crews to perform effectively in one-on-one engagements with enemy tanks. As a result, in 2014, training standards were changed to include the engagement of armoured targets at a distance of 2,200 metres.[8] There is also a greater emphasis on individual vehicles, rather than unit-level manoeuvres on the battlefield, on one-on-one tank engagements, and on revisiting proven but neglected tactics, such as tank ambushes.[9] For motor-rifle sections

---

[5] Khalitov and Khodarenok, 'Ideologiya boevoy systemy buduschego [Ideology of the Combat System of the Future]'.

[6] Alimov, 'Stalo izvestno o skrytykh vozmozhnostyakh Armaty [Armata's Hidden Capabilities become Known]'.

[7] *Ibid.*

[8] *ProGorod [AboutTown]*, 'Nizhegorodskie tankisty ZVO osvoyat bolee slozhnuyu programmu boevoy podgotovki [Western MD Tank Personnel from Nizhniy Novgorod will Master the New More Complicated Training Programme]', 21 January 2014, <http://progorodnn.ru/news/view/81632>, accessed 20 October 2016.

[9] Voenvideo [MilitaryVideo], 'Motostrelki YuVO uchatsya otrazhat nastuplenie vtroe prevoskhodyaschikh sil uslovnogo protivnika [Southern MD's Infantrymen Train to Repel Offensive of Three-times Superior Imitated Adversary]', 17 April 2013, <http://www.voenvideo.ru/news/motostrelki_juvo_uchatsja_otrazhat_nastuplenie_

fighting from individual IFV vehicles, preparedness to fight while being attacked from several different directions has also been a useful addition to core training.

The planned introduction of a UAV company as an organic element in every Russian motor-rifle, tank, reconnaissance and Spetsnaz brigade should substantially improve the situational awareness and EW capabilities of Russian forces. A UAV company for a motor-rifle brigade is equipped with three different types of drone. The Orlan-10 is designed to locate enemy command posts within a radius of 120 km by detecting and tracking their radio emissions, and can also carry day/night optical sensors. With the alternative Leer-3 payload, it is capable of emulating the base stations of and subsequently hijacking control of certain cell-network communications within a radius of 6 km. Takhion and Eleron-3, meanwhile, are designed for all-weather reconnaissance.[10] These capabilities provide a step change in tactical-level situational awareness for Russian forces and greatly complicate command and control for opposing forces, as Ukrainian forces have repeatedly discovered.

Russian military involvement in Syria encouraged revisiting the idea of the 'light' motorised brigades envisaged by Serdyukov's reform, but was later abandoned (the 56th Guards Air-Assault Brigade was experimentally reorganised as a 'light' brigade in July 2010, but restored to its previous structure two years later). *Tsentr-2015* (*Centre-2015*) strategic exercises proved that traditional armoured vehicles' mounted motor-rifle brigades are too 'clumsy' for operations in steppe, semi-desert and desert areas where jeep-mounted troops have tactical advantages due to much higher mobility, but it took the Russian political-military leadership one full year of combat operations in Syria to finally move ahead with this idea. Two new 'super-light' brigades will be established, one each in the Southern and Central MDs. These brigades will include: two jeep-mounted battalions (UAZ-3163 jeeps will be equipped to carry either an infantry section of seven soldiers and 12.7-mm machine gun or 30-mm automatic grenade launcher, or an anti-tank guided missile (ATGM) system, or 82-mm mortar); one battalion on BTR-82A armoured personnel carriers (APC); one artillery (with truck-mounted tube artillery systems and Grad MLR systems); and one anti-tank (with ATGM)

---

vtroe_prevoskhodjashhikh_sil_uslovnogo_protivnika/2013-04-17-932>, accessed 21 March 2017.

[10] Russian Ministry of Defence, 'V mirotvorcheskom soedinenii TsVO sformirovana rota bespilotnykh letatelnykh apparatov [UAV Company Established in the Peacekeeping Formation of the Central MD]', 17 December 2014, <http://function. mil.ru/news_page/country/more.htm?id=12003988@egNews>, accessed 21 March 2017.

battalion, plus other elements.[11] One 'super-light' jeep-mounted battalion was included, in order to prove the concept, in the 30th Motor-Rifle Brigade established in the Central MD on 30 November 2016.[12]

Territorial defence units – rear-area guard battalions and divisions (*Divizii Territorialnoy Oborony*, or DTO) – are another type of light-armoured formation being established by the Russian MoD. These parallel the role of the British Army Reserves (with the exception of air defence) but are manned by reservists coming from different, and not necessarily local, areas. The decision to move forward with DTOs seems to be driven by Russia's own experience of irregular warfare in Ukraine and Syria, where tighter control of rear areas proved to be both vital and difficult for armed forces.[13]

Finally, in terms of combined arms manoeuvre forces reforms, broader efforts to improve the tactical mobility of land forces have led to another important structural shift. Plans were set out in 2014 to establish army aviation (helicopter) regiments and brigades, replacing the current structure in which all aviation assets are under the command of the Air-Space Force. Under the new structure, every military district will have an army aviation brigade of 84–88 transport and fire support (gunship) helicopters.[14] Furthermore, every combined arms (and tank) army will have an army aviation regiment (66 helicopters) under its command. In 2014, these changes amounted to the establishment of four army aviation brigades and ten army aviation regiments;[15] the number of regiments will probably increase to twelve to equip the two new armies which have been established since then. It is also noteworthy that both brigades and

---

[11] Aleksey Ramm, 'Minoborony formiruet sverkhlegkie brigady [Ministry of Defence Establishes Super-light Brigades]', *Izvestiya*, 21 October 2016, <izvestia.ru/news/639226>, accessed 21 March 2017.

[12] *VolgaNjyus* [*VolgaNews*], 'V sostave nedavno sformirovannoy v gubernii motostrelkovoy brigady poyavilsya vysokomobilniy bataljon [High-mobility Battalion Created in the Motor-Rifle Brigade Recently Established in the Province]', 7 December 2016, <http://volga.news/article/426698.html>, accessed 12 December 2016; *VolgaNjyus* [*VolgaNews*], 'Samarskikh motostrelkov vooruzhat RSZO «Grad» [Samara Motor-Riflemen to be Armed with "Grad" Rocket Artillery System]', 8 December 2016, <http://volga.news/article/426848.html>, accessed 12 December 2016.

[13] Aleksey Ramm, 'V Krymu sozdali diviziyu dlya borby s diversantamy [Division to Fight Saboteurs Established in Crimea]', *Izvestiya*, 15 September 2016, <http://izvestia.ru/news/632465>, accessed 30 November 2016.

[14] *Vzglyad* [*Look*], 'V VVS Rossii resheno sformirovat 14 brigad armeyskoy aviatsii i vertoletnykh polkov [Russian Air Force to Establish 14 Army Aviation Brigades and Helicopter Regiments]', 26 July 2014, <http://vz.ru/news/2014/7/26/697375.html>, accessed 20 October 2016.

[15] *Ibid.*

regiments of this type will include one EW helicopter section of four Mi-8MTPS or Mi-8MTPR-1 aircraft.

Airborne Troops

Russia's airborne troops (*Vozdushno-Desantnye Voiska*, or VDV) – the separate branch of the armed forces directly subordinated to the General Staff – are the Supreme Commander's ultimate reserve for decisive response in rapidly changing operational situations. The necessity of such a role has been proven by the experience of Russia's operation in Ukraine. The VDV proved to be the force that was the most agile and professional and capable of delivering heavy blows at short notice during the conventional stage of the conflict (bearing in mind that Spetsnaz is destined for *non*-conventional tasks).

Recognition of the VDV's value led to the decision in 2014 to expand – rather than to halve, as was previously envisaged – the VDV, doubling their manpower from 36,000 to 72,000 uniformed servicemen by the end of 2017.[16] This was to have been achieved via the reintroduction of the previously disbanded third air-assault regiments into Russia's two air-assault divisions (which currently have two regiments each), as well as re-establishment of the 31st Detached Guards Air-Assault Brigade as the 104th Guards Air-Assault Division with three air-assault regiments in its structure. (The 31st Guards was the 104th Guards Airborne Division until 1998, when it was downgraded to a brigade.) The establishment of the 345th Detached Guards Air-Assault Brigade was planned for 2016 in Voronezh well before the events in Ukraine,[17] although this has now been postponed until 2018.

Unlike the situation with the re-establishment of Ground Troops divisions, the VDV HQ is taking a prudent approach to the task of expanding air-assault formations: re-establishment of the third regiments will happen as personnel become available, to avoid the creation of hollow units.[18] However, the economic situation in Russia is impeding the VDV's ambitious expansion plans. The establishment of the third

---

[16] Aleksey Nikolskiy 'Minoborony sobiraetsya udvoit chislennost Vozdushno-desantnykh voysk [Ministry of Defence to Double the Manpower of the Airborne Troops]', *Vedomosti* [*Statements*], 7 August 2014, <http://www.vedomosti.ru/politics/articles/2014/08/07/udvoenie-vdv>, accessed 12 January 2016.

[17] *TASS*, 'Novaya desantno-shturmovaya brigada VDV budet sformirovana v 2016 godu v Voronezhe [New Air-Assault Brigade of the Airborne Troops to be Established in 2016 in Voronezh]', 8 October 2013, <http://tass.ru/politika/687573>, accessed 12 January 2016.

[18] *TASS*, 'VDV mogut razvernut desantno-shturmovoy polk v Krymu [Airborne Troops Might Establish an Air-Assault Regiment in Crimea]', 30 July 2015, <http://tass.ru/armiya-i-opk/2153398>, accessed 12 January 2016.

regiments was postponed in early 2016 to after 2020; the VDV's overall target manpower was also revised down from 72,000 to 60,000.[19]

Air-assault, not traditional airborne, formations are the focus of the VDV as they are better suited to mobile infantry operations in Russia's near abroad. This reveals Moscow's preference for units capable of both dynamic defence and rapid offensive operations to create favourable conditions on the ground wherever required. The VDV have undergone doctrinal and structural changes. Their combat tasks have been expanded to reflect the modern reality that they are required to carry out some functions of regular ground troops under certain circumstances. For the first time in their history, VDV units have given up their determination to be fully air transportable and introduced MBTs – organised in tank companies, with planned expansion to tank battalions – into their air-assault formations. The change, which was accepted by the VDV high command in early 2015 as a result of experience in eastern Ukraine,[20] was deemed necessary due to the determination of the VDV to retain its new role as the spearhead of the Kremlin military machine. This role requires the capability to deliver a very heavy blow when the situation demands it.

Six new tank companies for the VDV were announced in May 2015. Two are likely to be expanded to battalion size by the end of 2018 and incorporated into the 76th Guards Air-Assault Division and the re-established 104th Guards Air-Assault Division.[21] The other four will be incorporated into four air-assault brigades[22] (one of which – the 31st Guards – is planned for expansion to division size in the near future). The 7th Guards Air-Assault Division will not receive tanks as it operates in mountainous areas.

---

[19] *TASS*, 'Istochnik: Rossiya na postoyannoy osnove razvernet bataljon VDV v Krymu v 2017-2018 godakh [Source: Russia to Establish an Airborne Battalion in Crimea in 2017–2018]', 18 February 2016, <http://tass.ru/armiya-i-opk/2677585>, accessed 13 December 2016.

[20] Aleksandr Staver, 'Zachem VDV bronevoy kulak – o zayavlenii komanduyuschego VDV RF [Why Do Airborne Troops Need an Armoured Fist? On the Russian Airborne Troops Commander's Statement]', *Voennoe obozrenie* [*Military Review*], 18 May 2016, <https://topwar.ru/95400-zachem-vdv-bronevoy-kulak-o-zayavlenii-komanduyuschego-vdv-rf.html>, accessed 20 October 2016.

[21] *Ibid.*

[22] Sergey Ishchenko, 'Tankovaya ataka generala Shamanova [General Shamanov's Tank Attack]', *Svobodnaya Pressa* [*Free Press*], 17 May 2016, <http://svpressa.ru/war21/article/148675/>, accessed 20 October 2016. The establishment of six tank companies has been announced; meanwhile, there are just two air-assault divisions. This implies that four more formations – which are inevitably air-assault brigades – will also receive tanks; see Staver, 'Zachem VDV bronevoy kulak – o zayavlenii komanduyuschego VDV RF [Why Do Airborne Troops Need an Armoured Fist? On the Russian Airborne Troops Commander's Statement]'.

These tank elements of air-assault formations will be equipped with the latest T-72B3M version of the venerable T-72 MBT, modified for VDV use.[23] A few senior airborne commanders have claimed that there are plans to equip formations with Armata-family tanks, but that seems to be an exaggeration. Taken as a whole, this plan will eventually generate six tank battalions/companies for the 76th and 104th Guards Air-Assault Divisions, as well as the 11th, 56th, 83rd and 345th Guards Air-Assault Brigades, with a total of 192–246 MBTs. This will enable Russia's air-assault formations to deliver a much heavier blow than currently possible.

This capability is being enhanced by the introduction into service of the heavily armed BMD-4M airborne combat vehicle (ACV), which carries a large 2A70 100-mm gun missile launcher paired with a coaxial 2A72 30-mm automatic cannon. As an interim measure, and to hurriedly improve the firepower of the two air-assault brigades deployed in the far east of Russia near the Chinese border (the 11th Guards and the 83rd Guards), these formations are taking delivery of BMP-2 IFVs,[24] which have better combat characteristics than the obsolete BMD-1 ACVs and BTR-80 APC, which the brigades had until recently. Taken together, these changes are evidence of the doctrinal transformation of Russian air-assault formations into a cross-breed between traditional air-assault and rapid-reaction infantry formations.

Radical expansion of the intelligence, surveillance and reconnaissance (ISR) capabilities of airborne and air-assault formations and elements is also under way. The introduction of reconnaissance battalions, expanded from the detached reconnaissance companies currently subordinated to brigades and divisions, has finally been set in motion as a result of experience gained during Russian operations in eastern Ukraine. One company in each new reconnaissance battalion will carry out diversionary reconnaissance actions (known as 'special reconnaissance', a term that has a different meaning in Russian military vocabulary than in Western), which means it will be a 'special purposes reconnaissance element', otherwise known as Spetsnaz (*razvedyvatelniye chasti SPETSialnogo NAZnacheniya*).

Until recently, the VDV were the only branch of the Russian armed forces that had an integral Spetsnaz unit formation – the 45th Guards Spetsnaz Regiment – before it was expanded to form the 45th Guards

---

[23] Ishchenko, 'Tankovaya ataka generala Shamanova [General Shamanov's Tank Attack]'.
[24] Aleksandr Staver and Roman Skomorokhov, 'O buduschem VDV [On the Future of the Airborne Troops]', *Voennoe obozrenie* [*Military Review*], 2 August 2016, <https://topwar.ru/98736-o-buduschem-vdv.html>, accessed 20 August 2016.

Spetsnaz Brigade as a result of the lessons learned in Ukraine. The brigade's ability to operate in three independent operational areas, instead of the regiment's two, was the immediate result of this structural change. These reforms – ISR units attached to brigades and divisions and the establishment of the 45th Guards Spetsnaz Brigade – triple the number of Spetsnaz companies in the VDV from six to eighteen.

The widespread introduction of reconnaissance UAVs for use by airborne and air-assault formations is another improvement to unit-level ISR capabilities as a result of experience gained in Ukraine. All reconnaissance units and elements will have drone elements/sub-elements in their structure. This also applies to the reconnaissance companies that are being established in every airborne/air-assault battalion in place of their corresponding 'A' companies (1st companies in Russian military jargon).

The decision to run all airborne formations through Arctic training to ensure they are capable of operating under such conditions is another doctrinal change for the VDV. Formations have traditionally been anchored to certain operational areas to sharpen operational skills for a specific environment. The decision to make all airborne formations Arctic-capable further signals the shift towards a more universal 'fire fighting' quick-reaction force role for these elite formations. It is also an indication of the General Staff's evolving plans for the defence of the Russian segment of the Arctic, which is discussed in more detail in Chapter III. Of further concern to military planners is the training of three regular airborne battalions to utilise the Arbalet-2 long-range, covert insertion parachute system, as well as universal training of airborne formations for landing on water (of particular value for taking islands in the Baltic Sea).[25]

Finally, it is worth noting that, of all branches of the Russian Ground Troops, the VDV have made the best progress in reorganising for network-centric combat operations. The Andromeda-D digital command-and-control system designed to VDV requirements has proved more successful than the problematic Sozvezdie-M2 equivalent used by the land forces. Sozvezdie is still struggling to achieve initial operational capability after many years of development and trials, while Andromeda-D is in service with Russian airborne formations as a standard feature.

---

[25] Anton Mardasov, 'VDV gotovyat massovuyu ataku novogo tipa [Airborne Troops Prepare Massive Attack of Innovative Type]', *Svobodnaya pressa* [*Free Press*], 29 December 2016, <http://svpressa.ru/war21/article/163448/>, accessed 21 March 2017.

Reconnaissance Units

The role of reconnaissance units in the Russian land forces differs from that of the British Army's ISR brigade. Russian units are a source of information for further analysis by higher headquarters and their intelligence elements, rather than integrated information-gathering and processing bodies.[26] Russian reconnaissance units are, therefore, better understood as a cross-breed between the US Army's reconnaissance, surveillance and target acquisition and long-range surveillance (LRS) elements in doctrinal terms.

At the same time, some specialist Russian reconnaissance units are tasked with 'special reconnaissance' – a combination of reconnaissance and target acquisition; and diversion actions ('direct actions' in NATO parlance) deep behind the forward line of troops (FLOT) in enemy rear areas against high-value targets. In this role, the Russian 'special reconnaissance' units perform a function similar to that of the British 22nd SAS Regiment. Units involved in these reconnaissance activities are formally referred to as 'special purpose reconnaissance units' or Spetsnaz. It is the obligatory doctrinal and operational element of direct action that differentiates Spetsnaz from 'regular' reconnaissance units/elements. Spetsnaz formations (except VDV Spetsnaz) are currently subordinated to the Chief Intelligence Directorate (recently renamed the Chief Intelligence Directorate for secrecy reasons) or the 2nd Chief Directorate of the General Staff. Spetsnaz operate deeper behind the FLOT in enemy territory in their reconnaissance and target-acquisition missions than US Army LRS units.

Experience gained during the conflict in eastern Ukraine has provided Russian military planners with plenty of evidence of the need to expand and improve all reconnaissance capabilities. The establishment and/or preservation of reconnaissance brigades in Russian combined arms armies is one of the first and most visible results. Former Minister of Defence Anatoliy Serdyukov considered establishing such brigades, which would be roughly equivalent to the US Army's 1st Armoured Cavalry Regiment (with several substantial differences that are discussed later in this paper), between 2009 and 2011, but the idea was met with hostility from most of the Russian military establishment. The only brigade established according to Serdyukov's plan was the 100th Detached Reconnaissance Brigade (Experimental) in the Southern MD in 2009; it was the target of constant attacks from the district's command and was on the verge of being disbanded by early 2013.

---

[26] See British Army, 'Intelligence Corps Role', <https://www.army.mod.uk/intelligence/32235.aspx>, accessed 12 January 2016.

Experience gained in Ukraine since February 2014 ended Russia's doubts about the need for dedicated reconnaissance brigades and their utility in combat, especially in operational scenarios short of open war. As a result, the long-delayed process of establishing reconnaissance brigades was resumed with the establishment of the 127th Detached Reconnaissance Brigade in Crimea in late 2014 and the 96th Detached Reconnaissance Brigade in Nizhniy Novgorod in late December 2015. Other brigades are expected for every Russian army.

Russian military thinkers have considered 'special reconnaissance' actions an increasingly important form of combat operations since the early 2000s.[27] 'Reconnaissance combat actions' is the term used to describe the activity of reconnaissance teams that look for targets of opportunity in an adversary's rear areas and destroy them.[28] This has become a dominant form of combat in eastern Ukraine in the periods between full-scale battles. The high density of Spetsnaz unit deployments during the preparatory stage of Russia's military incursions into Ukraine is evidence of the value placed on this form of warfare by the Russian military command (Figure 6).

Experience gained in Ukraine has been thoroughly incorporated into Russian military structures. As part of this process, Spetsnaz elements (those tasked for reconnaissance-diversion and reconnaissance-combat actions) have been widely introduced into the ground and airborne unit structures, as previously discussed. The decision to proceed with establishing reconnaissance brigades was also partly influenced by the recognition of the value of Spetsnaz troops, with every detached reconnaissance brigade benefiting from a Spetsnaz battalion as part of its permanent strength. As well as expanding a formation's combat capabilities due to the ability of the Spetsnaz elements to carry out reconnaissance-combat actions ahead of the FLOT, introducing Spetsnaz elements into brigade and division units improves the formation's situational awareness, especially in relation to the enemy's deep and rear areas.

The inclusion of a PsyOps (psychological operations) element in reconnaissance brigades is another distinctive feature that sets them apart from their US and British equivalents, and the importance and operational utility of these operations have also been demonstrated by events in eastern Ukraine. The decision to proceed with the full-scale introduction of reconnaissance brigades, including PsyOps elements, into the structure of combined arms armies is evidence of the importance attached to

---

[27] Vadim Udmantsev, 'Chto znachit razvedka dlya rossiyskogo desanta [The Role of Reconnaissance for Russian Paratroopers]', *Segodnya.ru* [*Today.ru*], 30 April 2009, <http://www.segodnia.ru/content/17940>, accessed 12 January 2016.

[28] *Ibid.*

Figure 6: Deployment of Spetsnaz Units during the Early Stage of the Russian Operation against Ukraine

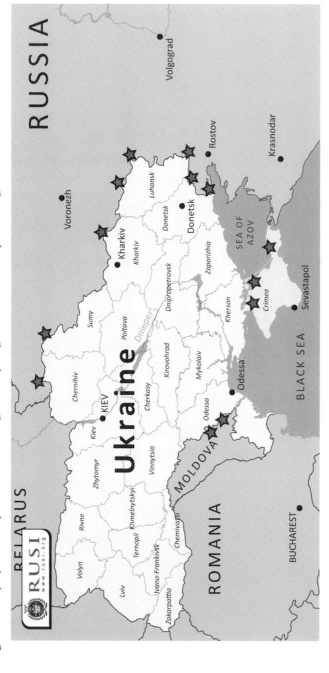

Source: Sutyagin and Clarke, 'Ukraine Military Dispositions'.
Each star represents a Spetsnaz battalion (*otdelniy otryad SpN*)

PsyOps as a core military task by Russian political–military planners. These additional capabilities of Russian reconnaissance brigades, and especially the PsyOps elements, tailored around establishing and controlling insurgent groups within enemy territory, as seen in the Ukrainian rebel provinces of Donestk and Luhansk, are evidence of their specifically offensive strategic role.

The evolution of Russia's land forces structure involves more than establishing reconnaissance brigades in combined arms armies. The reconnaissance companies of Russian combined arms brigades and divisions – as well as airborne and air-assault companies – are being expanded to full reconnaissance battalions. The first companies of these new reconnaissance battalions are being retrained to become Spetsnaz companies such as in their VDV counterparts. Once this is accomplished, every brigade or divisional commander will have an organic subordinated Spetsnaz company at his disposal. To accomplish this major reform, the overall Spetsnaz manpower of Russia's conventional forces (not including Spetsnaz elements of the Strategic Rocket Forces) will be almost doubled by 2018 (see Table 4).

One further change to note, on an issue somewhat removed from direct ground operations, is the transformation of combat divers who were traditionally tasked with defending Russian naval bases against underwater sabotage by US Navy SEALs and British Special Boat Service personnel. They are experimentally tasked with short-range direct action against adjacent shore territories and foreign counter-submersible

Table 4: Russian Special Operations Forces in 2013 and Planned for 2018

	Brigades	Regiments	Battalions	Companies
2013				
GRU	7	1	4	0
Airborne Troops	0	1	0	0
Ground Troops	0	0	1	0
Total	**7**	**2**	**5**	**0**
2018				
GRU	7	1	4	0
Airborne Troops	1	0	0	9
Ground Troops	0	0	12	50
Total	**8**	**1**	**16**	**59**

Source: Igor Sutyagin, 'Russia Confronts NATO: Confidence-destruction Measures', RUSI Briefing Paper, July 2016.

sabotage units; they are also intended to carry out littoral operations, paralleling the US Navy's 'brown water' forces. This is in line with the Russian military leadership's emphasis on Spetsnaz-style actions. Formerly purely defensive units are being converted into defensive-offensive ones in line with Russia's overall military reform ethos. There is a particular relevance to the Ukraine operation in that the first unit to undergo this conversion is what was once the anti-sabotage element of the Black Sea Fleet in Sevastopol (in the vicinity of Ukrainian shores). A unit in the Pacific Fleet is also being reorganised in a similar way.[29]

Missile and Artillery Units

The conflict in eastern Ukraine, and Russia's intervention in the Syrian civil war, have proved to the Russian military leadership the vital role of artillery in modern warfare. Approximately 80 per cent of the casualties on both sides in eastern Ukraine have been caused by artillery fire, illustrating the significant danger of neglecting an adversary's counter-battery fire, as well as the dramatic gains in artillery and counter-artillery effectiveness achievable through introducing reconnaissance UAVs to provide targeting information at unit level.

These lessons have led Russian military planners to focus on three main issues with regard to artillery reforms. First, there has been a relatively straightforward increase in the quantity of artillery for manoeuvre and specialist artillery forces. Russia's Ministry of Defence established several new artillery formations in 2016 alone, including at least one new heavy artillery brigade in Moscow province, and two independent artillery battalions with nuclear-capable artillery systems in the Southern MD. Meanwhile, existing units and formations have been reinforced with deliveries of potent heavy artillery systems that had previously been mothballed in strategic storage facilities.[30] The clear policy is to increase

---

[29] Alexey Mikhailov, 'V rossiyskom Voenno-morskom flote poyavilsya "pribrezhniy spetsnaz" [Coastal Spetsnaz Established in the Russian Navy]', *Izvestiya*, 25 July 2016, <http://izvestia.ru/news/623633>, accessed 20 October 2016.

[30] *Zvezda* [*Star*] (*Russian Ministry of Defence TV*), 'Novaya artilleriyskaya brigada razvernuta v Buryatii [New Artillery Brigade Deployed in Buryatiya]', 2 December 2015, <http://tvzvezda.ru/news/forces/content/201512021044-q8na.htm>, accessed 20 October 2016; *Rambler News Service*, 'Artilleriyskaya brigada v Moskovskoy oblasti poluchila partiyu ustanovok "Uragan" [Artillery Brigade in Moscow Region Gets Delivery of "Uragan" Rocket Systems]', 11 February 2016, <https://rns.online/military/artilleriiskaya-brigada-v-Moskovskoi-oblasti-poluchila-partiyu-ustanovok-Uragan-2016-02-11/>, accessed 20 October 2016; *Voenniy Promyshelennik* [*Military Industrialist*], 'Artilleristy VVO vpervye oprobovali novye SAU 2S7M "Malka" [Central MD's Artillerymen Try 2S7M "Malka" Self-propelled Gun for the First Time]', 4 April 2016, <http://military-industry.ru/artillery/4599>, accessed 20 October 2016;

both the number of artillery systems immediately available to manoeuvre force commanders and the potency of those systems.

Second, high priority is being given to the development of new and the modernisation of existing artillery systems to increase their mobility and improve battlefield survivability. It is planned to increase the mobility of artillery units and elements by replacing towed artillery systems with self-propelled equivalents in all units except for light infantry formations. For example, the new self-propelled 2S35–1 Koalitsiya-SV-KSh automated 152-mm gun-howitzer system[31] is intended to replace the towed 2A65 Msta-B 152-mm gun-howitzers in motor-rifle brigades, as well as potentially equipping air-assault and mountain brigades.[32]

Third, Russian military planners are pursuing measures to increase the firing range of artillery systems to further improve their survivability, flexibility and combat effectiveness. For example, the Koalitsiya-SV can engage targets up to 40 km away, compared to the 24 km maximum range of the Msta-B/Msta-S, which it is replacing. For rocket artillery, improved rockets have increased engagement ranges to 30 km for 122-mm MLR systems (Grad, Tornado-G) and to 120 km for 300-mm systems (Smerch, Tornado-S).[33] For the larger 300-mm systems, there are efforts to develop and field two-stage rockets which will allow engagements at up to 200 km.[34] Russian artillery systems are also being configured to deliver multiple rounds, simultaneous impact (MRSI)

Nikolai Gryshchenko, 'V voyskakh YuVO poyavyatsya gigantskie minomety i mortiry [Southern MD's Troops will be Armed with Gigantic Mortars]', *Rossiyskaya Gazeta* [*Russian Gazette*], 22 September 2016, <https://rg.ru/2016/09/22/reg-ufo/v-vojskah-iuvo-poiaviatsia-gigantskie-minomety-i-mortiry.html>, accessed 20 October 2016.

[31] *Vestnik Mordovii* [*Mordovia's Herald*], 'Kolesnaya 2S35-1 Koalitsiya-SV-KSh popala v Internet? [Has the Wheeled 2S35-1 "Koalitsiya-SV-KSh" Appeared on the Internet?]', 22 June 2016, <http://www.vestnik-rm.ru/news-4-16620.htm>, accessed 20 October 2016.

[32] *Voennaya tekhnika* [*Military Equipment*], 'SAU 2S35 Koalitsiya-SV – 152-mm samokhodnaya gaubitsa [2S35 Koalitsiya-SV – 152-mm Self-propelled Howitzer]', <http://kollektsiya.ru/artilleriya/724-sau-2s35-koalitsiya-sv-152-mm-samokhodnaya-gaubitsa.html>, accessed 20 October 2016.

[33] Up to 40 km for the 9M521 light rocket with increased solid-fuel charge. See *MilitaryArms.ru*, 'RSZO Tornado: opisanie i kharakteristiki [Tornado Multiple-launch Rocket System: Description and Characteristics]', <http://militaryarms.ru/voennaya-texnika/artilleriya/rszo-tornado/>, accessed 20 October 2016.

[34] Evgeniy Damantsev, 'Takticheskie preimuschestva 'gipezvukovogo drona' dlya "Smercha" [Tactical Advantages of the Hypersonic Drone for "Smerch"]', *Voennoe obozrenie* [*Military Review*], 23 October 2015, <https://topwar.ru/84515-prover-takticheskie-preimuschestva-giperzvukovogo-drona-dlya-smercha.html>, accessed 20 October 2016; *MilitaryArms.ru*, 'RSZO Tornado: opisanie i kharakteristiki [Tornado Multiple-launch Rocket System: Description and Characteristics]'.

capabilities in line with the latest NATO howitzer technology. MRSI capabilities contribute substantially to the survivability of artillery systems by reducing the time taken to deliver the necessary number of rounds to a target area and, therefore, reducing the time available for an adversary to react with counter-battery fire.[35] The higher fire rate (reportedly up to sixteen rounds per minute for a single-barrel design) that has been achieved by fully automating the reloading process (the Koalitsiya has an unmanned combat compartment) further contributes to this effect. The Koalitsiya was originally designed as a twin-barrel system, but that design has been deferred in favour of the less technically risky traditional single-barrel design.

Greater tactical and operational flexibility for artillery units is also being pursued through the standardisation of rocket artillery systems. To this end, 'multi-calibre' MLR systems are being introduced into service, in which launching tubes are integrated into modules that can be loaded on and off from the base vehicle. The modules can contain tubes of different calibres: for instance, the Uragan-1M system is designed to fire 122-, 220- or 300-mm artillery rockets.[36] This modular design is aimed at increasing the flexibility of rocket artillery since the same vehicles will be capable of delivering artillery fire with very different tactical characteristics in terms of range and potency, depending on the situation. A guided version of the 300-mm artillery rockets has been under development for a long time. If introduced into service, these will give artillery and combined arms unit commanders an alternative to the tactical ballistic missile-strike capability, which is currently the sole preserve of army-level missile brigades.[37]

Another advantage of multi-calibre MLR systems is a shorter reload time. Launch vehicles are rearmed and prepared for subsequent firing by reloading modules, rather than individual launcher tubes. This not only contributes to the vehicles' higher operational rate of fire, but also to higher survivability as vehicles will spend less time stationary during reloading. The Ministry of Defence plans to take delivery of around 660

---

[35] Vyacheslav Shpakovskiy, 'Dvustvolka na gusenitsakh snova v boyu [Twin-barrel [Gun] in Battle Again]', *Voennoe obozrenie* [*Military Review*], 22 December 2012, <https://topwar.ru/22363-dvustvolka-na-gusenicah-snova-v-boyu.html>, accessed 20 October 2016.

[36] Some as yet unconfirmed hints point to the possibility that Uragan-1M vehicles can launch cruise missiles of current (for the Iskander-M missile system) or longer-range type.

[37] The 120-km range of the new 300-mm guided variant of artillery rocket will match that of the currently deployed SS-21 Tochka-U tactical ballistic missile system, which itself is now being replaced by the Iskander-M system in Russian missile brigades. There is, however, a substantial difference in warhead weight between the SS-21 ballistic missile and 300-mm rockets.

modern MLR vehicles by 2020 to complete the rearmament of the rocket artillery formations.

A startling new innovation for the rocket artillery forces is the T90 (Item 9M61), a small drone that can be delivered to a target area by a standard 9M534 300-mm artillery rocket to provide a Smerch/Tornado-S battalion with fresh reconnaissance on a distant target, thus increasing the accuracy and agility of long-range artillery barrages. The T90 drone has a length of around 1.5 m, a wingspan when unfolded of 2.5 m, a diameter of 200-mm and a weight of 40 kg. The drone is equipped with a miniature pulsejet engine, giving it the capability to fly at 130 kmph for approximately 20–30 minutes at an altitude of around 3,000 m. When fired, it arrives over a target area at the maximum firing range of 120 km in approximately 110–150 seconds, and can immediately begin to supply the battery/battalion with reconnaissance data.[38]

A steady increase in the artillery firepower of combined arms manoeuvre units is also being achieved by the Russian military. Motor-rifle and airborne battalions are taking delivery of BMP-3 and BMD-4M tracked vehicles respectively, with a combination of 100-mm 2A70 gun/missile launchers and 2A72 30-mm automatic cannon in the 8BYa01 Bakhcha-U combat module.[39] Such heavy firepower in each infantry/paratrooper fighting vehicle substantially increases the cumulative firepower of the corresponding battalions. In addition, the Russian defence industry aggressively promotes BMPT fire support vehicles for integration into manoeuvre units of land forces. One option would be for tank support fighting vehicles with automatic cannons, automatic grenade launchers and anti-tank grenade launchers/flamethrowers to support MBTs against opposing infantry forces. However, the alternative envisages dedicated mobile artillery vehicles providing short-range, heavy artillery fire support to advancing motor-rifle elements. This concept can be traced back to early in the Second World War and the monstrous KV-2 Soviet heavy artillery tank with its 152-mm howitzer. The modern version would be a vehicle on the Armata chassis with a 152-mm low-velocity gun module,[40] or a variety of vehicles with an AU-220M Baikal combat module and a 57-mm automatic cannon. However, the Russian military is currently hesitant

---

[38] Damantsev, 'Takticheskie preimuschestva 'gipezvukovogo drona' dlya "Smercha" [Tactical Advantages of the Hypersonic Drone for "Smerch"]'.

[39] Dogs of War, 'Boevoy modul B8Ya01 "Bakhcha-U" (Rossiya) [B8Ya01 "Bakhcha-U" Combat Module (Russia)]', 4 October 2015, <http://www.dogswar.ru/artilleriia/pyshki-gaybicy/7589-boevoi-modyl-b8ia01-h>, accessed 9 December 2016.

[40] Khalitov and Khodarenok, 'Ideologiya boevoy systemy buduschego [Ideology of the Combat System of the Future]'.

about accepting the Baikal module for service due to the lack of proper modern ammunition for it, so the Armata derivative is more likely.[41]

Chemical, Biological, Radiological and Nuclear Defence (CBRN) Units

The establishment of a CBRN regiment in each of the eleven Russian field armies, which was leaked in mid-2014[42] and officially announced in June 2015,[43] has caused significant concern in the West, as it came against the backdrop of nuclear sabre-rattling by the Kremlin.

Until recently, there were CBRN elements at company strength in every brigade and/or division in the conventional Russian armed forces. There were also separate and more capable CBRN brigades with a greatly expanded range of combat tasks. After 2008, as part of the radical military reform started by Serdyukov for the 2008–20 period, one CBRN brigade was placed under the command of each of the four Russian MDs, while one was directly subordinated to the Commandant of the CBRN troops as a central reserve. In 2014, in the midst of the reform programme, it was also decided to establish a CBRN regiment in each of the eleven field armies.

The West is concerned because such a large-scale establishment of CBRN units – which are specifically designed to mitigate the effects of the combat use of weapons of mass destruction and to maintain the combat capacity of Russian troops during a nuclear exchange – could be interpreted as part of preparations for a nuclear war. Western observers cannot exclude the possibility that the move was a consequence of tectonic changes in the Russian leadership's assessment of the probability of a nuclear war.

Russia's preparedness to fight a nuclear war and its ability to maintain significant combat capability on the part of its ground forces in the event of a nuclear exchange is an important message that the Russian political-military

---

[41] *Livejournal*, 'A vot i ona: 57-mm pushka-avtomat dlya BMP i BTR [Here it is: 57-mm Automatic Cannon for IFV/APC]', 9 July 2015, <kerzak-1.livejournal.com/1892684.html>, accessed 21 March 2017.

[42] Russian Ministry of Defence, 'V polk RKhBZ Yuzhnogo voennogo okruga, dislotsirovanniy v Ingushetii, postupilo okolo 200 edinits novogo vooruzheniya [Around 200 Items of New Armaments Delivered to CBRN Regiment of the Southern Military District Stationed in Ingushetiya]', 30 October 2014, <http://function.mil.ru/news_page/world/more.htm?id=11997848@egNews>, accessed 14 January 2016; *ProGorod* [*AboutTown*], 'Noviy unikalniy polk sformirovali v Zapadnom voennom okruge [New Unique Regiment Formed in the Western Military District]', 24 December 2014, <http://progorodnn.ru/news/view/94951>, accessed 14 January 2016.

[43] Russian Ministry of Defence, 'V voyskakh RKhBZ sformirovany 10 novykh polkov [Ten New Regiments Established in CBRN Troops]', 29 June 2015, <http://structure.mil.ru/structure/forces/navy/news/more.htm?id=12044069@egNews&_print=true>, accessed 14 January 2016.

leadership has deliberately sent to the West. Unhappily for Western politicians and military planners, such preparedness lends credibility to the Kremlin's thinly veiled hints at its readiness to resort to nuclear weapons. The extent of Russian Ground Troops' CBRN capability reforms, therefore, complicates the already difficult process of separating the bluster from intention in terms of assessing the nuclear threat. With the characterisation of Putin as a risk-taker becoming ever more common among Western journalists and members of the political class,[44] Russia's ability to mitigate some of the immediate military consequences of nuclear war helps strengthen its policy of brinkmanship; a bluff, when backed by actual capability, however hypothetical, to wage nuclear war looks less like a bluff. The expansion of CBRN capabilities might be another way of making the Russian military an even more effective tool in the Kremlin's policy of trying to extract concessions from the West through threats and brinkmanship. These authors believe that such considerations played an important role in the Kremlin's decision to expand the CBRN capabilities of Russian forces, and to leak information about the decision in order to increase the pressure on Western decision-makers.

There are reasons to believe that the role of Russian CBRN units in a conventional conflict with NATO is at least as important as their role in the event of a nuclear exchange. The CBRN units of the Soviet Army were originally known as 'chemical troops' and were responsible for a much wider range of combat tasks than defending other troops against dangerous agents and reducing the destructive effects of nuclear weapons. 'Chemical troops' had responsibility for handling and offensively using chemical agents too, including (mixtures of) poisonous gases (chemical weapons, per se) and incendiary mixtures for flamethrowers. These combat tasks are fully preserved in Russia's modern CBRN units, although their responsibilities for chemical weapons use have been substantially modified. Thus, while the word 'defence' is in the official name (CBRN Defence Troops), the CBRN units of the modern Russian army are far from being exclusively defensive.

Supplying these troops with the most up-to-date equipment is clearly a high priority for the Ministry of Defence and CBRN troops HQ. This can be seen in the steady flow of modern equipment to CBRN units and their corresponding elements within combined arms formations. This equipment includes remote sensing systems for rapid and accurate detection of CBRN threats, as well as robotic systems specifically tailored

---

[44] See Gordon M Hahn, 'Putin the Risk-taker', Russian and Eurasian Politics, 24 November 2015, <http://gordonhahn.com/2015/11/24/putin-the-risk-taker/, accessed 14 January 2016; Jim Hoagland, 'Vladimir Putin, Failed Spy', *Washington Post*, 7 August 2015; Sarah Sloat, 'An Interesting Theory that Could Explain Vladimir Putin's Risky Behavior', *New Republic*, 19 March 2014.

to operate under fire and in high-risk areas, including areas with high levels of radioactive contamination.

In addition to CBRN threat detection and decontamination, CBRN units contain flamethrower elements that significantly contribute to the firepower of their parent formations. These are not only significant in terms of combat potential; since all Russian flamethrower-type weapons can fire projectiles which kill via incendiary effects – as opposed to blast overpressure with thermobaric munitions – their intended use against enemy personnel in cover is in violation of Protocol III of the Convention on Certain Conventional Weapons. Russian designers have updated the principle of handheld flamethrowers first seen during the First World War. The SPO Varna-S handheld flamethrower, which is in active service with flamethrower elements of CBRN units, is a shoulder-fired weapons system designed to project an enmeshed globule of an inflammable mixture over a distance of up to 120 metres. It avoids the backblast limitations associated with more powerful rocket-propelled launchers. Handheld versions of capsule flamethrowers use projectiles with 'pure' incendiary, smoke-generating and thermobaric warheads.

Flamethrower elements of CBRN forces also pioneered the use of projectiles with thermobaric warheads during the 1980s. These weapons, which are based on the principle of evaporating and then igniting chemical agents, kill predominantly through blast overpressure and are not considered exclusively 'chemical' in the Russian armed forces; they are widely used by ordinary troops and even riot police in Russia.[45] The use of chemical agents on the battlefield has not been fully abandoned by Russian forces either, as the agents used in the smoke-generating warheads fired by Russian handheld flamethrowers have a dual smoke/tear gas effect. This is designed to reduce the fighting capacity of enemy soldiers or force them to use gas masks.

The heavy flamethrower is also in service. This is an MRL system based on tank chassis, firing heavy artillery rockets with capsule-type incendiary or thermobaric warheads. The TOS-1 Buratino (Russian for

---

[45] Incendiary and thermobaric weapons in service with units other than the chemical troops include: the 9M55S 300-mm artillery rocket with thermobaric warhead (9K58 Smerch MRL system); rocket-assisted assault grenades RShG-1 and RShG-2 with thermobaric warhead; RMG rocket-assisted assault grenade with the combined shaped-charge thermobaric warhead, TBG-7V thermobaric grenades for RPG-7V grenade launcher; TBG-32V rocket-assisted grenades with combined fragmentation-thermobaric warheads for RPG-32 'Hashim' grenade launcher; rocket-assisted grenades with combined HE-thermobaric warhead for 'Bur' grenade launcher; VGM93.100 for GP-94/LPO-97 grenade launcher; BG-40TB thermobaric grenades for GP-25 under barrel grenade launcher; RG-60TB thermobaric hand grenades.

'Pinocchio') was the first of these heavy flamethrower systems and is based on the T-72 MBT chassis.[46] Equipped with a 30-tube 220-mm trainable and rotating launcher unit, the resulting vehicle is designated BM-1 (Boevaya Mashina-1 or Combat Vehicle, Model 1). Combat use of the TOS-1 revealed that BM-1 launcher tubes were susceptible to combat damage from artillery shell fragments and small arms fire due to the system's short maximum firing range of 3,600 metres. A variant has been developed, known as the TOS-1A Solntsepyok. It carries a 24-tube launcher unit with a layer of armour covering the tubes, mounted on a T-90 tank chassis. The TOS-1A also employs rockets with a maximum range of 6,000 metres and capable of carrying more powerful warheads. A TOS-2 heavy flamethrower system with the improved rockets and mounted on a TUGP Armata chassis is also planned for service in the future.

Every CBRN brigade includes one flamethrower battalion with three companies. The 1st and the 2nd flamethrower company in every battalion consist of three flamethrower platoons of three flamethrower sections each. Available data suggests that a CBRN regiment includes only one flamethrower company in its structure. One flamethrower section includes the section commander, seven flamethrower grenadiers, and a driver for the section's BMO-T combat vehicle. The BMO-T heavy APC, based on the T-72 tank chassis, is currently being supplied to flamethrower elements of CBRN units to replace the BMO-1 vehicle, based on the BMP-2, which was introduced in 2001. A next-generation BMO-2 vehicle, based on the T-15 IFV of the Armata family, is expected in the future.

Each BMO-T carries 30–32 assorted Shmel, Priz, MRO and Varna-S flamethrowers. The older BMO-1 carries a section commander, gunner, driver and four flamethrower grenadiers along with a complement of eighteen flamethrowers, with the option to load four more. The Armata-derived BMO-2 will carry a driver, section commander and six flamethrower grenadiers, with 42 flamethrowers. Company support vehicles carry a second load of flamethrowers for each BMO-T vehicle, meaning that each company has 540 rounds to use in combat.

---

[46] The new, highly classified TOS-1 weapons system was introduced for trial by Soviet troops in Afghanistan; the surname of the officer in charge of their combat use was Karlov. In the Russian-language version of Carlo Collodi's story of Pinocchio, adapted by Aleksey Tolstoy, the name Pinocchio is changed to Buratino and his creator's name is Dad Karlo. The story of Buratino was extremely popular in the Soviet Union and was reprinted 182 times between 1936 and 1986. It is also a widespread tradition in the Russian and Soviet armies to call the commanding officer 'Dad'. Therefore, Karlov was nicknamed 'Dad Karlo' – and his beasts were inevitably called Buratinos. The unofficial name has stuck to the weapons system so strongly that it has been accepted as its official codename.

One heavy flamethrower company in every flamethrower battalion is armed with the TOS-1/TOS-1A system. The company consists of three platoons; each platoon includes one BM-1/BM-1A combat vehicle and two TZM-T transporter-loader vehicles, each carrying one full load of rockets for the combat vehicle. Additional munitions are stored by the parent battalion. The TOS-1A system is designed to destroy a platoon defence position in a single salvo.[47] Indeed, one vehicle's full salvo, which takes twelve seconds, can destroy troops dug into trenches within an area of up to 10 acres.[48] This is sufficient to cover the majority of a typical British infantry platoon defence position, as envisaged by the Soviet military when the requirements for the system were under consideration (300–400 m along the front line and up to 200 m in depth).[49]

Another combat task for CBRN units is to disrupt hostile target detection and precision-guided munitions (PGMs) delivery by using smoke and aerosol screens to conceal friendly forces and positions.[50] The chemical compositions used are formulated to prevent observation by hostile forces in the ultraviolet, visual, infrared and radar bands.[51]

This ability to counter PGMs' targeting of friendly troops, as well as to conceal troop concentrations, preparations for advance and the early stages of an attack, was a dominant factor in the decision to expand existing CBRN units to regimental size. The widespread use of artillery and even PGMs by both sides in the Ukraine conflict emphasised the importance of these capabilities. The single CBRN company that is currently part of every

[47] Russian Ministry of Defence, 'Tyazhelaya ognemetnaya Sistema TOS-1A [TOS-1A Heavy Flamethrower System]', <http://structure.mil.ru/structure/forces/ground/weapons/rhbz/more.htm?id=10345028@morfMilitaryModel>, accessed 5 December 2015.
[48] Raketnaya Tekhnika [Missile Technik], 'Tyazhelaya ognemetnaya sistema TOS-1A [TOS-1A Heavy Flamethrower System]', <http://rbase.new-factoria.ru/missile/wobb/tos-1a/tos-1a.shtml>, accessed 5 December 2015.
[49] 'Pekhotnaya rota bataljona legkoy pekhotnoy divizii [An Infantry Company of a Light Infantry Division's Battalion]', Zarubezhnoe voennoe obozrenie [Foreign Military Survey], 1990, No. 11, p. 31. The development of the TOS-1 heavy flamethrower system was started in 1971 under the influence of the Sino–Soviet conflict of 1968, and fighting on the Damanskiy Island. See: M Knyazev, 'TOS-1 Buratino/TOS-1A Solntsepek, Boevye mashiny mira [Combat Vehicles of the World]', <http://coollib.com/b/296303/read>, accessed 5 December 2015.
[50] Viktor Khudoleev, 'Nakhimichit vragu ne dadim [We Won't Allow Enemy to Use Chemical Tricks]', Krasnaya zvezda [Red Star], 12 November 2014, <http://www.redstar.ru/index.php/component/k2/item/19846-nakhimichit-vragu-ne-dadim>, accessed 4 December 2015.
[51] Russian Ministry of Defence, 'Spetsialisty RKhB zaschity Zapadnogo voennogo okruga sorevnovalis v iskusstve maskirovki [NBC Defence Specialists of the Western Military District Compete in the Art of Disguise]', 29 August 2012, <http://function.mil.ru/news_page/world/more.htm?id=11325282@egNews>, accessed 13 January 2016.

Russian manoeuvre brigade includes an 'aerosol countering platoon'[52] that has the capability to screen only one of the brigade's combat elements at a time using its five TDA-U/TDA-2 K/TDA-2M smoke-generating vehicles.[53] Even with assistance from a decontamination platoon's TMS-65U vehicles to generate smokescreens – a secondary role for these vehicles[54] – screening capacity is still not sufficient to cover the full brigade.

This limited capacity to generate smokescreens for Russian manoeuvre brigades is the result of substantial neglect of CBRN capabilities during the first phases of the military reform programme after 2008.[55] The urgent establishment of CBRN regiments just three months after the start of the combat phase of the conflict in Eastern Ukraine in 2014 can therefore be seen as recognition by Russian military planners that such neglect had been a serious mistake in light of the dominance of long-range firepower in that and prospective future conflicts.

With CBRN regiments now being established under their command, commanders of Russian field armies will be able to substantially expand

---

[52] The official title of the element (*vzvod aerozolnogo protivodeystviya*) describes the 'platoon for countering [PGM strikes, adversarial surveillance and targeting] with use of aerosol screens'.

[53] Author notes from the Russian reserve officer training course (CBRN component) in 2015. This is ony the formal definition of combat capabilities of CBRN elements as taught to Russian officer cadets; 'advertising' (propaganda and misleading to a large extent) statements of the post-Soviet military press claim that one TDA-U/TDA-2K smoke-generating vehicle, which is the main armament of the aerosol countering platoon, is capable of generating a smoke screen to disguise one motor-rifle company. See Alexander Ivanov, 'Polyot "Shmelya" [Fight of "Bumblebee"]', *Belorusskaya Voennaya Gazeta* [*Belarus Military Gazette*], 23 April 2014, <http://vsr.mil.by/2014/04/23/polyot-shmelya-video/>, accessed 13 January 2016. In practice the task of covering one company/artillery battery requires two/three to five TDA-2K/M vehicles, depending on the wind; for instance an aerosol countering platoon is capable of generating a screen to cover two companies/batteries at best.

[54] Author conversation with an active service Russian CBRN officer in October 2015; Bolshaya promyshlennaya yarmarka Sibiri [Large Industrial Fair of Siberia], 'Mashina teplovaya TMS-65D [Thermal Equipment TMS-65D]', <http://www.techtorg.ru/product.asp?tid=872107&all=1&sort=1>, accessed 13 January 2016; *Armsdata – Oruzhie Rossii* [*Armsdata – Weapons of Russia*], 'Teplovaya mashina dlya spetsialnoy obrabotki TMS-65M [TMS-65D Thermal Equipment for Special Treatment]', <http://armsdata.net/russia/0226.html>, accessed 13 January 2016.

[55] Each combined-arms division of the Soviet and the pre-2008 Russian army had a separate CBRN battalion as its integral part, including one aerosol countering company with roughly three times the smoke screen-generating capacity compared with the current element of today's Russian manoeuvre brigades. See A Pokryshkin *Radiatsionnaya, khimicheskaya i biologicheskaya zaschita* [*Radiation, Chemical and Biological Defence*], edited by E Starshinov (Chelyabinsk: South-Urals State University Publishing House, 2007), p. 105.

concealment capabilities for their units according to operational priorities, and at their own discretion, without having to request additional CBRN capabilities from Operational-Strategic Command Headquarters.[56] It is important to note that aerosol countering operations are an important element of the preparation and execution of offensive actions for Russian forces, and are not used exclusively in a passive/defensive role. Hence, the expansion of CBRN aerosol capabilities helps strengthen formations' offensive potential as well as survivability.

The usefulness of CBRN units in conventional fighting is obvious, since they can limit enemy situational awareness as well as complicate the use of potentially devastating PGMs against Russian troops, command-and-control structures, and armaments and equipment. Equally, the flamethrower elements – handheld and heavy rocket artillery – significantly add to the offensive firepower of Russian land forces. CBRN units are an important force multiplier, enhancing troops' survivability, helping to gain and maintain tactical surprise and offering extended/multilayered area-denial capabilities. The fact that the 4th CBRN Regiment of the Black Sea Fleet coastal troops in Sevastopol was one of the first three Russian units established in Crimea after the annexation of the peninsula – when Russia expected Ukraine to try to recapture Crimea using military force, including artillery and missile fire – testifies to the importance the Russian military now attaches to CBRN troops.

In addition to the CBRN units of the MDs and field armies, which have active combat support roles in addition to the traditional CBRN protection role, the Ministry of Defence operates five units exclusively tasked with responding to accidents at Russian chemical weapons arsenals. These units are the 22nd, 24th, 27th, 28th and 29th Regiments of Disaster Recovery and Guard at the Leonidovka, Pochep, Schuchje, Mirniy/Maradykovo and Kizner chemical weapons storage and elimination sites. The five disaster recovery regiments will probably be reduced in size (and merged into three) before being transferred to the Ministry of Emergencies as disaster mitigation and recovery units (CBRN) after the completion of Russia's ongoing chemical weapons elimination programme as part of the Chemical Weapons Convention commitments. Ministry of Defence CBRN brigades also take part in disaster mitigation and recovery tasks. For example, the 27th CBRN Brigade in Kursk is tasked to react to potential accidents at the Kursk nuclear power station,[57] reinforcing disaster

---

[56] The Russian MDs will be transformed into the Operational-Strategic [Joint] Command in the event of war. The MDs' wartime role is to serve as a regional joint command in the corresponding theatre of military operations.

[57] Russian Ministry of Defence, 'Otdelnaya brigada RKhBZ Zapadnogo voennogo okruga prinimaet uchastie v protivoavariynom uchenii na Kurskoy AES [The

mitigation forces from the Ministry of Emergencies if necessary. Likewise, the 1st Mobile CBRN Brigade regularly participates in similar exercises at the Balakovo nuclear power station near Saratov.[58]

Combat Engineer Units

One of the primary goals of the 2008 military reform programme was to streamline the military structure, as outlined in the Introduction to this paper. All unnecessary duplication was to be avoided to save money and manpower while continuing to provide agile forces. This was the main reason for establishing a two-tier structure of combat engineer units.[59] Modernised motor-rifle brigades would have an organic engineer-sapper battalion included in their structure, while tank brigades would have an engineer-sapper company. In addition, each of the four MDs would have an engineer-sapper brigade to augment the combat engineer capabilities of subordinated units as required. The engineer-sapper regiments that had existed in 2008 in seven out of ten field armies (in addition to several units directly subordinated to the Commandant of the engineer troops, which also existed at that time) have been disbanded, and their personnel and equipment used to establish the new, enlarged district-subordinated engineer-sapper brigades.[60]

The engineer-sapper battalion contained in modernised motor-rifle brigades includes one pontoon company, which operates half of the standard PMP or PP-91/PP-2005 pontoon bridge set. Tank brigades, however, do not have an organic pontoon capacity and rely on external support from the MD's engineer-sapper brigade, which has a pontoon battalion (two pontoon companies) operating the full PMP/PP-91 bridge set. Before the 2008 reform, the Western MD's 66th Pontoon-Bridge

Separate CBRN Brigade of the Western Military District Takes Part in the Disaster-mitigation Exercise at Kursk NPS]', 4 October 2012, <http://structure.mil.ru/structure/forces/ground/news/more.htm?id=11390957@egNews>, accessed 3 December 2015.

[58] 'Vse o pozharnoy bezopasnosti' [All on Fire Safety], 'Voyska radiokhimbiozaschity uchatsya likvidirovat avarii na BAES [CBRN Defence Troops Train to Mitigate Accidents at Balakovo NPS]', 21 September 2010, <http://www.0-1.ru/?id=30641>, accessed 17 March 2017.

[59] This branch of the Russian armed forces is called Engineer Troops while the corresponding units and elements are designated as 'engineer-sapper' units.

[60] The 7th Guards (20th Army), 11th (58th Army), 27th (36th Army), 37th (35th Army), 56th (2nd Army), 58th (5th Red Banner Army), 60th (41st Army) Engineer-Sapper Regiments, as well as the 140th Guards Engineer-Sapper Regiment (Leningrad MD, currently part of the Western MD), the 66th Pontoon-Bridge Regiment, and the 45th Engineer-Camouflage Regiment (the latter two are directly subordinated to the Commandant of the engineer troops).

Regiment was a valuable addition to the river-crossing potential of its subordinated troops. However, this unit was disbanded and one of its pontoon battalions transferred to the new 45th Engineer-Sapper Brigade.

There are indications that the *Zapad-2013* strategic exercises suggested an urgent need to expand combat engineer capacities since district-subordinated assets proved inadequate to prevent bottlenecks at crossing points, which impeded the smooth progress of operations. The lesson was taken that in addition to the district-subordinated bridging capability, individual formations should receive their own organic bridging elements. It is unlikely to be a coincidence that, soon after *Zapad-2013*, the 30th Engineer-Sapper Regiment was re-established in the 6th Army's order of battle in 2013. During the Soviet era, pontoon-bridge units were pre-positioned according to the anticipated requirement for troops to cross waterways or swamps under combat conditions.[61] The 6th Army's main area of responsibility is in northwest Russia, near the border with Finland and the Baltic States, where there are rivers, lakes and swamps – precisely the sort of environment that requires pre-positioned pontoon-bridge and other combat engineer capabilities. *Zapad-2013* seems to have prompted a return to this Soviet practice.

Russian operations in eastern Ukraine during the summer of 2014, alongside the large-scale transfer of heavy armaments, including armour, to rebel forces, also appear to have revealed the inadequacies of existing combat engineer capabilities. The latest concept of combat employment involves BTGrs operating separately from their parent brigade, with the latter sometimes up to 7,000 km from the theatre of operations. In Ukraine, Russian troops regularly used pontoon-bridge river crossings to enhance operational flexibility, but BTGrs could not draw on the support of their parent brigades' pontoon-bridge companies. The rapid redeployment model used to generate forces in Ukraine from distant units did not include transporting bulky pontoon-bridge companies, and all units in the Ukrainian theatre had to rely on the support of the Western and Southern MDs' engineer-sapper brigades instead.

Extensive works to prepare field camps and defensive/fire positions for the BTGrs deployed far from their parent units (and frequently redeploying according to changes in the operational situation) also require substantial combat engineer support. Russian MD-subordinated engineer-sapper brigades – some elements of which operated on the Russian side of the Russia–Ukraine border, others on Ukrainian soil – appear to have

[61] Yuri Vereme, 'Inzhenernye voyska [Engineer Troops]', *Anatomy of the Army*, <http://army.armor.kiev.ua/engenear/ingener.shtml>, accessed 17 March 2017.

been overwhelmed by demand and could not provide the necessary tactical flexibility for all units in the operational area at the same time.

The expansion of Russian involvement in the Ukraine conflict dramatically increased the need for combat engineer support. Central reserves for the Engineer Troops have been expanded to include the 1st Guards Engineer-Sapper Brigade and the 28th Pontoon-Bridge Brigade, which are directly subordinated to the Commandant of the Engineer Troops. It is worth noting that the 28th Brigade is equipped with a new model of pontoon bridge, which can bear up to 120 metric tonnes, and span rivers up to 600 metres wide.[62] This level of bridging capability has not existed in front line Russian armed forces units since the 1990s.

It is noteworthy that while the new engineer-sapper regiments were originally destined for the Eastern MD, the 31st and 32nd Regiments were established in the 58th and 49th Armies of the Southern MD correspondingly, and were directly involved in generating forces for Russian operations in Ukraine and enhancing Russia's military posture in the European part of the country in general. This reveals a significant shift of priorities on the part of Russia's political-military leadership, from the long-term potential Chinese threat to the immediate need to conduct operations in Ukraine, and to oppose NATO.

Mine clearance and mine laying are two major combat tasks for engineer-sapper units. Mine clearance equipment is being improved in terms of speed of operation, and resistance to enemy fire is a high priority. To this end, the AIRM automated engineer reconnaissance vehicle – with remote-sensing equipment for mine- and other engineer-related threat detection capabilities, as well as automated reconnaissance data transmission to commanders – is being introduced. Alongside this, Prokhod-1 (Passageway-1) robotic heavy mine clearance vehicles, an optionally manned variant of the T-90-based BRM-3MA,[63] as well as several other vehicles, are being delivered to engineer-sapper units.[64]

New and more effective land mines, such as the POM-3 seismic sensor-activated anti-personnel mine and new M-225 and Temp-30 'Kleshch' (Mite) top-down attack anti-armour mines, are also being

---

[62] Aleksandr Pinchuk, 'Pervye na pole boya [First on the Battlefield]', *Red Star*, 18 January 2016, <http://redstar.ru/index.php/newspaper/item/27383-pervye-na-pole-boya>, accessed 17 March 2017.

[63] Anton Valagin, 'Tyazheliy robot-saper zavershil ispytaniya [Heavy Sapper Robot Has Passed Trials]', *Russkoe oruzhie/Rossiyskaya Gazeta [Russian Weapons/Russian Gazette]*, 15 July 2016, <https://rg.ru/2016/07/15/reg-cfo/tiazhelyj-robot-saper-zavershil-ispytaniia.html>, accessed 21 October 2016.

[64] Pinchuk, 'Pervye na pole boya [First on the Battlefield]'.

developed for the engineer units.[65] New UMZ-K vehicles are being delivered to the engineer-sapper elements of motor-rifle brigades to replace the obsolete UMZ. The UMZ-K can remotely lay a minefield up to 5 km long and 240 metres wide with a single load dispensed from rotary launchers on the launch vehicle,[66] providing motor-rifle brigades with a potent capability for defensive and offensive mine laying. VSM-1 heliborne and Smerch rocket artillery systems can also be used to quickly lay new minefields at range. Further development of the UMZ remote mine-laying vehicle family is planned using the heavy Armata chassis to create the UMZ-A. The UMZ-A, when introduced into service, will give Russian units the unique capability of mine laying alongside advancing troops, since the vehicle will have the same level of protection as the T-14 Armata MBT and will be capable of accompanying combat elements in areas of the highest threat. It will also be possible to operate the new mine laying vehicle remotely, in accordance with the overall design philosophy of the Armata family which incorporates remote controllability as part of its system architecture.[67]

Camouflaging troops, equipment and combat positions are other important combat tasks for Russian engineer units. In addition to the usual concealment methods, engineer-camouflage elements are responsible for operating inflatable and other types of high-fidelity equipment mock-ups,[68] including imitating motion through towing by an external vehicle.

---

[65] Anton Ryabov 'Perspektivnaya protivopekhotnaya mina POM-3 "Medaljon"' [POM-3 'Medalion' Perspective Anti-personnel Mine]', *Voennoe Obozrenie* [*Military Survey*], 30 November 2015, <https://topwar.ru/86566-perspektivnaya-protivopehotnaya-mina-pom-3-medalon.html>, accessed 18 May 2017; 'Protivovertoletnye i protivotransportnye miny razrabotany v Rossii' [Anti-helicopter and Anti-vehicle Mines Designed in Russia], *Zvezda* [*Star*] (*Russian Ministry of Defence TV*), 24 January 2016, <http://tvzvezda.ru/news/forces/content/201601240337-3bad.htm>, accessed 18 May 2017.

[66] ArmyRecognition.com, 'Russia Defense Industry Unveils New UMZ-K Multipurpose Mine-laying Vehicle at Army-2015', 27 June 2015, <http://www.armyrecognition.com/weapons_defence_industry_military_technology_uk/russia_defense_industry_unveils_new_umz-k_multipurpose_mine-laying_vehicle_at_army-2015_12706155.html>, accessed 16 May 2017. Note that anti-armour, anti-personnel and mixed minefields can be laid with this system.

[67] Yuliya Temereva and Olga Dedyaeva. '"Uralvagonzavod": "Armata" v perspective mozhet stat robotom ["Uralvagonzavod": "Armata" Can Become Robot in the Future]'. *TASS*, 10 December 2015, <http://tass.ru/armiya-i-opk/2515352>, accessed 18 May 2017.

[68] The armed forces requirement is that mock-ups imitate the features of vehicles so as to be barely distinguishable at a distance of more than 100 metres and to mimic radar and thermal emission characteristics with an accuracy within a few per cent (less than 10) of the genuine vehicle signature. In practice, approximately 80 per cent accuracy is more realistic.

The main goal of such activity is to imitate combat vehicles accurately enough to make reconnaisasance and target discrimination highly problematic for an adversary, in order to mislead adversary reconnaissance, undermine situational awareness, and force that adversary to waste expensive PGMs attacking mock-ups rather than combat vehicles. With this in mind, the expansion of combat engineer capacity is partly intended to enhance the survivability of Russian troops in the face of widespread use of PGMs and integrated sensor-shooter systems. These efforts, in parallel with the expanded capabilities of the CBRN and EW units, represent a concerted effort to make the Russian land forces competitive in high-end conventional warfare on the modern battlefield. Indeed, the use of high-fidelity mock-ups is considered a form of passive EW in Russian military theory.[69] According to the latest Russian assessments, their use increases the time taken for an enemy to obtain target data about Russian force elements via surveillance and reconnaissance by up to 100 per cent and therefore increases the survivability of friendly forces by 25 to 30 per cent.[70]

Engineer-camouflage elements of the Engineer Troops are also used to achieve strategic goals. In Ukraine, Russian forces have been imitating the tactics used by the Red Army during the Second World War – simulated troop movements, fake fortifications and mock-ups to distort the actual disposition of forces. For example, Russian engineer-camouflage elements were reportedly used after the first Minsk ceasefire agreement in September 2014 to imitate in a deliberately detectable way the withdrawal of heavy armaments from Donbass in accordance with Russian obligations. Mock-up tanks and heavy weapons were transported on trailers across the border back to Russia as 'evidence' of a withdrawal in full compliance with the Minsk deal.[71] Russia's strategic aim was to persuade the West to lift sanctions imposed after the shooting down of Malaysia Airlines flight MH17 without weakening the joint Russian-rebel military formations in eastern Ukraine. The mock-ups misled observers from the OSCE into initially releasing positive reports on the implementation of the Minsk agreement, providing ammunition

---

[69] Anatoliy Sokolov, 'Imitatsiya voennoy tekhniki – stariy metod s novymi tekhnologiyami [Mimicking of Military Equipment: The Old Method and New Technologies]', *Oruzhie Rossii* [*Weapons of Russia*], 10 September 2007, <http://www.arms-expo.ru/news/archive/anatoliy-sokolov-imitaciya-voennoy-tehniki-staryy-metod-s-novymi-tehnologiyami-10-09-2007-21-46-00/>, accessed 17 March 2017.
[70] *Ibid.*
[71] *Crime: Archive*, 'Rossiyskoe "naduvatelstvo". RF vyvozit iz Donbassa makety bronetekhniki [The Russian "Swindle": Russia Moves Mock-ups of Armour Vehicles out of Donbass]', 22 October 2014, <crime.in.ua/node/6795>, accessed 17 March 2017.

for those in Europe in favour of a 'business as usual' policy towards Moscow to press for the lifting of sanctions. This demonstrates the potential strategic impact of disinformation operations by Russian combat engineer elements.

The presence of an assault pioneer battalion[72] in the structure of the new 1st Guards Engineer-Sapper Brigade should attract particular attention.[73] This battalion is equipped and trained to carry out the demolition of obstacles and fortified positions as well as mine clearance tasks under fire as part of a first wave of advancing troops. The units are most valuable in urban area combat operations, where they provide advancing elements with much-needed firepower and obstacle-clearing capacity to deal with defensive positions at short range. Assault pioneer battalions will be established in every engineer-sapper brigade (at MD level, rather than in the engineer-sapper regiments of combined arms armies).[74]

Assault pioneer units were instrumental to the Red Army during the second phase of the Great Patriotic War, as the Soviet part of the Second World War is known in Russia. Soviet assault pioneers were equipped with body armour and flamethrowers, captured German Panzerfaust anti-tank grenade launchers, large quantities of hand grenades and Molotov cocktails, and formed the spearhead of the Red Army when storming Nazi defensive positions in European cities and towns.[75] By the end of the war, the Red Army had fielded ten pioneer armies and 25 specialist assault pioneer brigades.[76]

---

[72] ShISB was previously the official Russian military abbreviated name for this type of unit (Shturmovoy Inzhenerno-Saperniy Bataljon, assault engineer-sapper battalion). BShiR (Bataljon Shturma i Razgrazhdeniya, battalion for assault and obstacle clearing) has been chosen as the designator for the type of newly established element.

[73] *Zvezda* [*Star*] (*Russian Ministry of Defence TV*), 'V rossiyskoy armii poyavilsya perviy shturmovoy inzhenerno-saperniy bataljon [First Assault Pioneer Battalion Established in the Russian Army]', 2 December 2015, <http://tvzvezda.ru/news/vstrane_i_mire/content/201512020937-8t2f.htm>, accessed 17 March 2017.

[74] *Voennoe obozrenie* [*Military Review*], 'V rossiyskoy armii budut sozdany roty saperov-shturmovikov [Assault Pioneer Sapper Companies to be Established in the Russian Army]', 6 March 2016, <https://topwar.ru/91935-v-rossiyskoy-armii-budut-sozdany-roty-saperov-shturmovikov.html>, accessed 17 March 2017.

[75] Introduction of assault pioneer units into the Red Army began in early 1943 as the direct result of experience gained during the last stage of the Battle of Stalingrad, when Soviet troops experienced substantial difficulties storming Nazi forces in the urban districts of the destroyed city.

[76] *Murom24.rf*, 'V Murome sozdan perviy v Rossii shturmovoy inzhenerno-saperniy bataljon [First Russian Assault Engineer-Sapper Battalion Established in Murom]', 30 June 2015, <http://xn--24-7lcajlu.xn--p1ai/pervaya_polosa/476-v-murome-sozdan-

Modern Russian assault pioneers are grouped within an assault pioneer battalion. Each battalion includes an assault pioneer company, a heavy vehicles company equipped with rocket-propelled mine clearance vehicles (UR-77 Meteorit or UR-07M Peresortirovka) and IMR-3 armoured obstacle clearance vehicles based on an MBT chassis,[77] as well as a company of robotic systems equipped with robotic mine-clearing and firefighting capabilities.[78] One of these robotic vehicles is the Uran-6 (Uranium-6) multifunctional, remote-controlled mine clearance system, a Russian copy of the Croatian MV4 DOK-ING[79] tracked mine-clearing vehicle,[80] similar in basic design to the Sherman Crab flail tanks used by Britain in the D-Day landings. The Uran-6, like the MV4, makes use of alternatively installed flail, tiller or segmented roller demining tools. The Uran-14 robotic firefighting vehicle can also mitigate mine- and obstacle clearance risks, and is a copy of the Croatian MVF-5 firefighting vehicle.[81] Used by the Russian Ministry of Emergencies, the vehicle was known as El-10 (Fir Tree-10). Currently, it appears that the 'robotic company' of assault pioneer battalions will include three vehicles of

---

pervyy-v-rossii-shturmovoy-inzhenerno-sapernyy-batalon.html>, accessed 17 March 2017.

[77] *Voennoe obozrenie [Military Review]*, 'V rossiyskoy armii budut sozdany roty saperov-shturmovikov [Assault Sapper Companies to be Established in the Russian Army]'.

[78] Mikhail Mikhin, 'Pro gvardeyskoe shturmovoe podrazdelenie inzhenernykh voysk [On the Guards' Assault Element of the Engineer Troops]', *Livejournal*, 25 February 2016, <http://onepamop.livejournal.com/1140514.html>, accessed 17 March 2017. It is worth mentioning that Russian sources tend to exaggerate new Russian military equipment's technological sophistication, regularly calling new remote-controlled systems 'robotic' or 'robots', which assumes artificial intelligence, missing in the systems, rather than just their remote-controlled operations.

[79] *MForum.ru*, 'Nazemnye voennye roboty [Land-based Military Robots]', 23 April 2015, <http://www.mforum.ru/news/article/111879.htm>, accessed 17 March 2017; MV-4 DOK-ING website, <http://dok-ing.hr/products/demining/mv_4>, accessed 17 March 2017.

[80] *Novosti VPK [Military-Industrial Complex News]*, 'V inzhenernykh voyskakh sformirovana inzhenerno-sapernaya brigada, osnaschennaya unikalnoy robototekhnikoy [Engineer-sapper Brigade, Equipped with Unique Robotic Systems, Established in the Engineer Troops]', 13 January 2015, <http://vpk.name/news/124513_v_inzhenernyih_voiskah_sformirovana_inzhenernosapernaya_brigada_osnashennaya_unikalnoi_robototehnikoi.html>, accessed 17 March 2017.

[81] *MForum.ru*, 'Pozharnye roboty [Firefighting Robots]', 21 April 2015, <http://www.mforum.ru/news/article/113693.htm>, accessed 17 March 2017; MVF-5 DOK-ING website, <http://dok-ing.hr/products/firefighting/mvf_5>, accessed 17 March 2017.

each type.[82] It is not clear whether Russia has a licence from Croatia to produce MV-4 and MVF-5 vehicles or if it has illegally copied vehicles and started mass production at the 766th Directorate of Production and Processing Equipment ('UPTK 766') plant in Nakhabino near Moscow; the former seems the most likely. The new Uran-10 is a heavier variant of the Uran-6 mine clearance vehicle, which is capable of dealing with anti-tank mines (Uran-6 is only capable of dealing with anti-personnel mines). The Uran-10 is currently being introduced into Russian service.[83]

Despite the absence of assault pioneer battalions in army-level engineer-sapper regiments, these regiments will still receive one company of Uran-family robotic vehicles, which are intended to become standard equipment for all engineer-sapper formations (brigades) and units (regiments).[84] This large-scale introduction of robotic vehicles into service with Russian troops is representative of a significant shift in Russian military planning. For the first time, Russian military doctrine is looking exclusively to technological developments, rather than the bravery of soldiers, to ensure success in a critical capability area.

Assault pioneers are armed with thermobaric grenade launchers and thermobaric hand grenades of varying types and power, as well as handheld mine clearance equipment. Their tactics include elements of special operations forces' tactics, and cooperation on training with the Russian Special Operations Command is planned for the near future.[85] It is noteworthy that the assault of heavily fortified positions in urban areas is the main operational task of assault companies within BShiRs – the designator for these newly established assault battalions. Obstacle clearance is the task of another element of these battalions, making BShiRs evidently offensive-oriented units. Assault pioneers will wear the OVR-3Sh Kaspiy (Caspian Sea) body armour suits,[86] which have an

---

[82] *RIA Novosti*, '"Rota robotov" sformirovana v brigade inzhenernykh voysk v Murome ["Robotic Company" Established in the Murom Engineer Troops Brigade]', 23 January 2016, <http://ria.ru/defense_safety/20160123/1364018185.html>, accessed 21 March 2017.

[83] Ivan Kapustin 'Yuzhniy voenniy okrug pervym poluchit kompleks "Uran-10" [Southern Military District will be the First to Get Delivery of "Uran-10" System]', *RIA Novosti*, 20 January 2017, <https://ria.ru/arms/20170120/1486132306.html>, accessed 21 March 2017.

[84] *RIA Novosti*, 'Inzhenernye voyska VS RF poluchat v 2016 godu ne odin desyatok robotov [Russian Armed Forces' Engineer Troops Will Get Delivery of Dozens of Robots in 2016]', 23 January 2016, <http://ria.ru/defense_safety/20160123/ 1364040328.html>, accessed 21 March 2017.

[85] Mikhin, 'Pro gvardeyskoe shturmovoe podrazdelenie inzhenernykh voysk [On the Guards' Assault Engineer Element of the Engineer Troops]'.

[86] Kirill Ryabov, 'V voyska postupayut komplekty zaschity OVR-3Sh [Troops Get Delivery of OVR-3Sh Protective Suits]', *Voennoe obozrenie* [*Military Review*], 27

innovative liquid cooling system (similar to that used in space suits) to provide extended durability. In its most protected areas, the suit is capable of protecting the wearer from a 7.62×54r steel-cored round from an SVD sniper rifle fired from 10 m away.[87] Close-quarter combat, including use of throwing knifes and sapper shovels, remains an integral part of assault pioneer training.

Lieutenant General Yuri Stavitsky, Commandant of the Russian Engineer Troops, referred to experience gained during combat operations against separatists in Chechnya – which revealed the Russian army's substantial deficiencies in urban-fighting capabilities[88] – when he announced the establishment of the first such battalion in early December 2015. However, the unsuccessful siege of Donetsk Airport by a combination of Ukrainian rebel, Russian 'volunteer' and regular Russian forces from May 2014 to January 2015 seems to be the main reason for the Russian military planners' decision to re-establish assault pioneer units. There was no precedent during the Chechen campaign, nor since the beginning of the Second World War, of Russian troops being unable to seize just two large buildings (the old and new terminals of Donetsk Airport) for more than eight months.[89] The repeated failed attempts to capture the airport, regardless of the various measures undertaken since the Chechen campaign experience, revealed the inefficiency of Russian units' structures and training for urban assault actions.

The inclusion of assault pioneer elements in the formations of advancing troops, therefore, appears to be a natural response, since assault pioneer battalions' main combat task is to facilitate the advance of

January 2016, <https://topwar.ru/89829-v-voyska-postupayut-komplekty-zaschity-ovr-3sh.html>, accessed 21 March 2017.

[87] *Livejournal*, 'Zaschitniy kostyum "Kaspiy" pod obstrelom ["Caspian Sea" Protective Suit Under Fire]', 4 November 2015, <samoletchik.livejournal.com/83502.html>, accessed 21 March 2016.

[88] *Voennoe obozrenie* [*Military Review*], 'V kazhdoy obschevoyskovoy armii budet sformirovana inzhenernaya brigada [Engineer Brigades Will be Established in Every Combined Arms Army]', 3 December 2015, <http://topwar.ru/87274-v-kazhdoy-obschevoyskovoy-armii-budet-sformirovana-inzhenernaya-brigada.html>, accessed 21 March 2017.

[89] Joint Russian and rebel forces unsuccessfully assaulted Donetsk Airport terminals for 242 days and captured them only when Ukrainian troops were ordered to pull out. The defence of Stalingrad, by contrast, lasted 200 days. See *Joinfo*, 'V shtabe podschitali, skolko 'kiborgov' pogiblo za vremya oborony Donetskogo aeroporta' [Headquarters Have Counted Number of "Cyborgs" [the nickname rebels gave to Ukrainian soldiers defending Donetsk Airport] Lost in Action During Defence of Donetsk Airport]', 11 April 2015, <http://joinfo.ua/sociaty/1083821_V-shtabe-podschitali-skolko-kiborgov-pogiblo.html>, accessed 21 March 2017.

combined arms combat troops in urban environments.[90] It can be inferred from Stavitsky's announcement that the structure of the MD-subordinated engineer-sapper brigades will be adjusted to include assault pioneer battalions in each one.

Assault pioneer elements per se are not unique to Russian Ground Troops, as the Airborne Troops also include them in their formations.[91] However, the range of combat tasks assigned to airborne assault pioneers differs significantly from those of assault and obstacle-clearing land forces.[92] Airborne assault pioneers are equipped and trained mainly for clearing drop zones under fire as opposed to urban-assault combat operations.

Russian assault pioneer training and equipment, along with their role in the Second World War, gives clues to their probable tactics in combat.[93] First, engineer-sapper reconnaissance teams will covertly identify the structure of defences, with a particular focus on weak points, firing positions and minefields. Then, assault pioneers – generously equipped with light machine guns, grenade launchers with thermobaric grenades and light flamethrowers – will lead an advance through precleared passages in minefields to suppress and, if possible, destroy strong points with close-range firepower many times heavier than that of ordinary infantry. Demolition charges carried by assault elements will be used to suppress and destroy fortified firing positions and to break through walls and other obstacles to open up new paths to attack the enemy.

The Second World War proved that assault pioneer units alone do not guarantee the successful storming of prepared urban or fortified defensive positions. Therefore, artillery and, if necessary, tank support will be provided. Infantry elements are also likely to provide cover against possible flanking counterattacks by enemy forces against assault pioneer elements spearheading an assault.

---

[90] *Zvezda* [*Star*] (*Russian Ministry of Defence TV*), 'V rossiyskoy armii poyavilsya perviy shturmovoy inzhenerno-saperniy bataljon [First Assault Engineer Battalion Established in the Russian Army]'.
[91] There are assault pioneer companies in the 661st, 388th, 629th and 656th Detached Guards Engineer-Sapper Battalions of Russia's two airborne (98th and 106th) and two air-assault (7th and 76th) divisions respectively; air-assault brigades, which are also in the structure of the Russian airborne troops, do not have engineer-sapper battalions.
[92] *TASS*, 'Kazhdaya obschevoyskovaya armiya poluchit k 2020 godu inzhenerno-shturmovuyu brigadu [Every Combined Arms Army Will Receive an Assault Engineer Brigade by 2020]', 2 December 2015, <http://tass.ru/armiya-i-opk/2492454>, accessed 21 March 2017.
[93] Mikhail Mikhin, 'Pro gvardeyskoe shturmovoe podrazdelenie inzhenernykh voysk [On the Guards' Assault Engineer Element of the Engineer Troops]'.

Improvements in troops' survivability against PGMs, operational flexibility and assault potential in urban operations are the primary effects of the revitalisation of engineer-sapper units and the re-establishment of disbanded engineer-sapper regiments in each field army, alongside the re-establishment of the centrally subordinated engineer-sapper brigades as a reserve force. The current plan is to ensure that every field army has its own engineer-sapper regiment, which will itself contain a company of assault pioneers, by 2020.[94] Additional engineer-sapper units will be established during the same period, subordinated to the central command rather than MDs or field armies,[95] but it is not yet clear whether these will be of regimental or brigade size.[96]

One further, seemingly minor but noteworthy detail of these recent developments is the presence of amphibious elements in the structure of the new 28th Pontoon-Bridge Brigade in addition to its pontoon-bridge and bridge-construction elements.[97] Amphibious elements are configured for assault river crossings under combat conditions. This not only underlines the greater emphasis on enhancing the mobility of Russian troops, but also discloses a shift in planning towards offensive operations. This is a substantial departure from reductions in the offensive potential of Soviet, and then Russian, forces common in military planning practice since 1988.

The current reforms in engineer-sapper unit capabilities shed light on the thinking of Russia's political-military decision-makers, which can best be described as a persistent inclination to increase Russian armed forces'

---

[94] *Voenno-promyshlenniy kurjer* [*Military-Industrial Courier*], 'Shturmovye inzhenernye brigady k 2020 godu budut v kazhdoy obschevoyskovoy armii [Assault Engineer Brigades will be Included in Every Combined Arms Army by 2020]', 2 December 2015, <http://vpk-news.ru/news/28321>, accessed 21 March 2017.

[95] *Ibid.*

[96] As Stavitsky said: 'My nadeemsya sformirovat esche neskolko polkov do 2020 goda v sostave kazhdoy obschevoyskovoy armii i v sostave chastey tsentralnogo podchineniya [We hope to establish several more regiments in each combined arms army and under Central Command by 2020]'. See *ibid.* On the one hand, the other engineer-sapper units currently subordinated to central command (to the Commandant of the Engineer Troops) are brigades – the 1st Guards Engineer-Sapper Brigade and the 28th Pontoon-Bridge Brigade. On the other, there is a precedent that the Commandant of the Engineer Troops was in direct command until recently (2010) of the 66th Pontoon-Bridge Regiment and the 45th Engineer-Camouflage Regiment.

[97] *Voennoe obozrenie* [*Military Review*], 'V inzhenernykh voyskakh VS RF formiruetsya pontonno-mostovaya brigada s uchebnym tsentrom v Murome [The Pontoon-bridge Brigade, with a Training Centre in Murom, is Being Established in Russia's Armed Forces]', 16 July 2015, <http://topwar.ru/78947-v-inzhenernyh-voyskah-vs-rf-formiruetsya-pontonno-mostovaya-brigada-s-uchebnym-centrom-v-murome.html>, accessed 21 March 2017.

offensive potential in high-end conventional conflicts. The reintegration of modern, capable river-crossing equipment into manoeuvre formations and the larger, centrally subordinated brigades provide increased mobility for advancing troops. Safer (in terms of reduced risk of personnel losses) and more efficient obstacle- and mine-clearing hardware also contributes to this goal. Most notably, perhaps, the new assault pioneer battalions bring with them the capability to advance swiftly in the most densely defended urban areas.

Electronic Warfare Units

Russian forces have made extensive use of electronic warfare (EW) in the conflict in eastern Ukraine, underlining the emphasis placed on EW to counter enemy military capabilities by Russian military planners. Indeed, EW units manned by Russian regulars and reporting to Russian commanders have been established in every rebel military formation in Donbass.[98] This alone proves that even the specialist Russian EW units deployed on both sides of the Russia–Ukraine border in direct support of the combat in Donbass were unable to provide sufficient EW support to satisfy operational requirements.

A fundamental feature of the Russian approach to EW units is that they are integrated into every Russian manoeuvre formation;[99] they are not viewed as 'magicians' sitting deep in the rear and coming to the front line for specific tasks. The tactical integration of EW force elements increases the flexibility and effectiveness of combat operations. It also allows a much better understanding of the value and proper use of EW capabilities on the part of mid-level Russian commanders, which further enhances their combat efficiency. Every MD has its own EW brigade directly

[98] Numerous examples can be found documenting the presence of these specialists, including: *InfoNapalm*, 'Vozle DAP vyyavlen noveyshiy kompleks radiorazvedki VS RF "Torn"' [The Russian Armed Forces' "Torn" Newest SIGINT System is Identified near Donetsk Airport]', 1 September 2015, <https://informnapalm.org/12200-kompleks-radyorazvedky-torn-dap/>, accessed 18 May 2017; also *InfoNapalm*, 'VS RF ispolzovali stantsiyu R-330Zh v boyakh za Debaltsevo. Snimki rabochego terminala' [Russian Armed Forces Employed the R-30Zh Station in Combat at Debaltsevo. Screenshots of the Station's Terminal]', 21 April 2015, <https://informnapalm.org/22085-reb-r-330zh-zhitel/>, accessed 18 May 2017; also *InfoNapalm*, 'Pod Luganskom obnaruzhena rossiyskaya stantsiya R-934UM. Radioperekhvat peregovorov' [Russian R-943UM Station is Detected near Lugansk: Radiointercept]', 28 April 2015, <https://informnapalm.org/22638-stantsiya-r-934um-pod-luganskom/>, accessed 18 May 2017.
[99] *TASS*, 'Den spetsialista radioelektronnoy borby. Dosje [Electronic Warfare Specialists' Day: Dossier]', 15 April 2016, <tass.ru/info/3204583>, accessed 21 March 2017.

subordinated to its commandant.[100] Furthermore, one enlarged EW brigade is maintained as a strategic reserve, directly subordinated to the Commandant of Russia's EW troops.[101] EW elements are also being incorporated into those army aviation regiments/brigades subordinated to MD and combined arms armies.[102]

The technical capabilities of EW units are tailored to the operational needs and responsibilities of their parent formations. The standard EW company of a Russian manoeuvre brigade operates equipment capable of jamming both tactical command-and-control networks, including those used by hostile tactical aviation forces, and GPS signals to counter local use of GPS-guided munitions,[103] and can also prematurely activate the radio proximity fuses of incoming munitions to defend friendly forces against artillery, rocket and missile attacks.[104] District-subordinated EW brigades (and fleet-subordinated detached EW centres) are responsible for jamming operational- and strategic-level communications networks, as well as jamming AWACS and JSTARS/ELINT-type aircraft to impede an enemy's surveillance and operational control capabilities.

Electronic countermeasures against UAVs – reconnaissance and armed – are being introduced at all levels, from EW companies of manoeuvre brigades to General Staff-subordinated EW brigades. This impetus is in part fuelled by experience gained in eastern Ukraine, where the use of small UAVs for reconnaissance and artillery spotting was widespread on both sides.

A triple role is envisaged for EW units in the Russian land forces. The first is the disruption of enemy command-and-control networks and communications channels. The second is countering an adversary's intelligence, reconnaissance and surveillance activities with active and/or passive radar-based techniques. The third is defending friendly forces against enemy artillery, missile and air-dropped munitions. Interestingly,

---

[100] *Ibid.*

[101] Alexey Ramm, 'Elektronnaya voyna – mify i pravda – chast 1 [Electronic Warfare – Myths and Truth – Part 1]', *Voenno-promyshlenniy kurjer* [*Military-Industrial Courier*], 30 September 2015, <http://vpk-news.ru/articles/27272>, accessed 21 March 2017.

[102] *Vzglyad* [*Look*], 'V VVS Rossii resheno sformirovat 14 brigad armeyskoy aviatsii i vertoletnykh polkov [Russian Air Force Decides to Establish 14 Army Aviation Brigades and Helicopter Regiments]'.

[103] NVP Protek, 'Avtomatizirovannaya stantsiya pomekh R-330Zh' [R-330Zh Automated Jamming Station]', <http://www.protek-vrn.ru/production/avtomatizirovannaya-stantsiya-pomeh-r-330zh/>, accessed 18 May 2017.

[104] Kirill Ryabov, 'Mashina REB 1L262 "Rtut-BM"' [1L252 "Rtut-BM" EW Vehicle]', *Voennoe Obozrenie* [*Military Survey*], 30 July 2014, <https://topwar.ru/55269-mashina-reb-1l262-rtut-bm.html>, accessed 18 May 2017.

the second and third roles link EW units to the previously discussed roles of engineer-camouflage and CBRN units, creating a capability triad that enhances the survivability and combat effectiveness of Russian land forces in defensive and offensive scenarios. While all three roles are very much part of defence, they also contribute substantially to troops' offensive potential, mitigating the threat of enemy opposition to a Russian advance. It is noteworthy that the newest EW equipment (the Mi-8MTPR-1 Rychag-AV heliborne EW designed to suppress enemy air defences, for instance) is being delivered to the units of the Southern and Western MDs bordering Ukraine.[105]

Impact of Sanctions and Reduced Government Revenues on Reforms

Substantial restrictions have been imposed on the military reform process by the economic difficulties Russia is experiencing as a result of low oil prices and the economic sanctions imposed following its annexation of Crimea and military involvement in eastern Ukraine. These have contributed to a range of difficulties. For example, the ambitious helicopter rearmament programme has been hit by chronic shortages of engines, due to previous reliance on imports from Ukraine. Difficulties in establishing adequate alternative sources of helicopter engines is just one of numerous examples of the impact of sanctions on the implementation of Russia's ambitious rearmament programme. After more than two years of bravado, Putin reluctantly admitted in October 2016 that sanctions are having a serious impact, stalling development due to restrictions on technology transfer that significantly impeded the Russian defence industry's activities.[106]

Another noteworthy effect of Russia's economic and structural difficulties is the descision to establish several fully female-crewed motor-rifle battalions,[107] due to the demographic gap and lack of sufficient resources to attract male candidates for professional military service. This is an unprecedented move for the Russian military. Mass employment of women in front line units has been a taboo for the Soviet and Russian

---

[105] *Livejournal*, 'Vertolety Mi-8MTPR-1 [Mi-8MTPR-1 EW Helicopters]', BMPD blog of the Centre for Analysis of Strategies and Technologies, 3 September 2015, <http://bmpd.livejournal.com/1458627.html>, accessed 21 March 2017.
[106] Vladimir Putin, 'Investitsionniy forum VTB Kapital 'Rossiya zovyot!' [VTB Capital's Investment Forum "Russia Calling!"]', speech given to 8th Annual VTB Capital Investment Forum, 12 October 2016, <http://www.kremlin.ru/events/president/news/53077>, accessed 21 March 2017.
[107] Anton Valagin, 'Pod Khabarovskom nachalis ucheniya zhenskogo bataljona [Female Battalion Exercises Begin Near Khabarovsk]', *Russkoe oruzhie/ Rossisyskaya Gazeta* [*Russian Weapons/Russian Gazette*], 25 July 2016, <rg.ru/2016/07/25/reg-dfo/pod-habarovskom-nachalis-ucheniia-zhenskogo-batalona.html>, accessed 21 March 2017.

armies since the end of the Second World War. While it might be interpreted as evidence of modernising attitudes to women in Russia, the highly conservative nature of the Russian military suggests that it is driven by demographic and financial necessity.

However, given the priority attached to the military reform programme by the Kremlin, equipment development programmes are likely to remain cushioned wherever possible from the worst effects of the economic crisis.[108] In the wake of 10 per cent budget cuts imposed by the Kremlin on other state departments, the defence budget was increased from the expenditure originally planned by law for the 2016 defence budget (see Table 5) by RUB 739.7 billion[109] ($11.84 billion as of October 2016), or 23.5 per cent, to RUB 3.888 trillion[110] ($62.26 billion) in October 2016.[111] This additional money has been allocated to pay in advance loans that defence firms had to take out in order to fulfil the State Armament Programme's contracts. This October 2016 repayment of the loans from the federal budget to enterprises was originally planned for a later period – but this seemed less possible due to the seemingly inevitable financial difficulties that the Russian government will encounter in the not-too-distant future. Since the situation is not expected to improve significantly, Russian political-military planners are attempting to maintain unsustainable levels of investment in the short term in order to get the ground forces into a sufficiently powerful condition, with stocks of reasonably up-to-date weapons large enough to last through the anticipated period of severe austerity while still remaining a useful tool of state power.

Moscow wishes to avoid at any cost a situation such as that of the Russian land forces in Georgia in 2008, when equipment reserves were exhausted and Russian weapons were technologically inferior to those of its adversaries. Prospective delays and reductions in the delivery of Armata-series vehicles (70 tanks to be delivered by 2020 instead of 2,300 tanks as originally planned, and the programme fulfilment delayed until 2025[112])

---

[108] *RBC*, 'U pravitelstva obnaruzhilsya neuchtenniy 1 trillion rubley [Government Finds 1 Trillion Roubles of Unaccounted Money]', 15 January 2016, </www.rbc.ru/ economics/15/01/2016/5697f6e79a794701f110b8ce>, accessed 21 March 2017.

[109] *Interfax*, 'Gosduma odobrila v pervom chtenii popravki v byudzhet na 2016 god [State Duma Approves First Reading of Amendments to the 2016 Budget]', 21 October 2016, <http://www.interfax.ru/business/533475>, accessed 21 March 2017.

[110] *Ibid.*

[111] *RBK*, 'Minfin predlozhil urezat raskhody na oboronu [Finance Ministry Proposed Cuts to Defence Spending]', 9 September 2016, <www.rbc.ru/economics/09/09/ 2016/57d1ecd09a79475217227650>, accessed 21 March 2017.

[112] *TASS*, 'Istochnik: armiya RF k 2020 godu poluchit okolo 70 seriynykh tankov "Armata" [Source: Around 70 "Armata" Tanks Will be Delivered to the Russian

Table 5: Russian Defence Expenditure, Billions of Russian Roubles

	2008	2013	2014	2015	2016
Nominal military expenditure ('National defence' article of budget)	1,136[a]	2,104[b]	2,479[c]	3,181[d]	3,888[e]
Increase year-on-year, %	25.1	16.1	17.9[f]	28.3[g]	22.2
Military expenditure as reported to the UN[h]	1,065.8	1,709.9	1,959.9	2,903.3	*Not Available*
Military expenditure via civilian articles of the consolidated budget[i]	0.426	0.887	0.922	1.075	≈1.0[j]
Total military expenditure	1,562	2,991	3,401	4,256	4,888[k]
% of GDP, 'National defence'/Total expenditure	2.75/3.78	3.15/4.48	3.49/4.79	3.94/5.27	4.62/5.81

Source: Authors' calculations based on multiple sources. More information available on request.
Notes:
[a] CAST, 'Gosudarstvennye programmy vooruzheniya Rossiyskoy Federatsii: problemy ispolneniya i potentsial optimizatsii [The Russian Federation's State Armament Programmes: Problems of Implementation and Possibilities for Optimisation]', 2015, <http://www.cast.ru/files/Report_CAST.pdf>, accessed 21 March 2017; and in compliance with *RBK*, 'Zasekrechennye trilliony: skolko Rossiya na samom dele tratit na armiyu [Classified Trillions: How Much Russia Actually Spends on its Army]', 27 July 2016, <www.rbc.ru/economics/27/07/2016/5797ed069a79475ab72f84bb>, accessed 21 March 2017.
[b] Calculated using figures found at *Informing.ru*, 'SMI: v 2016 godu RF sokratila voennye raskhody na 100 mlrd rubley [Media: Russian Federation Reduced Defence Expenditure by 100 Billion Roubles in 2016]', 13 October 2016, <informing.ru/2016/10/13/smi-v-2015-godu-rf-sokratila-voennye-rashody-na-100-mlrd-rubley.html>, accessed 21 March 2017, in compliance with 'CAST, 'Gosudarstvennye programmy vooruzheniya Rossiyskoy Federatsii: problemy ispolneniya i potentsial optimizatsii [The Russian Federation's State Armament Programmes: Problems of Implementation and Possibilities for Optimisation]' and *RBK*, 'Zasekrechennye trilliony: skolko Rossiya na samom dele tratit na armiyu [Classified Trillions: How Much Russia Actually Spends on its Army]'.
[c] *Ibid.*
[d] *Informing.ru*, 'SMI: v 2016 godu RF sokratila voennye raskhody na 100 mlrd rubley [Media: Russian Federation Reduced Defence Expenditure by 100 Billion Roubles in 2016]'.
[e] *Interfax*, 'Gosduma odobrila v pervom chtenii popravki v byudzhet na 2016 god [State Duma Approves First Reading of Amendments to the 2016 Budget]'.
[f] On the basis of 'SMI: v 2016 godu RF sokratila voennye raskhody na 100 mlrd rubley [Media: Russian Federation Reduced Defence Expenditure by 100 Billion Roubles in 2016]', in compliance with 'Gosudarstvennye programmy vooruzheniya Rossiyskoy Federatsii: problem ispolneniya i potentsial optimizatsii [The Russian Federation's State Armament Programmes: Problems of Implementation and Possibilities for Optimisation]', and 'Zasekrechennye trilliony: skolko Rossiya na samom dele tratit na armiyu [Classified Trillions: How Much Russia Actually Spends on its Army]'.
[g] *Ibid.*
[h] Calculated based on UN Report on Military Expenditures, 'Russian Federation Country Profile', <www.un-arm.org/MilEx/CountryProfile.aspx?CountryId=163>, accessed 21 March 2017.
[i] See for instance analysis by Vasiliy Zatsepin, Head of the Laboratory of Military Economy at the Gaidar Institute, in *RBK*, 'Zasekrechennye trilliony: skolko Rossiya na samom dele tratit na armiyu [Classified Trillions: How Much Russia Actually Spends on its Army]'.
[j] On the assumption that 2016 expenditure will roughly equal that of 2015.
[k] This figure is an estimate.

suggest a pattern whereby equipment programmes are preserved wherever possible, but the timeframes have been shifted. Furthermore, delivery of new assets is prioritised for those units most likely to be involved in combat, deterrence or 'intimidation' operations in the Western and Southern MDs near Ukraine and the Baltic States.

In other words, despite Russia's economic woes, the Kremlin is going to great lengths to ensure that the military reform programme delivers the kind of forces described in this paper. The atmosphere of imminent danger from NATO encirclement and aggression – fed by an unrelenting tide of state media propaganda – means there are fewer domestic pressures on Putin to divert scarce resources to other purposes than there might be in Western countries. Even active supporters of the Kremlin's policy now admit that 'fear and apathy are seizing Russia; people are afraid to say what they think, they have become indifferent to what is happening [for fear of endangering themselves if they speak up]'.[113] It is likely, therefore, that while the sanctions regime and continuing low oil prices will slow the pace of Russian land forces restructuring and rearmament – and potentially affect the universal distribution of new equipment in the short term – it will not immediately change the underlying trends described in this section. The Russian leadership is doing its best to guarantee that its land forces get better equipment and tactical concepts of employment, and will continue to become stronger in this regard for the foreseeable future.

However, geopolitics might still prove disruptive. The Kremlin's ambitious rearmament programme was based on the assumption that Russia would have unimpeded opportunities to capitalise on Western technologies, parts, machine tools and advances in materials science in order to produce modern armaments and to base innovative/sophisticated tactics on the capabilities provided by such modern systems. In this regard, Russia has evidently followed a similar path to the Soviet Union during its desperate rearmament programme of the 1920s and 1930s, when extensive imports of Western technologies and weapons system designs were critical to the rapid development of the (then) modern Red Army. There are currently at least 826 Russian weapons systems that depend on parts from NATO and EU member states,[114] with Russian government officials stating that they want

---

Army by 2020]', 10 September 2016, <tass.ru/armiya-i-opk/3610673>, accessed 21 March 2017; *Lenta.ru* [*Tape.ru*], 'Rossiyskaya armiya poluchit na vooruzhenie 2300 tankov "Armata" [Russian Army Will Get Delivery of 2,300 "Armata" Tanks]', 15 September 2015, <lenta.ru/news/2015/09/15/armata/>, accessed 21 March 2017.
[113] Aleksandr Gorniy, 'Strakh [Fear]', *Ekho Moskvy* [*Moscow's Echo*], 16 October 2016, <echo.msk.ru/blog/amountain/1856530-echo/>, accessed 21 March 2017.
[114] *Novosti VPK* [*Military-Industrial Complex News*], 'Importozameshenie: blesk i nischeta rossiyskogo oboronno-promyshlennogo kompleksa [Import Substitution: The Brilliance and Poverty of Russia's Military-industrial Complex]', 20 January

to end import dependence for those specific systems by 2025.[115] In addition, 1,070 weapons systems are dependent on supplies from Ukraine,[116] which has banned by law any directly military-related exports to Russia as a result of its aggression in eastern Ukraine. Across the military as a whole, an average of between 8 and 10 per cent of the components in Russian weapons systems are imported.[117] In particular, the new Armata family of vehicles depends on imported Western optics and electronics.[118]

However politically embarrassing this situation is for Moscow, it is merely a symptom of a greater underlying problem – Russia's technological and material dependence on the West and its inability to overcome its own technological underdevelopment for the foreseeable future (see Table 6). Russian officials openly showed their concern when, in 2014, they admitted that import dependence in the economy's strategic sectors exceeded 80 per cent.[119] Between 40 and 90 per cent of electronic components in any Russian weapons system, with the exception of naval electronics, are imported.[120] Naval electronic systems are 100 per cent dependent on imported electronic components.[121]

Even with traditionally strong Russian industries, such as space-vehicle manufacture and launch, there is a strong dependence on imports. Some 25–

2016, </vpk.name/news/147993_importozameshenie__blesk_i_nisheta_rossiis kogo_oboronnopromyishlennogo_kompleksa.html>, accessed 21 March 2017.

[115] *Ibid.*

[116] Andrey Frolov, 'Svoy vmesto chuzhikh [Ours, Not Foreign]', *Rossiya v globalnoy politikve [Russia in Global Policy]* (No. 6, 2016), <www.globalaffairs.ru/number/ Svoi-vmesto-chuzhikh-18493>, accessed 21 March 2017.

[117] *TASS*, 'Minoborony: voennoe vedomstvo RF gotovo k slozhnostyam pri vypolnenii gosoboronzakaza [MoD: Russian Defence Ministry is Prepared for Difficulties with the Execution of the State Military Acquisition Programme]', 13 January 2015, <http://tass.ru/armiya-i-opk/1694063>, accessed 18 May 2017

[118] *Virtual Encyclopedia of Armour*, 'Tanki "Armata" prevzoydut analogy na 25-30 protsentov ["Armata" Tanks will Outmatch Rivals by 25 to 30 Per Cent]', 10 November 2014, <http://pro-tank.ru/blog/1407-armata-the-fifth-generation-tank>, accessed 18 May 2017.

[119] Sergey Tsyb, 'Dolya importa v strategicheskikh otraslyakh prevysila 80 protsentov [Share of Imports in Strategic Industries Exceeds 80 Per Cent]', *Lenta.ru [Tape.ru]*, 10 July 2014, <lenta.ru/news/2014/07/10/import/>, accessed 21 March 2017.

[120] Sergey Boev, 'Rossiya ostro nuzhdaetsya v pervoocherednom razvitii sobstvennoy elektronnoy komponentnoy bazy [Russia Badly Needs to Develop its Own Electronic Components Industry]', *Vremya elektroniki [Electronics' Time]*, 23 September 2016, <http://www.russianelectronics.ru/leader-r/32149/doc/64526/>, accessed 23 October 2016.

[121] *Novosti VPK [Military-Industrial Complex News]*, 'Importozameshenie: blesk i nisheta rossiyskogo oboronno-promyshlennogo kompleksa [Import Substitution: The Brilliance and Poverty of Russia's Military-industrial Complex]'.

Table 6: Current and Planned Dependence of Russian Industries on Imports

	Shipborne gas turbine engines	Helicopter engines	Electronics and optronics	Chipsets	Telecommunication equipment	Aircraft parts	Ship parts	Truck and car parts	Tractors	Machine-tools production	Medicines
% imports 2015	100	60	80–90	85	89	92	55 (95[a])	44	98	88.4	85
Planned % imports 2020	0	5	10	45	40	71	30	38	53	58	40

Source: *Vzglyad* [*Look*], 'Kak vyglyadyat plany po zamescheniyu importnykh tovarov rossiyskimi [How Are Plans Progressing to Substitute Imported Goods with Russian Ones]', 21 July 2015, <http://vz.ru/infographics/2015/7/21/757291.html>, accessed 21 March 2017.
Notes: [a] Up to 95 per cent of sub-units and components for ship general systems and devices are imported by Russia. *Novosti VPK*, 'Importozameshenie: blesk i nisheta rossiyskogo oboronno-promyshlennogo kompleksa [Import Substitution: The Brilliance and Poverty of Russia's Military-industrial Complex]'.

75 per cent of the electronic components used in Russia's legacy space systems are imported,[122] while the share of imported components exceeds 90 per cent in the newest ones, such as the 14F17 Uragan-K (also known as GLONASS-K) global positioning system satellites.[123] The continuation of sanctions has the potential to very negatively affect the deployment, maintenance and further use of the Uragan/GLONASS system.[124]

Therefore, the Kremlin's current assertive policy and its intensification of confrontation with the West threaten the very foundation on which the Russian rearmament programme is built – namely unrestricted access to modern Western technologies and goods. The Kremlin will be unable to resolve this dilemma without a fundamental change in its current paradigm. Even if there were such a change, it would probably be a long time before the trust necessary to restore the pre-2014 level of technological exchange between the West and Russia could be achieved. This is one potentially long-lasting impact of the seismic change in Western attitudes towards Moscow that has been provoked by Putin's aggressive policies since 2014.

The loss of access to modern technologies threatens the continuation of the (so far) fairly successful reform and rearmament of the Russian military. Structural, tactical and doctrinal changes alone cannot fulfil the Kremlin's aspirations for Russian land forces, since many of the crucial changes discussed in this paper will be seriously impeded, at best. It should be concluded, therefore, that reform of Russian land forces is facing a turbulent period and it is the Kremlin's geopolitical strategy that represents the largest obstacle to fulfilling its ambitious plans.

---

[122] *Ibid.*
[123] *Ibid.*
[124] *Vremya elektroniki* [*Electronics' Time*], 'Sanktsii Zapada mogut privesti k serjeznym problemam s razvitiem GLONASS [Western Sanctions Could Lead to Serious Problems with the Development of the GLONASS System]', 4 April 2014, <www.russianelectronics.ru/leader-r/news/29536/29541/doc/67417/>, accessed 21 March 2017.

III. GEOGRAPHICAL DISTRIBUTION AND MISSION ASSIGNMENTS OF RUSSIAN MILITARY UNITS

The deployment patterns of military forces can unwittingly (or wittingly) reveal national threat perceptions and military planning priorities. In the case of Russia, they strongly suggest that the Kremlin acts from a position of relative weakness and perceives potential dangers from all directions. This perception leads the Russian military to prioritise high readiness and strategic mobility on the part of its limited available forces, while retaining concurrent, substantial strike potential in every theatre of military operations. As this section shows in detail, the deployment pattern currently being pursued suggests that the Kaliningrad area, Crimea, Ukraine and the Russian segment of the Arctic are perceived as the main threat axes. At the same time, Russian deployments designed to mitigate the most urgent dangers are simultaneously used to intimidate the West and deter it from intervention inside what Russia perceives as its 'sphere of influence', primarily Ukraine. This section also shows that the deployments portrayed as threatening NATO member states are mainly oriented against Ukraine.[1]

Western Military District

The Western MD of the Russian armed forces includes land and air forces deployed in the western part of Russia, as well as the Baltic Fleet. The Western MD will generate Operational-Strategic Command (OSC) West in the event of hostility, which will cover two main areas – the Baltic region and Russia's continental western and southwestern border. The Western MD's land forces currently include three armies: the 20th Guards and 6th

---

[1] For the sake of brevity, individial units' coded designators (field post office numbers) and individual footnotes for specific unit information are not provided here, but can be obtained on request from the authors.

Combined Arms Armies (*Obschevoyskovaya Armiya*, or OA); and the 1st Guards Tank Army (TA). The land forces also include the 11th Army Corps. There are also numerous other formations and units either directly subordinated to the MD's commandant or operating to fulfil its operational needs.

The Baltic Region
Russian military posture in the Baltic region inevitably attracts the particular attention of Western observers, since it is one of only two regions in the world where Russian land forces are in direct contact with those of NATO member states (the other similar region – the Russia–Norway border – is much calmer). The Western MD's land forces are represented in this area by the 6th Combined Arms Army and the forces of the Kaliningrad Special Defence Region.

The 6th Combined Arms Red Banner Army
While proudly called an 'army', the 6th Red Banner, with its headquarters in St Petersburg, is the rough equivalent of a British or US Army division. It includes just two manoeuvre brigades stationed on the northern and southern shores of the Gulf of Finland, as well as fire support, combat support and logistics formations. Although the combat potential of the Russian forces permanently stationed in this area is not impressive, it must be noted that the Russian military has the ability to relocate its reserves on a grand scale, as demonstrated during operations in and around Ukraine in 2014–16. The 76th Guards Air-Assault Division, which has 6,200 airborne troops, is permanently deployed in Pskov – only 100 km from the Estonian border – within easy reach for the Western MD's commandant.

The 6th Combined Arms Red Banner Army includes:

- The 25th Detached Guards Motor-Rifle Brigade (Strugi Krasnye, Pskov province).
- The 138th Detached Guards Motor-Rifle Brigade (Kamenka, Leningrad province).
- The 26th Guards Missile Brigade (Luga, Leningrad province).
- The 9th Guards Artillery Brigade (Luga, Leningrad province).
- The 5th Zenith-Rocket (air defence) Brigade (Lomonosov/Nenyumyaki, Leningrad province).
- The 30th Engineer-Sapper Regiment (Kerro village, Leningrad province).
- The 6th CBRN Regiment (Sapernoe, Leningrad province).
- The 10th Detached CBRN Battalion (Sertolovo, Leningrad province).
- The 95th Command and Control Brigade (*brigada upravleniya*, Chyornaya Rechka St Petersburg suburb).

- The 51st Detached Logistics Brigade (St Petersburg).

There is a significant gap in deployed forces between the northernmost unit of OSC West and the southernmost unit of OSC North (Russian Northern Fleet), with both brigades sitting on the Russia–Finland border. This gap means that Russia does not possess sufficient forces to invade Finland at short notice without significant preparatory reinforcement. It is also strong evidence that Finland is not high on the threat-priority list of Russia's political–military leadership.

Kaliningrad Special Defence Region
The situation in Kaliningrad differs significantly from that on the Russia–Finland border. The Kaliningrad Special Defence Region (*Kaliningradskiy Osobiy Oboronitelniy Rayon*, or KOOR) is one of the most heavily militarised areas in the world. Even so, the Ministry of Defence has declared that strengthening Russia's military posture in the Kaliningrad area is among its top priorities, alongside Crimea and the Arctic.[2]

All land formations in the KOOR are directly subordinated to the Baltic Fleet. Ground troop formations in the region used to be organised under the 11th Combined Arms Army, but this was disbanded in 1997, when overall command passed from Ground Troops Headquarters to the Baltic Fleet. The KOOR was then established as a parent organisational structure under which to merge the fleet (with its organic coastal defence forces) and the locally deployed land forces. The 11th Army Corps has recently been re-established in Kaliningrad as a further intermediate structure subordinate to the fleet in order to directly control the land force. Currently, the KOOR military grouping includes:

- The 11th Army Corps, which includes:
  - The 79th Detached Guards Motor-Rifle Brigade (Gusev, Kaliningrad province).
  - The 7th Detached Guards Motor-Rifle Regiment (Kaliningrad) – reportedly uprated to brigade level by May 2015.[3]

---

[2] *Rossiyskaya Gazeta* [*Russian Gazette*], 'Rossiya ukrepit voyska v Krymu, Kaliningrade i Arktike [Russia Will Reinforce Troops in Crimea, Kaliningrad and the Arctic]', 13 January 2015, <https://rg.ru/2015/01/13/voiska-anons.html>, accessed 21 March 2017.

[3] The *Krasnaya zvezda* [*Red Star*] Russian Ministry of Defence daily newspaper referred to this formation as the 7th Brigade, rather than 7th Regiment, in an article in May 2015; Olga Vorobjeva and Dmitriy Semenov, 'Muzey eto zvuchit gordo [Museum is the Proud Name]', *Krasnaya zvezda* [*Red Star*], 15 May 2015, <redstar.ru/index.php/component/k2/item/23691-muzej-eto-zvuchit-gordo>, accessed 21 March 2017.

- o The 152nd Guards Missile Brigade (Chernyakhovsk, Kaliningrad province).
  - o The 244th Guards Artillery Brigade (Kaliningrad).
  - o The 22nd Detached Guards Zenith-Rocket (air defence) Regiment (Kaliningrad).
  - o The 214th Detached EW Regiment (Kaliningrad).
- The Baltic Fleet's coastal troops (all deployed in Kaliningrad province), which include:
  - o The 336th Detached Guards Marines Brigade (Baltiysk (Pilau)).
  - o The 25th Detached Coastal Missile Regiment (Donskoe).
  - o The 561st Naval Reconnaissance (naval Spetsnaz) Unit (Parusnoe).
  - o The 69th Detached Guards Naval Engineer Regiment (Primorsk).
  - o The 841st Detached EW Centre (Yantarniy).
  - o The 302nd Detached EW Regiment (Gvardeysk).
- Troops of the 44th Air Defence Division, which include:
  - o The 183rd Guards Zenith-Rocket (air defence) Regiment (Gvardeysk).
  - o The 1545th Zenith-Rocket (air defence) Regiment (Znamensk).
  - o The 81st Radio-Technical (radars) Regiment (Pereslavskoe).

A Russian National Guard (formerly Ministry of Interior Internal Troops) unit organised and equipped to the standards of a light infantry regiment (to be subordinated to the Baltic Fleet headquarters in the event of hostility):

- The 136th Detached Special Motorised Regiment (Kaliningrad).

One potentially noteworthy development is the possible appearance of an air-assault brigade and special operations units, not currently present in Kaliningrad province. During exercises between 5–10 December 2015, the Western MD tested its ability to rapidly redeploy troops between the Russian mainland and Kaliningrad with two full brigades, including an air-assault brigade and elements of the 26th Missile Brigade armed with Iskander-M short-range ballistic missile systems.[4] Statements made publicly six days after the exercise ended deserve particular attention: the Russian Ministry of Defence publicly stated that the creation of a *self-sufficient* grouping had been achieved as a result of the redeployment of these two brigades.[5]

---

[4] *Rugrad.eu*, 'S 5 po 10 dekabrya v Kaliningradskoy oblasti byla provedena vnezapnaya proverka boegotovnosti voysk [Snap Test of the Troops' Combat Readiness Carried Out in Kaliningrad Province from 5 to 10 December]', 16 December 2014, <http://rugrad.eu/news/733482/>, accessed 21 March 2017.

[5] Dmitriy Neratov, 'Voyska v Kaliningrade podnyali po trevoge [Troops Suddenly Alerted in Kaliningrad]', *Utro.ru* [*Morning.ru*], 16 December 2016, <http://www.utro.ru/articles/2014/12/16/1226073.shtml>, accessed 21 March 2017.

That statement suggests that the Russian military command regards the presence of an air-assault formation/unit as a precondition for the KOOR's self-sufficiency. An air-assault brigade/regiment would certainly be a valuable high-readiness mobile reserve force for the Russian commander in Kaliningrad to react to unexpected developments in the NATO member states that surround the enclave. Such a force could certainly fulfil an active defensive role, making it harder for NATO to try to cut Kaliningrad off from the rest of Russia. However, it would also be capable of mounting a deep incursion into Polish or Baltic territories in a crisis. While difficult to sustain indefinitely, such a lightning strike from Kaliningrad would divert NATO forces in the region, providing relief to Russian troops defending against an all-out NATO offensive or forcing NATO to defend on two fronts in the east against a Russian attack.

The same reasoning applies to the military grouping established by the Ministry of Defence in Crimea. This grouping of forces is also declared to be self-sufficient, but includes the planned 97th Guards Air-Assault Regiment,[6] whose parent unit, the 7th Guards Air-Assault Division, remains deployed on the Russian mainland. There are obvious parallels between the strategic situation for Russian forces in Crimea and Kaliningrad. Both territories are isolated from the Russian mainland in terms of defence infrastructure, since the ferry lane across the Kerch Strait is the only way for Russian military units with heavy armaments to reach Crimea. It is only logical that the Russian military might assume similar requirements for forces defending Kaliningrad and Crimea.

The announced plans to establish a third air-assault regiment – the 237th Guards – in the 76th Guards Air-Assault Division attract attention in this regard.[7] Although the regiment will initially be established in Pskov, it will be redeployed almost immediately. While Pushkin in Leningrad province rumoured to be a destination for this redeployment,[8] according to official announcements there are other options, the most obvious of which is Kaliningrad. The Crimean precedent shows that deployment of an air-assault regiment from a division deployed nearby

---

[6] Konstantin Bogdanov, 'Osinoe gnezdo [Wasps' Nest]', *Novosti VPK* [*Military-Industrial Complex News*], 17 March 2016, <http://vpk.name/news/151517_osinoe_gnezdo.html>, accessed 21 March 2017.

[7] *PAI – Pskovskoe Agentstvo Informatsii* [*PAI – Pskov Information Agency*], 'Vnov sozdanniy desantno-shturmovoy polk 76-y divizii VDV poluchit naimenovanie «237-y DShP» [The Newly Established Air-Assault Regiment of the 76th Airborne Division Will be Named the 237th Air-Assault Regiment]', 31 July 2015, <informpskov.ru/news/183743.html>, accessed 21 March 2017.

[8] *Ibid.*

on the mainland is a viable option for strengthening Kaliningrad. Therefore, the redeployment of the 237th Guards to Kaliningrad after it has been established in Pskov cannot be ruled out, and would considerably change the nature of Russia's already complex military posture in this region.

It is uncertain whether plans to establish reconnaissance brigades in every combined arms army (detailed in Chapter II) apply to the KOOR. Kaliningrad's strategic importance might lead Russian military planners to demand that a full combined arms army, including a reconnaissance brigade, be stationed there. However, the KOOR land forces sit one level below combined arms armies, and the 561st Naval Reconnaissance Unit – a naval Spetsnaz battalion – might be judged as adequately fulfilling the reconnaissance requirements of the Baltic Fleet. In this situation, adding a reconnaissance brigade is likely to be judged excessive. Given the manpower limitations facing the Russian land forces and the reform ethos to avoid unnecessary duplication of forces, the latter option is probably the more likely outcome for Kaliningrad.

However, if establishing a separate reconnaissance brigade is approved as part of the KOOR's land forces, it would be a strong indicator that the Russian political-military leadership is determined to use the Kaliningrad area for offensive military purposes. Such a brigade would be capable of carrying out long-range reconnaissance and surveillance patrols, as well as direct action, as far as 350 km from Kaliningrad. It would, therefore, substantially increase a KOOR commander's situational awareness and ability to project military power far beyond the borders of Kaliningrad.

Overall, Russian military forces in the Kaliningrad region are sufficient to create considerable problems for Poland and the Baltic States in areas with significant populations of ethnic Russians through destabilisation efforts along the same lines as those used in eastern Ukraine, backed by threatening Russian military deployments over the border and covert military operations in destabilised areas. They are not sufficient, however, for any extended conflict with NATO or for attempting to occupy any significant territory in the Baltic States or Poland. Unfortunately for NATO planners, Russia has proved that it can rapidly reinforce its forces in Kaliningrad; such efforts might be disguised as 'snap exercises', as was common practice during the spring 2014 phase of the Russian operation against Ukraine.

With the prospective addition of an air-assault regiment, and possibly a reconnaissance brigade structured to operate at up to 350 km beyond the FLOT, the Kaliningrad grouping could quickly be transformed from a defensive orientation to one much more offensive in nature and capable of direct action operations deep inside NATO territory.

The 1ˢᵗ Guards Tank and 20ᵗʰ Guards Combined Arms Armies

The 1ˢᵗ Guards TA and the 20ᵗʰ Guards OA are the most visible examples of Russia's efforts to strengthen its military muscle. Russia portrayed the establishment of these two field armies in 2014–15 as a direct response to alleged NATO 'provocations'. This is how Russian propaganda, and the officials echoing it, have characterised the measures taken by NATO to reassure its eastern member states in the face of Russia's increasing assertiveness and aggressive rhetoric.

Both armies will have a standardised structure, including a number of manoeuvre formations, and artillery, missile, reconnaissance, air-defence and logistics brigades, as well as helicopter, combat engineer and CBRN regiments.[9]

A closer look at the deployments of these two new armies, however, suggests that, contrary to the official line, their main weight is not directed against NATO but against Ukraine.

The 1ˢᵗ Guards Tank Army

The 1ˢᵗ Guards TA was re-established on 13 November 2014 with its headquarters in the Moscow suburb of Bakovka.[10] The headquarters is responsible for the units deployed around Moscow and in Nizhniy Novgorod, which were previously part of the 20ᵗʰ Guards OA (currently relocated). The current 1ˢᵗ Guards is the only tank army in the Russian Ground Troops' order of battle since 1999, and is a formation with an evocative combat history. The 1ˢᵗ Guards TA was established in April 1944 when the 1ˢᵗ TA was awarded Guards status. It participated in the Battle of Berlin in 1945 and was deployed as part of Soviet forces in Germany between 1945 and 1992 as the 1ˢᵗ Guards Tank Red Banner Army, with its headquarters in Dresden, East Germany. The army was withdrawn from Germany to the city of Smolensk in western Russia in 1992 and was disbanded seven years later.

Endowing this newly re-established formation with such heritage can be seen as a clear political message intended to intimidate and to draw attention to its specific, overtly offensive operational role within the

---

[9] *TASS*, 'Istochnik: tankovaya armiya pod Moskvoy budet sformirovana k zime [Source: Tank Army Will be Established Near Moscow By Winter]', 29 July 2015, <tass.ru/armiya-i-opk/2150702>, accessed 21 March 2017; Alexey Ramm, 'Reformy i resultaty [Reforms and Results]', *Voenno-promyshlenniy kurjer* [*Military-Industrial Courier*], 24 December 2015, <http://vpk.name/news/146871_reformyi_i_rezultatyi.html>, accessed 21 March 2017.

[10] *LiveJournal*, 'Sformirovana 1-ya gvardeyskaya tankovaya armiya [The 1ˢᵗ Guards Tank Army Has Been Established]', 1 June 2015, <http://bmpd.livejournal.com/1324525.html>, accessed 16 January 2016.

military. The 1st Guards TA takes responsibility for the units that were controlled by the 22nd OA, which had its headquarters in Nizhniy Novgorod until it was disbanded in 2010. However, it was not the 22nd OA that the General Staff chose to resurrect but the TA – which traditionally fulfilled the main offensive strike role in the Soviet army.

The newly established 1st Guards TA will take command of the following formations, most of which were previously under the command of the 22nd OA (pre-2010) or the 20th Guards OA between 2010 and 2014, when the 20th OA was located in Nizhniy Novgorod:

- The 2nd Guards Tamanskaya Motor-Rifle Division (Kalininets, Moscow province).
- The 4th Guards Kantemirovskaya Tank Division (Naro-Fominsk, Moscow province).
- The 144th Guards Motor-Rifle Division (Elnya, Smolensk province).[11]
- The 6th Detached Tank Brigade (Mulino, near Nizhniy Novgorod).
- The 112th Guards Missile Brigade (Shuya, Ivanovo province).[12]
- An artillery brigade (designated number unknown at time of writing) (Moscow province).[13]

---

[11] *Lenta.ru* [*Tape.ru*], 'Istochnik soobschil o razvertyvanii Elninskoy divizii v sostave 1-y tankovoy armii [Source Reported Establishment of Elnya Division in the 1st Tank Army's Structure]', 5 July 2016, <https://lenta.ru/news/2016/07/05/elninskaya/>, accessed 21 March 2017. While some Russian sources report subordination of the 144th Guards to the 20th Guards OA, this seems unlikely. It is located in Smolensk province, but Russian sources specified that the 20th Guards OA's formations would be located in Belgorod, Kursk, Lipetsk, Tambov, and Voronezh provinces, and not in Smolensk province. See *TASS*, 'Istochnik: pereformiruemuyu 20-yu armiyu razvernut v pyati regionakh na zapade Rossii [Source: Redefined 20th Army Will be Deployed in Five Regions in Western Russia]', 13 August 2015, <tass.ru/armiya-i-opk/2184493>, accessed 21 March 2017; Aleksandr Khrolenko, 'Priuchenie k miru: chto 20-ya armiya delaet u zapadnykh granits Rossii [Acclimatising to Peace: What the 20th Army is Doing Near Russia's Western Borders]', *RIA Novosti*, 18 November 2016, <https://ria.ru/defense_safety/20161118/1481665537.html>, accessed 21 March 2017.
[12] The subordination of the 112th Guards Missile Brigade to the 1st Guards Tank Army is not clear. The 112th Guards was directly subordinated to the Western MD command, being the reserve of the District's Commandant. The 448th Missile Brigade, which was previously subordinated to the 20th Guards Army (when the army's headquarters was located in Nizhniy Novgorod) will likely remain in the structure of the 20th Guards after the army's relocation to Voronezh as the 448th Brigade's location in Kursk, near Voronezh, makes it possible to keep the brigade under the command of the Voronezh-based army.
[13] The artillery brigade did not exist in Moscow province until it was established in early 2016. See *Rambler News Service*, 'Artilleriyskaya brigada v Moskovskoy oblasti poluchila partiyu ustanovok "Uragan" [Artillery Brigade in Moscow Province Gets Delivery of "Uragan" Rocket System]', 11 February 2016, <https://rns.online/

- The 49th Zenith-Rocket (air defence) Brigade (Krasniy Bor, Smolensk province).
- The 96th Detached Reconnaissance Brigade (Nizhniy Novgorod).
- An engineer regiment (designated number unknown at time of writing) (Mulino, near Nizhniy Novgorod)[14] or the 45th Engineer-Sapper Brigade (Nakhabino, Moscow province, and Murom, Vladimir province).[15]
- The 60th Detached Command Brigade (Selyatino, Moscow province).
- The 20th CBRN Regiment (Nizhniy Novgorod).
- The 69th Logistics Brigade (Mulino, near Nizhniy Novgorod).

The 1st Guards will also probably assume command of at least some of the reserve formations raised as active service brigades in the period immediately preceding any large-scale war, including the 99th Guards armaments and equipment storage and maintenance base (the wartime 13th Detached Guards Motor-Rifle Brigade) in Tver.

There is ambiguity regarding the 144th Guards' subordination, which is probably deliberately supported by the Russian side to mislead analysts: there are reports that the 28th Brigade is subordinated to the 20th OA.[16] However, those 28th Brigade elements redeployed to Klintsy were used to re-establish the 488th Motor-Rifle Regiment[17] – which was in the structure of the 144th Guards Division until the latter was disbanded in 2003. The re-established 488th is also situated near the 144th Guards Division's main camp in Elnya, Smolensk province. Other 28th Brigade force elements are being used in Elnya and Shatalovo to lay the foundation for the 144th Guards' other units. Taking all of this together, it is reasonable to conclude that the 488th Regiment is subordinated to the 144th Guards Division, which, in turn, is in the structure of the 1st Guards TA, as the 20th OA does not have any of its

---

military/artilleriiskaya-brigada-v-Moskovskoi-oblasti-poluchila-partiyu-ustanovok-Uragan-2016-02-11/>, accessed 21 March 2017.

[14] To be established on the base of the existing engineer battalion military unit 11364-2.

[15] The military unit 11361 – allegedly the 45th Engineer-Sapper Brigade – did exist as late as mid-December 2015 regardless of the earlier information that it had been disbanded. See *Prizyvnik* [*Conscript*], 'Inzhenernye voinskie chasti g.Murom [City of Murom's Engineer Military Units]', 15 December 2015, <http://www.prizyvnik. info/threads/134266-injenernyie_voinskie_chasti_gmurom_v_ch_11361-4_v_ch_ 11105_v_ch_45445/page19>, accessed 21 March 2017.

[16] Ekaterina Zgirovskaya, 'Shoygu ukreplyaet bryanskiy rubezh [Shoigu Reinforces the Bryansk Frontier]', *Gazeta.ru* [*Gazette.ru*], 1 June 2016, <https://www.gazeta.ru/ army/2016/06/01/8276903.shtml#>, accessed 21 March 2017.

[17] *GorodBRYANSK24* [*City-of-Bryansk24*], 'V Klintsakh stroitsya voenniy gorodok dlya 488-go motostrelkovogo polka [The 488th Motor-Rifle Regiment's Camp is Under Construction in Klintsy]', 18 August 2016, <www.gorodbryansk.info/2016/ 08/klintsy_warfare/>, accessed 21 March 2017.

subordinated formations in Smolensk province. Therefore the plans to subordinate the 488th Regiment to the 20th OA, which existed up until early April 2016, were probably abandoned.

Earlier reports on the resubordination of the 27th Guards Motor-Rifle Brigade to the 1st Guards TA[18] were not confirmed – which probably points to the cancellation of plans to resubordinate. Since 1983, the 27th Guards has always been directly subordinated to the Moscow and then the Western MD headquarters, rather than to any of the field armies in the structure of the 'capital city military district'.

There are good reasons for keeping the 27th Guards Brigade under the direct command of the 'capital city military district' commandant. Since it was established in 1983, the 27th Guards has a comparable status to the British Army's Household Division, tasked to serve as a last reserve for the Soviet (and then Russian) government in a national emergency. In 1990, the brigade was even placed under the KGB's command structure (alongside the 103rd Guards Airborne Division, the 75th and 48th Motor-Rifle Divisions, and the 15th Detached Spetsnaz Brigade) to deal with separatist threats to state security. These formations were withdrawn from KGB command after the failed coup d'état in August 1991. During the attempted coup, the 27th Guards troops guarded all the most important state installations in the capital under the orders of the State Committee on the State of Emergency. The government's decision to resubordinate such a valued and loyal state asset (and security tool) to a field army would therefore be made unwillingly, due to severe manpower shortages.[19] Stripping down the Central MD, whose brigades have been hurriedly redeployed to western Russia, was probably a solution to the manpower problem while not depriving the Kremlin of its unit of last resort.

---

[18] *TASS*, 'Istochnik: tankovaya armiya pod Moskvoy budet sformirovana k zime [Source: Tank Army Will Be Established Near Moscow by Winter]'.

[19] If transferred to the 1st Guards TA command, the 27th Guards will lose part of its appeal as a 'weapon of last resort' for the Kremlin, as extra links in the chain of command add time to the execution of urgent decisions. At the same time, an indirect chain of command of the unit being used as the last resort in an emergency leads to questions about the unit's reliability. The Russian political elite has not forgotten the experience of 1991, when commanders of two units not subordinated directly to the top Russian military hierarchy – one battalion each of the 137th Airborne Regiment (106th Guards Airborne Division) and the 1st Guards Tank Regiment (2nd Guards Tamanskaya Motor-Rifle Division) – switched loyalty and defended the then Russian President Boris Yeltsin and his people instead of preparing to storm them by the order of the Soviet government. Therefore, any unit not permanently under central control at the highest levels is not considered reliable by the Kremlin.

The 20ᵗʰ Guards Combined Arms Army

The 20th Guards OA was relocated from Nizhniy Novgorod to Voronezh in early June 2015.[20] Russian sources make no attempt to conceal the fact that coordination of Russian troops deployed against Ukraine was the main task driving this relocation.[21] The 20th Guards OA will probably take command of the following formations:

- The 3rd Guards Motor-Rifle Division (Boguchar, Voronezh province).[22]
- The 23rd Guards Detached Motor-Rifle Brigade (Valuyki, Belgorod province).[23]
- (Probably) the 288th Artillery Brigade (Mulino, but probably relocated to the southern region of Russia).
- The 448th Missile Brigade (Durnevo, Kursk province).
- The 53rd Zenith-Rocket (air defence) Brigade (Kursk).
- The 20th CBRN Regiment (Nizhniy Novgorod).
- The 456th Detached CBRN Battalion (Kursk)[24] or the 564th Detached CBRN Battalion (Kursk).
- The 9th Guards Command (C3) Brigade (Voronezh).

---

[20] *RIA-Voronezh*, 'Minoborony perebrosilo shtab 20-y armii v Voronezhskuyu oblast [Ministry of Defence Relocates 20th Army Headquarters to Voronezh Province]', 2 June 2015, <http://riavrn.ru/districts/bogucharsky/minoborony-perebrosilo-shtab-20-y-armii-v-voronezhskuyu-oblast/>, accessed 21 March 2017.

[21] *Ibid.*; *LiveJournal*, 'SMI objyasnili prichinu sozdaniya tankovoy armii v Rossii [Media Explained the Reasons for the Establishment of a Tank Army in Russia]', 4 June 2015, <http://birserg-1977.livejournal.com/340441.html>, accessed 16 January 2016.

[22] Ivan Petrov, 'Shoigu rasskazal o postuplenii novoy tekhniki v voyska [Shoigu Told about Arrival of New Equipment to the Troops]', *Russkoe oruzhie/Rossiyskaya Gazeta* [*Russian Weapons/Russian Gazette*], 21 October 2016, <https://rg.ru/2016/10/21/shojgu-rasskazal-o-postuplenii-novoj-tehniki-i-vooruzhenij-v-vojska.html>, accessed 21 March 2017.

[23] Gulnara Tagirova, 'SMI: V Belgorodskoy oblasti razmestyat motostrelkovuyu brigadu [Media: A Motorised Rifle Brigade Will be Deployed in Belgorod Province]', *Fonar.tv* [*Flashlight.tv*], 15 September 2015, <http://fonar.tv/news/2015/09/15/smi-v-belgorodskoy-oblasti-razmestyat-motostrelkovuyu-brigadu>, accessed 21 March 2017. The camp in Valuyki ('Object T-42/15-122') accommodates up to 1,500 conscripts and 2,000 professionals as privates/sergeants, plus an unknown number of officers; the planned completion date for construction work was 29 April 2016. See *AllTenders*, 'Tender: Vypolnenie proektno-izyskatelskikh rabot po pervomu i vtoromu etapam i stroitelno-montazhnykh rabot pervogo etapa po objektu "Kapitalnoe stroitelstvo objektov voennogo gorodka" [Tender: Design and Survey Work on the First and Second Stages of Construction and Installation Works of the First Phase of the Objects of Capital Construction of a Military Camp]', <www.alltenders.ru/tender_podrob_new.asp?KodTendera=12963611>, accessed 21 March 2017. In practice internal finishing of buildings was still underway in mid-November 2016.

- The 2728th CBRN Armaments and Equipment Storage and Maintenance base (Frolovo, Volgograd province) may be transferred from the Southern MD and used to establish the 20th Army's CBRN regiment.
- An engineer-sapper Regiment being established in Voronezh province.
- Other combat support and support formations.

It should be noted that the 23rd Guards and 28th Motor-Rifle Brigades from the Central MD have been redeployed to Belgorod and Bryansk provinces respectively on the Russia–Ukraine border. This move reveals the urgent nature of measures being adopted by the Russian military command to establish the two new armies. Instead of waiting for new formations to be established in the corresponding locations, the Russian leadership has redeployed brigades from the Asian part of the country, depriving the Central MD of a quarter of its available manoeuvre formations.

It is reported that the 1st Guards TA and 20th Guards OA will be the first in the Russian armed forces to receive Armata armoured vehicles. T-14 Armata next-generation MBTs will replace the T-80 and T-90 MBTs currently in service,[25] while T-15 Bagulnik heavy IFVs will equip the motor-rifle units and elements of the 'heavy' divisions and brigades of the two armies. T-16 BREMs (*Bronirovannaya Remontno-Evakuatsionnaya Mashina*, or armoured repair-and-recovery vehicles) will augment combat support elements. Both armies are also reported to receive the new Kurganets-25 family of medium-armoured personnel carriers (APC and IFV variants).

While these formations would be an impressive force in potential operations against NATO, the newly established armies are not exclusively oriented against the Alliance. The deployment pattern of the new armies shows that their immediate purpose is to legitimise and maintain constant military pressure on Ukraine. This is being achieved through the permanent deployment of Russian troops near the Russia–Ukraine border (Figure 7). The new and relocated formations are stationed in a wide arc that bears a strong resemblance to the deployment patterns used during the spring and summer of 2014. This pattern would not be expected if Russia was preparing for an imminent operation against NATO. Nor does it imply an imminent Russian attack on Ukraine, as political considerations have

---

[24] Currently in the structure of the 27th CBRN Brigade, assigned to the 20th Combined Arms Army as its CBRN unit.

[25] Anton Valagin, 'Pervymi 'Armatu' poluchat tankisty Voronezha i Podmoskovja [Tankmen in Voronezh and Moscow Regions Will be First to Receive Armata Tanks]', *Rossiyskaya Gazeta* [*Russian Gazette*], 29 July 2015, <http://www.rg.ru/2015/07/29/armata-site-anons.html>, accessed 21 March 2017.

Figure 7: Deployment of the New and Relocated Russian Formations in Western Russia

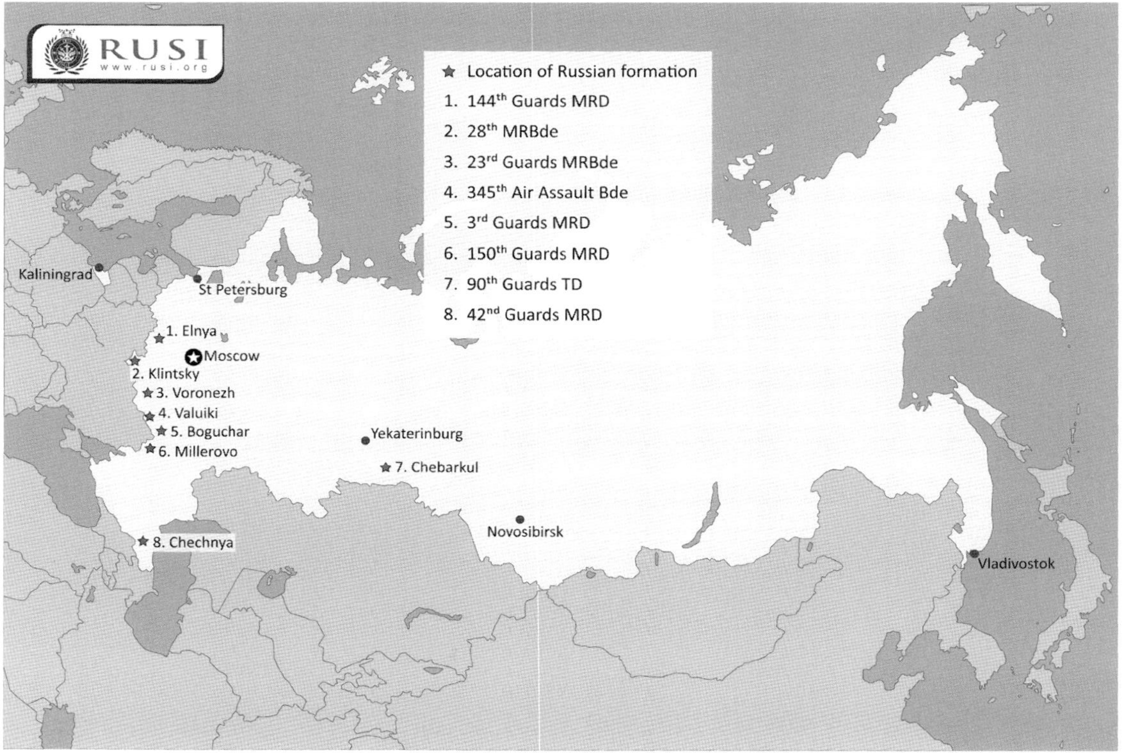

Source: Igor Sutyagin, 'Russia Confronts NATO: Confidence-Destruction Measures', RUSI Briefing Paper, July 2016, p. 8.

changed since 2014 and the Kremlin is now interested in getting Western sanctions lifted, which an invasion would make impossible. A frozen conflict in Ukraine, with permanent military forces exerting psychological pressure through large-scale deployments along the Russian border, appears to be sufficient for Moscow at this point.

To give an idea of the scale of these enduring deployments, semi-official 'leaks' from the General Staff state that every new division will have manpower levels of around 10,000.[26] If this is to be believed, the establishment of three divisions and one brigade (the 345th Air-Assault Brigade), as well as numerous combat support units, will give Russian military planners approximately 42,000 troops in the region – similar to the levels of spring/ early summer 2014. The deployment of troops in permanent camps rather than temporary field camps would make such a deployment more sustainable and affordable. This combination of factors strongly suggests that Moscow plans to maintain pressure on Ukraine in the long term. While this pressure will be mainly political, it will also involve the use of military tools to ensure that Ukraine cannot make sovereign choices without a high level of risk if those choices are unwelcome in Moscow.

The anti-Ukrainian nature of these recent Russian deployments is clear. However, Moscow also aims to exploit Western concerns about its offensive capabilities and to cast doubt over the affordability and feasibility of any attempt by NATO or the EU to contain Russia. The Kremlin seeks to create an over-inflated impression among Western observers that Moscow is willing to use military force (the 'aura of power' described by then US Secretary of Defense Harold Brown in January 1980),[27] such that this becomes a substitute for the possession of power itself. Concentration of offensive military capabilities in the west of Russia is intended to compensate for the Kremlin's overall shortage of resources, thereby reducing the likelihood of the West standing up to Russian adventurism in its 'near abroad'. In other words, these deployments are intended to enable the Kremlin to achieve foreign policy goals through military force that it lacks the resources to pursue under 'normal' circumstances.[28] This perfectly

---

[26] *Vzglyad* [*Look*], 'Istochnik: Divizii 1-y tankovoy i 20-y armiy budut imet po shest polkov [Source: Divisions of the 1st Tank and 20th Armies Will Have Six Regiments in their Structure]', 1 April 2016, <http://vz.ru/news/2016/4/1/802954.html>, accessed 21 March 2017.

[27] Harold Brown, *Department of Defense Annual Report: Fiscal Year 1981*, (Washington, DC: US Government Printing Office), pp. 99–100.

[28] For further discussion of the 'aura of power' phenomenon and its implications for Russian policy, see Igor Sutyagin, 'Driving Forces in Russia's Strategic Thinking', in Janne Haaland Matlary and Tormod Heier (eds), *Ukraine and Beyond: Russia's Strategic Security Challenge to Europe* (London: Palgrave Macmillan, 2016), pp. 85–100.

fits the observed general trends in Moscow's use of military force to achieve political goals without resorting to hostilities.

Western MD-subordinated and Other Western MD-deployed Formations and Units

In addition to the formations and units that are part of the 1st Guards TA, the 20th Guards/6th OAs and the 11th Army Corps, there are formations and units directly subordinated to the MD's Commandant. There are also formations deployed within the territory of the Western MD but which are not operationally related to it, or which are included in a different chain of command but operating in coordination with the Western MD.

The following formations are directly subordinated to the Western MD Commandant:

- The 27th Detached Guards Motor-Rifle Brigade (Mosrentgen in the southwestern suburb of Moscow).
- The 79th Guards Rocket-Artillery Brigade (Tver).
- The 202nd Zenith-Rocket (air defence) Brigade (Naro-Fominsk, Moscow province).
- The former 45th Artillery Brigade – divided into the 18th Detached Self-Propelled Artillery Battalion (2S7M 203-mm guns) and the 19th Detached Self-Propelled Mortar Battalion (2S4 240-mm mortars) (Tambov).
- The 49th Zenith-Rocket (air defence) Brigade (Smolensk).
- The 27th Detached CBRN Brigade (Kursk).
- The 1st Red Banner Command (C3) Brigade (Sertolovo, Leningrad province).
- The 16th Detached EW Brigade (Kursk).

There is also an Operational Group of Russian forces in Transnistria in Tiraspol, Moldova, which includes the 82nd Detached Motor-Rifle Battalion and the 113th Guards Detached Motor-Rifle Battalion and is administratively subordinated to the Western MD's Commandant. Formations under the command of the Baltic Fleet in Kaliningrad province are discussed in the corresponding sub-section.

The combat formations deployed on the territory of the Western MD but not operationally subordinated to it are the airborne and air-assault divisions and brigades of the Russian Airborne Troops:

- The 76th Guards Air-Assault Division (Pskov).
- The 98th Guards Airborne Division (Ivanovo).
- The 106th Guards Airborne Division (Tula).
- The 45th Guards Airborne Spetsnaz Brigade (Kubinka, Moscow province).

- The 38th Guards Airborne Communications Brigade (Medvezhjiy Ozera, Moscow province).
- The 345th Guards Air-Assault Brigade (Voronezh, planned for 2020).[29]

Those formations that are deployed in the Western MD under a different chain of command but operating in accordance with its operational needs are two Spetsnaz brigades, two engineer brigades and one EW brigade:

- The 2nd Detached Spetsnaz Brigade (Promezhitsy, near Pskov).
- The 16th Detached Spetsnaz Brigade (Tambov).[30]
- The 1st Guards Engineer-Sapper Brigade (Murom, Vladimir province) – Engineer Troops Commandant's central reserve.
- The 28th Pontoon-Bridge Brigade (Murom, Vladimir province) – Engineer Troops Commandant's central reserve.
- The 15th Detached EW Brigade (Stroitel, Tambov province) – directly subordinated to the Commandant, Electronic Warfare Troops, Ministry of Defence.

There are also numerous smaller specialist support and reserve units and formations deployed within the territory of the Western MD which are not listed here.

Southern Military District

The Southern MD was originally designed to counterbalance NATO forces in Turkey. Its secondary role was to contribute to Russia's influence over three former Soviet Union Caucasian republics – Georgia, Armenia and Azerbaijan. Unexpectedly, the Southern MD has obtained great political importance in view of the deterioration of Russia–Georgia relations and the Nagorno-Karabakh conflict between Armenia and Azerbaijan. Both the frozen conflicts in the former Soviet Union Caucasus and tensions on NATO's southern flank have direct implications for European security.

The Southern MD has another, unanticipated, responsibility: to coordinate Russia's military pressure on Ukraine and to maintain control over the Russian-controlled 'rebel' territories in the Donbass region of

---

[29] Establishment of the 345th Guards Air-Assault Brigade was announced in 2013 to be completed by the end of 2016; this was delayed until 2017–18 and then until 2020.
[30] The 2nd and 16th Detached Spetsnaz (special purpose) Brigades are directly subordinated to the 2nd (Main Intelligence) Directorate (GRU) of the General Staff, but operate in the area of responsibility of the Western MD in the latter's interests. They are responsible for the western and southwestern sectors of the Western MD's operational area, respectively; one battalion of the 2nd Spetsnaz Brigade is deployed on a rotational basis to the Northern Fleet's area to cover the reconnaissance/Spetsnaz tasks on the Russia–Finland border.

eastern Ukraine. Moscow's ultimate political goal there is to insert the rebel 'republics' back into the fabric of the Ukrainian state while maintaining full control over them. This would force Kiev to accept the rebel territories' de facto right of veto over Ukrainian policy, allowing Moscow to block unwelcome national policies through its control over Donbass. This remains the ultimate goal of the campaign Russia is waging in eastern Ukraine. However, 'hybrid' operations do not work if they lack the backing of sizeable conventional military power, and the Southern MD – alongside the Western MD's 20th Guards OA – is tasked with that role. The Southern MD provides military forces to support Russia's operations in Ukraine and, therefore, plays a central role in this bitter conflict. The Southern MD also controls the Russian military in post-annexation Crimea.

The Southern MD includes the 49th and 58th OAs, the 22nd Army Corps, the 102nd, 7th and 4th Military bases beyond Russia's borders (in Armenia, Abhkazia and South Ossetia, respectively), as well as formations and units directly subordinated to the MD's Commandant. It also includes the 25th Spetsnaz Regiment, the 22nd Guards, 10th and 346th Spetsnaz Brigades, which are subordinated to the General Staff but operate according to the interests of the Southern MD. The 8th Guards OA is being established in the district.

The 49th Combined Arms Army

The 49th Combined Arms Army, which has its headquarters in Stavropol, is deployed to defend the Russian Black Sea coast and the western spurs of the Caucasus range as well as the western sector of Russian territories near the northern slopes of the Caucasus Mountains. While not in direct territorial contact with Turkey, the 49th OA is responsible for defence against a potential offensive by Turkish or joint NATO forces from Turkish territory. Defence against Georgia (that is, military intimidation of Georgia) is another operational task of this army, which explains the inclusion of Russian troops deployed in Abkhazia within its command structure. Russian troops in the unrecognised republic, separated from Georgia as a result of the Russia–Georgia war of August 2008, are organised as the 7th Military base – with the role of the wartime 131st Motor-Rifle Brigade. The 33rd Detached Motor-Rifle Brigade (Mountain), previously subordinated to the 49th OA, was recently redeployed to Novocherkassk to lay the foundations of the 150th Motor-Rifle Division, subordinated to the newly established 8th Guards OA, thus ending the 33rd Brigade's history within the 49th OA.

The 49th OA includes the following formations and units:

- The 34th Detached Motor-Rifle (Mountain) Brigade (Storozhevaya, Zelenchuk district of Karachay-Cherkessia).
- The 205th Detached Motor-Rifle Brigade (Budennovsk, Stavropol province).

- The 7th Military base (Gudauta in Abkhazia, Georgia).
- A detached reconnaissance brigade (designated number unknown at time of writing) (being established in Korenovsk, Krasnodar province).
- The 1st Guards Missile Brigade (Molkino, Krasnodar province).
- The 227th Artillery Brigade (Maykop, Adygeya).
- The 90th Zenith-Rocket (air defence) Brigade (Rostov-on-Don, newly established in 2015).
- The 32nd Engineer-Sapper Regiment (settlement of Afipskiy, Rostov province).
- The 66th Command (C3) Brigade (Stavropol).
- The 99th Logistics Brigade (Maykop, Adygeya).

All of these formations and units (except the 90th Zenith-Rocket Brigade and the reconnaissance brigade that is still being established) took part in the generation of battalion and/or company tactical groups for Russian operations in Ukraine or on the Russia–Ukraine border. It is also important to note that the 7th Military base contains the 100th Guards Zenith-Rocket (air defence) Regiment in its structure. The 100th Guards is equipped with two battalions of the formidable SA-20 Gargoyle (S-300PM) surface-to-air missile system with a maximum engagement range of up to 150 km. It can, therefore, effectively block any air approaches to Georgia from the Black Sea in the event of fresh Russia–Georgia hostilities, contributing to its isolation from supporters in the West.

The 8th Guards Combined Arms Army

The re-establishment of the 150th Motor-Rifle Division, with its headquarters at Kadamovskiy Range near Rostov-on-Don[31] (on the base of the 33rd Motor-Rifle Brigade relocated from Maykop), is surely the most visible and important development in the Southern MD in recent years. The division is another formation with an extremely evocative history. It is named after the 150th Rifle Division of the Red Army, which stormed the Reichstag in Berlin in April–May 1945 and marked the building with the red flag, which remains the official symbol of the Soviet victory over Nazi Germany. The domestic propaganda message of re-establishing a division under this specific name is clearly that Russia's current confrontation with the West will end in another victory. The propaganda

---

[31] The divisional camps will be at the Kadamovskiy, Kuzminskiy and Millerovo training grounds. The 150th Motor-Rifle Division's units will also be deployed in two other locations – in camps in the town of Millerovo and at the Kadamovskiy training range, all in Rostov province. Kadamovskiy is the major rear base of Russian troops operating in eastern Ukraine.

slogan 'We can repeat!', which was associated with the announcement of this new division, is an obvious allusion to the Red Army's 1944–45 European campaign.

Furthermore, the 150th Division will be under the command of the new 8th Guards OA in Volgograd and Rostov provinces.[32] The intention is evidently to draw parallels with the glorious past of the Soviet Army. During the Cold War, the role of the 8th Guards OA was to attack NATO forces via the Fulda Gap in Germany, until it was relocated to Volgograd in 1992 and subsequently disbanded there. The establishment of a new army (with at least one division in its structure) in the Southern MD, and the 20th Guards OA and 1st Guards TA in the Western MD, represents a dramatic increase in the combat potential of Russian troops deployed around Ukraine. The 20th Guards OA is officially tasked with coordinating Russian troops deployed against Ukraine, while the 1st Guards TA constitutes a heavy force which can threaten a breakthrough towards Kiev and Kharkiv. The 8th Guards OA fits into this strategy by putting additional pressure on Ukraine's defences via a permanent deployment of a large military formation near the southeastern section of Ukraine's border. The overall announced deployments of new Russian formations (Figure 7) provide clear evidence of plans to maintain the threat of Russian military action to isolate the eastern part of Ukraine if the Kremlin deems it necessary. Russian military units encircle Ukrainian territory with overwhelming forces to the north, east and south.

There is no credible information on the order of battle of the new 8th Guards OA, except that the 150th Motor-Rifle Division and probably 20th Guards Motor-Rifle Brigade are both in its structure.[33]

The Crimean Defence Region
As in Kaliningrad, the Russian land forces permanently deployed in Crimea are currently under the command of the Black Sea Fleet, with the recently established 22nd Army Corps as the intermediate structure. These forces include the following formations and military units:

- The 126th Coastal Defence Brigade (Perevalnoe).
- The 127th Detached Reconnaissance Brigade (Pargolovo, Sevastopol).

---

[32] *RIA56*, 'Kiev zanervnichal: Rossiya vossozdala 8 armiyu na yugo-zapade [Kiev Got Nervous: Russia Has Re-established the 8th Army in the Southwest]', 17 March 2017, <http://www.ria56.ru/posts/495694569546946955469.htm>, accessed 21 March 2017.
[33] *Ibid.*

- The 97th Air-Assault Regiment of the 7th Guards Air-Assault Division (Dzhankoy)[34] – this will be established as a permanently stationed battalion in 2017–18 at first, and then expanded to regimental size after 2020.[35]
- The 8th Artillery Regiment (formally Perevalnoe, in practice Dzhankoy and Armyansk).
- The 47th Territorial Defence Division (Simferopol).
- The 4th CBRN Regiment (Inkerman, Sevastopol).
- The 68th Naval Engineer Regiment (Evpatoria).
- The 219th EW Regiment (Sevastopol).
- The 133rd Logistics Brigade (Bakhchisarai).
- The 810th Detached Marines Brigade (Sevastopol).
- The 501st Detached Marines Battalion (Feodosiya).
- The 15th Coastal Missile Brigade (Sevastopol).
- The 388th Naval Reconnaissance (naval Spetsnaz battalion) Point (Sevastopol).
- The 475th Detached EW Centre (Cape Fiolent, near Sevastopol).

In addition, a Russian National Guard (formerly the Ministry of Interior's Internal Troops) formation will carry out rear areas defence tasks in the event of hostility:

- The 112th Detached Motorised Operational Brigade.

The overall strength of the Russian military grouping permanently deployed on the Crimean Peninsula is estimated at up to 40,000 troops. In addition, there are elements deployed on a rotational basis from mainland Russia to the north of the peninsula, tasked with defending two narrow isthmuses connecting Crimea to mainland Ukraine. These are usually represented by two battalion tactical groups. Originally, these were land troops drawn from the Southern MD, but are currently mainly composed of airborne troops and, sometimes, marines.[36] They are supported by up to one

---

[34] *Newsland*, 'VDV mogut razvernut desantno-shturmovoy polk v Krymu [Airborne Troops May Establish an Air-Assault Regiment in Crimea]', 30 July 2015, <http://newsland.com/news/detail/id/1582597/>, accessed 21 March 2017. See *Kherson tipichniy* [*Typical Kherson*], 'Rossiya perebrasyvaet shturmovikov v Severniy Krym – SNBO [Russia Relocating Assault Troops to the Northern Crimea – NSDC]', 24 November 2015, <www.t.ks.ua/rossiya-perebrasyvet-shturmovikov-v-severnyy-krym-snbo>, accessed 21 March 2017.

[35] Bogdanov, 'Osinoe gnezdo [Wasps' Nest]'.

[36] *!NFormer*, 'Voennaya infrastruktura Kryma – vse pod kontrolem! [Crimean Military Infrastructure – Everything is Under Control!]', 4 September 2015, <ruinformer.com/page/voennaja-infrastruktura-kryma-vsjo-pod-kontrolem>,

artillery regiment/brigade equivalent and one or two tank companies, with forces divided between the two. Near the peninsula's northern boundary there is also a near-permanent presence of reconnaissance/Spetsnaz elements, coming from Spetsnaz brigades on the Russian mainland and/or the 127th Reconnaissance Brigade in Crimea.

Given that the combined width of the isthmuses does not exceed 10 km, these forces are perfectly adequate to prevent an attempt by Ukrainian troops to recapture the Crimean Peninsula. The Russian forces covering the two northern entrances to Crimea are considered sufficient to repel a prospective offensive by up to three Ukrainian mechanised brigades, especially with the comparatively high density of deployed Russian artillery. That the Russian military command considers it necessary to maintain this level of deployment reveals the Kremlin's insecurity regarding the annexed peninsula. However, the replacement of motor-riflemen by paratroopers on the border with Ukraine in Crimea might signal to Kiev that Moscow is willing to undertake offensive actions, thus intimidating Ukraine's leadership into making whatever concessions the Kremlin might consider desirable.

Plans were discussed soon after the annexation of Crimea in 2014 to permanently deploy much larger Russian forces to the peninsula.[37] However, since then, fears have diminished and it is more likely that further deployments will be limited to establishing additional artillery and rocket artillery units, in addition to the announced air-assault regiment. The current composition of the Russian grouping on the peninsula, being the de facto equivalent of Russia's modern combined arms armies, lacks the missile firepower that is standard for other Russian field armies. However, establishing a missile brigade in Crimea can probably be ruled out on the basis that there is no operational need.

Such a powerful military grouping on the southern borders of Ukraine would force Kiev's military planners to divert substantial forces to defend against a breakout by Russian troops from Crimea if full-scale hostilities erupted. The Russian military grouping in Crimea, therefore, serves a dual purpose. First, it is Moscow's hedge against any attempt by Kiev to retake the peninsula by force, and second, it is a deterrent force to complicate Ukrainian military plans. Russian marines and air-mobile units, as well as naval special operations forces deployed in Crimea, can operate well along the Ukrainian coast to the west of the peninsula. These 'coastal Spetsnaz elements', with the task of infiltrating sabotage groups into nearby coastal areas, provide a capability specifically oriented against

accessed 21 March 2017; *Kherson tipichniy* [*Typical Kherson*], 'Rossiya perebrasyvaet shturmovikov v Severniy Krym – SNBO [Russia Relocating Assault Troops to Northern Crimea – NSDC]'.
[37] One or two tank brigades, one or two additional brigades of marines, and so forth.

Ukraine.[38] This ability to bring war to the Ukrainians' backyard makes the troops deployed in Crimea an important factor when examining the conflict in and around Ukraine, and has implications for the security environment in Europe as a whole.

'Luhansk/Donetsk People's Republics' Armed Formations
Russian quasi-independent military formations in eastern Ukraine are another force with a similar role – to intimidate Ukraine and constrain its freedom of action through deployment of military assets. The first Minsk deal, signed by the representatives of the OSCE, Russia, Ukraine and two rebel Ukrainian territories (Luhansk and Donetsk) on 19 September 2014, led to a new situation in which the Kremlin deemed it necessary to establish strict control over the separatist armed units in eastern Ukraine. These separatist units were manned by locals and Russian volunteers, supported by Russian regular troops disguised as volunteers. The reorganisation of these militias into a more regular military-style force started in early September 2014, and brought the scattered rebel formations under centralised command, executed by active service Russian military officers generically designated 'military advisers' according to Moscow's will. As Alexander Khodakovsky, Secretary of the Security Council of the Donetsk People's Republic, admitted in an interview with Russian media, these 'advisers' had established full control over rebel forces' operations at battalion level and above by mid-October 2014.[39]

Khodakovsky even named the Russian officer responsible for operational control over the rebels as Lieutenant General Alexander Lentsov, Deputy Commander-in-Chief of Russian Ground Troops. According to Khodakovsky, Lentsov was the permanent head of the 'corps of advisers' in eastern Ukraine even before the decision was made to put rebel units under their control.[40] The important role played by active service Russian officers in the command structures of the rebel forces is confirmed by other sources, and is an ongoing feature of the 'people's militias' of the rebel territories.[41] The general officer in charge of

[38] Mikhailov, 'V rossiyskom Voenno-morskom flote poyavilsya "pribrezhniy spetsnaz" [Coastal Spetsnaz Established in the Russian Navy]'.
[39] Alexander Vasilyev, 'My pritormazhivaem protsess ekspansii na Ukrainu [We are Slowing Down the Process of Expansion to Ukraine]', *Lenta.ru*, 14 October 2015, <http://lenta.ru/articles/2015/10/14/khodakovski/>, accessed 12 January 2016.
[40] *Ibid.*
[41] *Seabreeze,* 'Raskryty imena ofitserov vooryzhennykh sil Rossiyskoy Federatsii – koordinatorov DNR i LNR [The Names of the Russian Federation Armed Forces' Officers Coordinating DNR and LNR are Disclosed]', 27 April 2015, <http://seabreeze.org.ua/raskryityi-imena-ofitserov-vooruzhyonnyih-sil-rossiyskoy-federat sii-koordinatorov-dnr-i-lnr/>, accessed 12 January 2016; *Gulyay Pole [Gulyay Pole]*,

the rebels' military formations is currently Deputy Chief of the General Staff Colonel General Sergey Istrakov, who was appointed in late November 2015, according to Ukrainian military intelligence.[42] The authors have no information on who might succeed Istrakov.

The rebel armed forces have been reorganised since September 2014 into two Russian-style army corps – the 1st Army Corps of People's Militia in the rebel-controlled territories of Donetsk province and the 2nd Army Corps in the territories of Luhansk province. In early May 2016, the plan to reorganise the 1st Corps into Operational Command Donetsk was announced by one of the leaders of the 'Donetsk Republic'.[43] This might suggest further expansion of the corps structure to the level of a combined arms army, with a corresponding increase in Russian-controlled forces in Donbass.

The rebel armed forces in eastern Ukraine are regarded as reserve formations of the Russian armed forces (probably at the formal rank of auxiliary territorial defence troops in order to differentiate them from regular Russian troops), and it was the 12th Reserve Components Command of Russia's Southern MD that was originally responsible for establishing/reorganising the armed units, as well as manning (through provision of recruitment teams) and supplying them with armaments and equipment.[44] This is in line with the role for which

'Rossiya ispolzuet na Donbasse model fashistskoy Germanii – Waffen SS [Russia Uses Nazi Germany's Waffen SS Model for Donbass]', 30 August 2015, <http://politua.su/2015/08/30/3984/>, accessed 12 January 2016; *Informatsioonoe Soprotivlenie* [*Informational Resistance*], 'Svodka IS: rossiyskie kuratory proveryat «2-y armeyskiy korpus LNR» [The IC Report: Russian Military Curators Check the "2nd Army Corps of the LNR"]', 4 November 2015, <http://sprotyv.info/ru/news/kiev/svodka-rossiyskie-kuratory-proveryat-2-y-armeyskiy-korpus-lnr>, accessed 12 January 2016; *Liga.Novosti*, 'Identifitsirovan esche odin ofitser RF, komanduyuschiy boevikami – GRU [Another Russian Federation Officer, the Commander of Rebels, Identified – Main Intelligence Directorate]', 7 January 2016, <http://news.liga.net/news/politics/8214038-identifitsirovan_eshche_odin_ofitser_rf_komanduyushchiy_boevikami_gur.htm?utm_source=bigmir&utm_medium=blocknovostei&utm_campaign=informer>, accessed 12 January 2016.

[42] *Khvylya* [*Wave*], 'V "DNR" i "LNR" pomenyalos voennoe rukovodstvo – razvedka [Military Commanders of the "DNR" and "LNR" Have Been Changed – Intelligence]', 24 November 2015, <http://hvylya.net/news/digest/v-dnr-i-lnr-pomenyalos-voennoe-rukovodstvo-razvedka.html>, accessed 12 January 2016.

[43] *Novosti Donetskoy Respubliki* [*Donetsk Republic News*], 'Forma upravleniya voyskami v DNR izmenena na operativnoe komandovanie [Command and Control of the DNR Troops Changed to Operational Command]', 3 May 2016, <dnr-news.com/dnr/32301-forma-upravleniya-voyskami-v-dnr-izmenena-na-operativnoe-komandovanie.html>, accessed 21 March 2017.

[44] *Espreso*, 'Polnaya rasshifrovka dopsosa SBU rossiyskogo ofitsera, zaderzhannogo na Donbasse [Full Transcript of the Interrogation of Russian Officer Taken Prisoner in

the MDs' reserve component commands were established in 2013 – to mobilise and establish new formations and military units in the event of hostilities. The reserve component commands were established according to the otherwise secret Russian 'Country's Defence Plan';[45] their establishment has been confirmed in the Southern and Eastern MDs.[46] There are also reports that the 12th Reserve Component Command, Southern MD, has been reorganised into the Territorial Troops Centre.[47]

According to some reports, the establishment of an Information Warfare Directorate was part of the command's reorganisation.[48] Colonel Konstantin Karpov has been appointed head of the new directorate. His task is to carry out psychological operations (PsyOps) against Ukraine, isolate eastern Ukraine from the influence of Ukrainian information operations and create a favourable image of Russia in the Russian and international media. The directorate's personnel have reportedly been involved in creating false evidence that the Ukrainian state has committed war crimes in order to create a pretext for international legal procedures

Donbass by Ukraine's Security Service (SBU)]', 29 July 2015, <http://ru.espreso.tv/article/2015/07/29/polnaya_rasshyfrovka_doprosa_sbu_rossyyskogo_ofycera__zaderzhannogo_na_donbasse>, accessed 12 January 2016.

[45] President of Russia, 'Presidentu Rossii predstavlen plan oborony Rossiyskoy Federatsii [Russian Federation Defense Plan Presented to President of Russia]', 29 January 2013, <http://www.kremlin.ru/events/president/news/17385>, accessed 12 January 2016.

[46] The Southern MD's press service, 'V Yuzhnom voennom okruge naznachen komanduyuschiy 12-go komandovaniya reserva [Commander of the 12th Reserves Command Appointed in the Southern Military District]', in *Armyman.Info*, 25 July 2014, <http://armyman.info/novosti/29646-v-yuzhnom-voennom-okruge-naznachen-komanduyuschiy.html>, accessed 12 January 2016; Alexander Pasmurtsev, 'Tankist v tretjem pokolenii [Third-Generation Tankmen]', *Krasnaya zvezda [Red Star]*, 22 August 2014, <http://www.redstar.ru/index.php/syria/item/18128-tankist-v-tretem-pokolenii?tmpl=component&print=1>, accessed 12 January 2016; *Interfax-AVN*, 'V Rossii na strategicheskikh napravleniyakh sozdayutsya komandovaniya rezerva [Commands of Reserves Established in Russia on the Strategic Axis]', 20 January 2015, <http://www.militarynews.ru/Story.asp?rid=1&nid=363477>, accessed 12 January 2016.

[47] *Gordon.ua*, 'Ukrainskie razvedchiki identifitsirovali polkovnika is Tuly, commanduyuschego boevikami "DNR" v Novoazovske [Ukrainian Intelligence Services Have Identified the Russian Colonel from Tula as the Commander of the "DNR" Rebels in Novoazovsk]', 7 January 2016, <gordonua.com/news/war/Ukrainskie-razvedchiki-identificirovali-polkovnika-iz-Tuly-komanduyushchego-boevikami-DNR-v-Novoazovske-114411.html?utm_source=bigmir.net&utm_medium=informer&utm_campaign=gordon_on_bigmir#>, accessed 12 January 2016.

[48] *Khvylya [Wave]*, 'V "DNR" i "LNR" pomenyalos voennoe rukovodstvo - razvedka [Military Commanders of the "DNR" and "LNR" Have Been Changed – Intelligence]'.

against it. These operations are in line with the Russian military's broad incorporation of information warfare as a key part of its warfighting arsenal.[49]

The order of battle of both 'rebel' army corps is shown below.

Operational Command 'Donbass'

The 1st Army Corps of the People's Militia (Donetskaya Narodnaya Respublika (DNR), Donetsk People's Republic):[50]

- The 1st Detached Motor-Rifle Brigade, 'Slavyanskaya'.
- The Detached Brigade of Special Destination, 'Kalmius' (artillery).
- The 3rd Detached Motor-Rifle Brigade, 'Berkut'.[51]
- The 5th Detached Motor-Rifle Brigade, 'Oplot'.
- The 100th Detached Motor-Rifle Brigade (Republican Guard).[52]
- The 9th Detached Motor-Rifle Regiment.[53]
- The 11th Detached Motor-Rifle Regiment, 'Enakievo-Dunayskiy' (established on the base of the Detached Spetsnaz Brigade 'Vostok' elements).
- The Detached Commandant's Regiment.
- The 2nd Detached Tank Battalion, 'Umanskiy' (formerly the 2nd Detached Mechanised (tank) Battalion, 'Dizel').
- The Detached Tank Battalion (formerly the 1st Detached Mechanised Battalion, 'Somali').
- The 3rd Detached Tank Battalion.
- The Detached Air Defence Battalion.

---

[49] For more detailed discussions on Russian incorporation of information warfare into military operations, see authors' other publications, for example Igor Sutyagin, 'Russian Forces in Ukraine', RUSI Briefing Paper, March 2015.

[50] For the DNR, the sources, if not stated otherwise, are: *Garmata,* 'Sostav i struktura terroristicheskoy armii DNR/LNR [Composition and Structure of the DNR/LNR's Terrorist Army]', 21 March 2015, <http://garmata.org/razvedka/info/item/321>, accessed 12 January 2016; *LiveJournal*, 'Noviy oblik VSN (uslovno, 2-e pereformirovanie) v zimney kampanii 2015 goda, na osnove fotosvidetelstv [The New Face of the VSN (Relatively Speaking, the 2nd Reorganisation) in the 2015 Winter Campaign, Based on Visual Evidence]', 26 February 2016, <http://ce48. livejournal.com/3073.html>, accessed 12 January 2016.

[51] Anna Gromova, 'Zdes net mesta nesoglasnym [There is No Place For Dissenters Here]', *Rosbalt News Agency*, 12 January 2016, <http://www.rosbalt.ru/exussr/2016/ 01/12/1478772.html>, accessed 14 January 2016.

[52] *Ibid.*

[53] *Gordon.ua*, 'Ukrainskie razvedchiki identifitsirovali polkovnika is Tuly, commanduyuschego boevikami "DNR" v Novoazovske [Ukrainian Intelligence Services Have Identified the Russian Colonel from Tula as the Commander of the "DNR" Rebels in Novoazovsk]'.

- The 1st Detached Spetsnaz Battalion, 'Khan' (established on the base of the Detached Spetsnaz Brigade 'Vostok' elements).
- The 3rd Detached Spetsnaz Battalion.
- The Detached Marines Reconnaissance Battalion, 'Sparta-Prazhskiy'.
- The Detached Repair Battalion, 'Kongo'.
- The Detached Communications and Headquarters Guard Battalion.
- The Detached Logistics Battalion.
- The Detached Engineer-Sapper Company.
- The Detached EW Company.
- The 1st Battalion of the Territorial Defence.
- The 2nd Battalion of the Territorial Defence, 'Shakhterskaya diviziya' (established on the base of the Detached Spetsnaz Brigade 'Vostok' elements).
- The 3rd Battalion of the Territorial Defence.
- The 4th and the 5th Battalions of the Territorial Defence.

The 2nd Army Corps of the People's Militia (Luganskaya Narodnaya Respublika (LNR), Luhansk People's Republic):[54]

- The 2nd Detached Motor-Rifle Brigade.
- The 4th Detached Motor-Rifle Brigade.
- The Detached Artillery Brigade of Special Destination.
- The Detached Commandant Regiment.
- The 1st or 6th Detached Cossack Regiment (named after chieftain Matvey Platov).
- The 4th Detached Tank Battalion.
- The Detached Reconnaissance Battalion.
- The Detached Air Defence Battalion.
- The Detached Repair Battalion.
- The Detached Communications and Headquarters Guard Battalion.
- The Detached Logistics Battalion.
- The Detached Engineer-Sapper Company.
- The Detached EW Company.
- CBRN Service.
- The 4th Territorial Defence Battalion (established in March 2015 on the base of the 3rd Mechanised Brigade, 'Prizrak').
- The 11th, 12th, 13th, 14th, 15th, 16th and 17th Battalions of the Territorial Defence.

---

[54] For the composition of the LNR 2nd Army Corps, the source, if not stated otherwise, is *Livejournal*, 'Istoriya armii LNR [History of the LNR Army]', 7 April 2015, <http://yadocent.livejournal.com/697892.html>, accessed 12 January 2016.

There is also information on other possible units, subordinated to the 2nd Army Corps, in the territory of Luhansk province controlled by separatists:[55]

- The Detached Brigade of Special Destination (mechanised), 'Odessa' (probably a battalion-size unit).[56]
- The Cossack National Guard (acts as a territorial defence battalion).

The composition of the brigades in the structure of the rebel republics' armed forces is similar to that of Russian army brigades in terms of their manoeuvre elements, but without the majority of combat support elements. It is noteworthy that all brigades have organic air-defence elements, composed of a few Strela-10 (SA-9) vehicles. The engineer elements in rebel brigades are predominantly basic 'ditch diggers' that lack specialist army-style engineer equipment. EW elements are proudly marked in brigades, but are either non-existent or manned by Russian regulars and kept separate from the corresponding rebel brigades.

The full payroll strength of the 1st and 2nd Army Corps of the rebel republics is estimated at approximately 35,000 troops.[57] However, in practice, the majority of units are manned at between two-thirds and three-quarters of their full strength. Therefore, the armed formations established in eastern Ukraine with Russian assistance and under the command of Russian officers (at the level of battalion and above) provide Russian military commanders with additional combat potential roughly equivalent to one Russian combined arms army in terms of its manoeuvre forces, but without the combat support formations/support units typically found in those armies. This is a very substantial addition to the forces available to Russia in the Western and Southern MDs with which it can pressure Ukraine, although it also imposes a burdern on the already stretched manpower and supply resources of the Russian land forces.

---

[55] *StopTerror*, 'Svodniy spisok nezakonnykh vooruzhennykh formirovaniy na okkupirovannoy territorii Luganskoy oblasti [Summary of Illegal Armed Groups in the Occupied Territory of Luhansk Province]', 12 January 2016, <https://stopterror. in.ua/info/2016/01/svodnyj-spisok-nezakonnyh-vooruzhennyh-formirovanij-na-okkupirovannoj-territorii-luganskoj-oblasti/>, accessed 12 January 2016.

[56] *StopTerror*, 'Otdelnaya mechanizirovannaya brigada osobogo naznacheniya «Odessa» [The "Odessa" Special Purpose Mechanised Brigade]', 28 November 2015, <https://stopterror.in.ua/info/2015/11/otdelnaya-mehanizirovannaya-brigada-osobogo-naznacheniya-odessa/>, accessed 12 January 2016.

[57] *Gulyay Pole*, 'Rossiya ispolzuet na Donbasse model fashistskoy Germanii – Waffen SS [Russia Uses Nazi Germany's Waffen SS Model for Donbass]'.

Private Military Companies

Russian private military companies (PMCs)[58] are sometimes referred to by Russian sources as military provider companies (MPCs) as they are considered to provide overtly military services, including participation in combat, the sort of activities banned for PMCs. This situates the envisaged Russian MPCs closer to mercenaries rather than to their legitimate counterparts, PMCs. The term MPCs will be used in this section to differentiate them from PMCs operating within internationally recognised legal frameworks. MPCs have played an important role in the conflict between Russia and Ukraine.

Russian MPCs reportedly took part in the covert actions leading up to the annexation of Crimea, as well as sparking hostilities in eastern Ukraine by participating in the seizure of public buildings. These activities evolved into direct participation in combat after the outbreak of open hostilities in Donbass and, especially, after Russia's military intervention in the late summer of 2014. The 'MAR' MPC was reported by Ukrainian sources as taking part in combat actions around Ilovaisk,[59] while another MPC – Dmitriy Utkin's *'Wagner-Chastnaya voennaya kompaniya'* ('Private military company', 'Wagner-ChVK') – is often referred to as one of the most influential military actors in Donbass and is directly controlled from Moscow.[60] Local observers have repeatedly compared Wagner-ChVK to a mechanised brigade-size unit, participating in combat throughout eastern Ukraine.[61]

Using MPCs in the interests of the Russian state was first mentioned publicly in spring 2012 by then Prime Minister and President-elect Putin in a Q&A session following his address to parliament on the government's performance in 2011. Hardline MP Aleksey Mitrofanov of the A Just Russia party asked Putin about the prospects of using PMCs to promote Russia's influence abroad; 'I believe that such companies are a way of implementing national interests *without the direct involvement of the state,'*

---

[58] While not formally in the composition of the Southern MD, PMCs are discussed here in the interest of consistency as they participate in the operations centrally controlled and executed according to the plans of the Russian military command, including those of the Southern MD.

[59] *StopTerror*, 'Chastnye Voennye Kompanii Rossii na Donbasse [Russian Private Military Companies in Donbass]', 18 January 2016, <https://stopterror.in.ua/info/2016/01/chastnye-voennye-kompanii-rossii-na-donbasse/>, accessed 19 January 2016.

[60] Sergey Gulyaev, 'Donbass. Gryaz i krov «bratskoy voyny» [Donbass. Mud and Blood of "Fratricide War"]', *Rosbalt*, 19 January 2016, <http://www.rosbalt.ru/exussr/2016/01/19/1481267.html>, accessed 19 January 2016; Gromova, 'Zdes net mesta nesoglasnym [There is No Place For Dissenters Here]'.

[61] *Ibid.*

Putin replied. 'Yes, I think we could consider this option.'[62] Since then, the use of proxy forces, established under the state's control and acting on behalf of the Kremlin without direct attribution, has been enthusiastically adopted and will probably continue for the foreseeable future.

The value of MPCs for Russia's political-military leadership lies in three interrelated spheres. First, the use of private companies' personnel in areas in which there is a high risk of the participating force's nature and origin being exposed allows the Kremlin to deny direct and immediate responsibility. That buys Moscow time while rules-based Western politicians try to establish beyond reasonable doubt the links between the mercenaries and their masters; by the time the link is proven, it may be too late to punish the perpetrators as new 'facts' favourable to Russia will have been established on the ground. The delay in Western decision-making caused by the unclear nature of Russian MPCs distinguishes them from disguised Russian regulars whose origin can be established with relative ease (as the story of the two Spetsnaz officers captured by Ukrainian troops in May 2015 has proved).[63] This feature makes MPCs a useful tool in Moscow's foreign policy.

Second, the material motivation of mercenaries makes them easier to manipulate. They are often willing to accept the role of cannon fodder, especially since many volunteers to Russian MPCs, such as Wagner-ChVK, lack professional training or experience and underestimate the dangers of what they are being asked to do.

Third, the use of mercenaries allows the government to avoid popular discontent about combat losses. The contracts signed by privateers often include a provision that their bodies will not be recovered in the event of death in combat. Although Russian casualties have so far had only a limited immediate influence on public opinion, news of large-scale losses as a result of operations abroad generates inevitable associations with the traumatic Soviet experience in Afghanistan in 1979–89. The Kremlin's desire to avoid such parallels is another driver of the continued use of MPCs.

Thus, MPCs are becoming an increasingly popular military tool of adventurist Russian policy. It is not surprising, therefore, that reports of Wagner-ChVK (and probably other MPC companies) participating in Russian operations in Syria have appeared in Russian and international media. MPCs are set to be an enduring feature of Russian military policy abroad.

---

[62] *Sputnik International*, 'Russia May Consider Establishing Private Military Companies', 13 April 2012, <http://sputniknews.com/analysis/20120413/172789099.html>, accessed 12 January 2016. Emphasis added.

[63] Reid Standish, 'Captured Russian Special Forces Soldier Describes His Unit Fighting in Eastern Ukraine', *Foreign Policy*, 18 May 2015, <http://foreignpolicy.com/2015/05/18/captured-russian-special-forces-soldier-describes-his-unit-fighting-in-eastern-ukraine/>, accessed 18 May 2017.

The 102nd Military Base

In discussing the Southern MD's posture, its capabilities and operational tasks, it is important to keep in mind that Ukraine is not the only operational forcus for the Russian military grouping in the western part of the Southern MD. Russian involvement in the Syrian civil war has exacerbated tensions between Russia and Turkey, which have widely divergent goals in the conflict. It is these differences, and not isolated crisis events, that have led to increased tensions between Moscow and Ankara, and they are not going to disappear. The warming of relations between the two in July–August 2016 is more of a rapprochement between two powers that have found themselves isolated in the international arena than a sincere alliance.

In this context, the establishment of the 150th Motor-Rifle Division increases the Southern MD Commandant's room for manoeuvre in the event of an operation against Turkish or allied NATO/Turkish forces, either in the form of brinkmanship or overt confrontation. At the same time, the 102nd Military base in Armenia (which should become the 73rd Motor-Rifle Brigade in the event of hostilities) – a Russian military formation deployed in Armenia very close to the Turkish–Armenian border – will have a much more visible role in any potential contest between Moscow and Ankara. At the end of November 2015, there was a sudden surge of articles in the Russian tabloid media concerning the 'leaked' Kremlin plan to deploy up to 7,000 troops to the 102nd base.[64] These rumours surfaced just under a week after the Turkish air force shot down a Russian Su-24M Fencer bomber on 24 November 2015, only to disappear without trace in the following days – suggesting an emotion-driven move by Russian policymakers that was cooled by military and diplomatic advisers soon after. Nevertheless, the preparation of military tools to intimidate Ankara if necessary has become a significant part of Kremlin policy relating to the Southern MD. This has significance for the rest of Europe as Turkey remains an important member of NATO.

---

[64] *Newsli.ru*, 'Molniya! Rossiaya srochno razvorachivaet 58-yu armiyu. Ukraina i Turtsiya gotovyat provokatsiyu [Flash! Russia Urgently Deploys the 58th Army. Ukraine and Turkey are Preparing for Conflict]', 29 November 2015, <http://www.newsli.ru/news/world/politika/18807?utm_campaign=transit&utm_source=mirtesen&utm_medium=news&from=mirtesen>, accessed 12 January 2016; *Political kaleidoscope*, 'SMI: tysyachi rossiyskikh voennykh razvertyvayutsya na armyano-turetskoy granitse [Media: Thousands of Russian Troops are being Deployed to the Armenian–Turkish Border]', 29 November 2015, <http://k-politika.ru/smi-tysyachi-rossijskix-voennyx-razvyortyvayutsya-na-armyano-tureckoj-granice/>, accessed 12 January 2016; *News2.ru*, 'Na turetsko-armyanskoy granitse razvernuta 58-ya rossiyskaya armiya – bolee 7000 voennosluzhaschikh [The Russian 58th Army is Deployed on the Armenian–Turkish Border – More than 7,000 Troops]', 30 November 2015, <http://news2.ru/story/477736/>, accessed 12 January 2016.

The Kremlin's determination to use intimidation as an important tool in international relations is evident in the following events: snap exercises of the 102nd base's air component (the 3624th AB (*Aviatsionnaya basa*, air force base)) – eighteen MiG-29s, five Mi-8 Hip transport helicopters and two Mi-8MTPR-1 electronic warfare helicopters – just 10–15 km from the Turkish border;[65] a surge deployment of an additional helicopter squadron comprising eighteen gunships and transport helicopters to the 3624th AB with the option of further expansion of its helicopter force; modernisation of the Russian MiG-29 air-superiority fighter jet deployed at the 3624th AB to provide land-attack capability; and steps being taken to establish an operationally questionable Russian airbase in Qamishli on the Syria–Turkey border.[66] Periodic rumours of an official expansion of the 102nd Military base from brigade to division size would fit with this trend.

Therefore, the re-establishment of the 127th Red Banner Motor-Rifle Division in Armenia within the 102nd Military base cannot be excluded. This would parallel earlier developments in the composition of Russian forces deployed abroad, including the transformation of the brigade-size 201st Military base in Tajikistan into the 201st Motor-Rifle Division.[67] So, the 'leaked' information on the 'relocation' of up to 7,000 Russian troops to Armenia might have some substance, as the combined strength of the 102nd Military base after such reinforcement would correspond to the standard manpower level of a full-strength (six regiments) Soviet-era motor-rifle division.

At the same time, the Azeri–Armenian conflict over Nagorno-Karabakh shows signs of heating up. Domestic instability in Armenia, the location of Russia's 102nd Military base, is another reason for Moscow's concern. In both cases, Moscow might be interested in increasing its political-military presence in the region. A 'Crimea scenario' might be a consideration, given the presence of Russian capital in the republic and widespread pro-Russian sentiment among Armenians (which could be mistaken for a desire to be controlled by Moscow), that might see the establishment of a regime fully controlled by Moscow in the event of any unrest directed at the current government, which is loyal to Russia. The likelihood of such a development is considered low, however.

---

[65] *Minval.az*, 'V Armenii usilivaetsya strakh pered Turtsiey – zakulisje vnezapnoy suety vraga [Fear of Turkey Intensifies in Armenia – Behind the Scenes of the Enemy's Sudden Activity]', 18 January 2016, <http://minval.az/news/123536729>, accessed 21 January 2016.

[66] Jennifer Griffin and Lucas Tomlinson, 'Russians Survey New Airbase on Syria–Turkey Border, US Officials Concerned', *Fox News*, 21 January 2016.

[67] The base, expanded to division size, was reduced back to brigade size less than a year later.

The 102nd base includes the 988th Zenith-Rocket (air defence) Regiment with one battalion of the SA-12 Gladiator/Giant long-range air-defence system and one battalion of the SA-17 Grizzly medium-range air-defence system, with ranges of up to 150 km and 42 km, respectively. Deployed in Gyumri, the 988th Regiment's Gladiators cover the central part of Georgia, augmenting the operational capabilities of the 100th Guards Zenith-Rocket Regiment in the structure of the 49th OA's 7th Military base. The resulting ability of Russian forces to deny Georgia and its allies use of Georgian airspace should not be underestimated.

The 58th Combined Arms Army
The 58th Combined Arms Army, with headquarters in Vladikavkaz in North Ossetia, is responsible for operations in the eastern part of the Caucasus Ridge and includes the following formations and units:

- The 8th Guards Motor-Rifle (Mountain) Brigade (Borzoy, Chechnya).
- The 17th Guards Motor-Rifle Brigade (Shali, Chechnya).
- The 18th Guards Motor-Rifle Brigade (Khankala, Chechnya).

  – The 8th, 17th and 18th Guards Brigades will be merged into the 42nd Guards Motor-Rifle Division, with its re-establishment planned for 2017.[68]

- The 19th Detached Motor-Rifle Brigade (Vladikavkaz, North Ossetia).
- The 136th Guards Motor-Rifle Brigade (Buynaksk, Dagestan).
- The 4th Guards Military base (the wartime 131st Motor-Rifle Brigade, Tskhinvali, South Ossetia).
- The 12th Missile Brigade (Mozdok, North Ossetia).
- The 291st Artillery Brigade (Troitskaya, Ingushetiya).
- The 100th Reconnaissance Brigade (Mozdok, North Ossetia).
- The 67th Zenith-Rocket (air defence) Brigade (Vladikavkaz, North Ossetia).
- The 40th CBRN Regiment (Troitskaya, Ingushetiya).
- The 31st Engineer-Sapper Regiment (Prokhladniy).
- The 34th Command (C3) Brigade (Vladikavkaz, North Ossetia).
- The 78th Logistics Brigade (Budennovsk, Stavropol province).

---

[68] *SKFO News*, 'V Chechne budet vossozdana legendarnaya 42-ya motostrelkovaya diviziya [Legendary 42nd Motor-Rifle Division to be Re-established in Chechnya]', 30 September 2016, <http://skfonews.info/news/6462>, accessed 23 October 2016.

The 58th OA also probably includes:

- The 15th Guards Motor-Rifle Brigade (current location not known, might be relocated from the Central MD[69]).

The 4th Guards base includes one battalion with the SA-17 Grizzly air-defence system, which covers airspace up to halfway from Tskhinvali to Tbilisi, the capital of Georgia. In addition, one battery of the Iskander-M missile system is deployed at the 4th Guards base, putting the whole of Georgia within the strike range of missiles launched from Tskhinvali. The 12th Missile Brigade is the first new missile brigade established in the Russian armed forces since 1998;[70] it took delivery of the Iskander-M missile system when it was established.

The District-subordinated Units
In addition to the units and formations subordinated to the 8th, 49th and 58th armies, as well as the Black Sea Fleet in Crimea, the Southern MD includes the following formations subordinated to the Commandant:

- The 439th Guards Rocket Artillery Brigade (Znamensk, Astrakhan province).
- The 77th Zenith-Rocket (air defence) Brigade (Korenovsk, Krasnodar province).
- A Zenith-rocket (air defence) brigade (designated number unknown at time of writing and location unknown; the first brigade that got delivery of the newest Buk-M3 air-defence system).
- The 28th CBRN Brigade (Kamyshin, Volgograd province).
- The 176th Command (C3) Brigade (Aksay, near Rostov-on-Don).
- The 19th EW Brigade (Aksay).
- The 11th Guards Engineer-Sapper (combat engineer) Brigade (Kamensk-Shakhtinskiy, Rostov province).
- Other support and reserve units.

---

[69] There are contradicting ideas on the fate of the 15th Guards. On the one hand, it was permanently located in Samara (Central MD) and its presence there was confirmed by local publications as late as September 2016. However, General Major Andrey Gurulev, the 58th OA Commander, reported about the 15th Guards as one of the 58th OA's formations participating in the Southern MD's exercises in February 2016. The authors lean towards the conclusion that the 15th Guards are still permanently deployed in the Central MD. Russian President, 'Doklad Ministerstva oborony o khode ucheniy v Yuzhnom voennon okruge [Ministry of Defence Report on the Progress of Exercises in the Southern Military District]', 1 February 2016, <http://special.kremlin.ru/events/president/transcripts/51300>, accessed 12 August.
[70] *Ibid.*

The Southern MD also includes two formations of the Airborne Troops:

- The 7th Guards Air-Assault Division (Novorossiysk – HQ and two out of four regiments).
- The 56th Guards Air-Assault Brigade (Kamyshin, Volgograd province).

These latter two formations are both subordinated to the Commandant of the Russian Airborne Troops but are located within the territory of the Southern MD and would probably be employed in support of the district's operations in the event of hostilities. However, as part of the Supreme Commander's reserve, these formations might also be used elsewhere.

- The 10th Detached Spetsnaz Brigade (Molkino, Krasnodar province).
- The 22nd Guards Detached Spetsnaz Brigade (Aksay, Rostov province).
- The 346th Detached Spetsnaz Brigade (Prokhladniy).
- The 25th Spetsnaz Regiment (Stavropol).

These Spetsnaz formations are deployed in the Southern MD and although they are part of a different chain of command, they also serve the operational needs of the Southern MD.

The Arctic

The Arctic is becoming an area of increasingly bitter competition between the eight Arctic nations (Russia, the US, Canada, Denmark, Iceland, Sweden, Finland and Norway), as well as other nations which do not have direct access but are interested in exploiting the opportunities provided in this region. Russia feels insecure over its hitherto unchallenged access to the vast natural resources of the Arctic Ocean shelf in the sector traditionally claimed by the Soviet Union, and then the Russian Federation. This sector stretches from the westernmost point of the Russian Arctic coast on the Kola Peninsula to the North Pole and back to the easternmost point of the Russian coast on Chukotka Peninsula.

The melting of Arctic sea ice is making it increasingly likely that the Northeast Passage (Severmiy Morskoy Put, SMP) will become permanently open for navigation. The passage would mean international waters beyond the 12 nautical miles limit were open to anyone. Such a development would expose Russia to incursions from the north via its undefended Arctic coast, a problem scenario for Moscow given that the Russian Arctic generates approximately 12–15 per cent of Russia's GDP and 25 per cent of its exports,[71] and 80 per cent of Russian gas is produced there.[72] Russia is therefore spending a great deal on improving its northern defences, including improvements to the Northern Fleet. The duty to generate the Operational-Strategic Command (OSC) North in the event of hostilities was given to the Northern Fleet on 22 December 2014,[73] with responsibility for the territories of five northwestern provinces of the Russian Federation,[74] as well as islands along the Russian Arctic up to 152 degrees East. The Eastern MD is responsible for the islands further east, with the Central and Eastern MDs responsible for the Arctic mainland defences within their corresponding boundaries, beyond the limits of the Northern Fleet's area of responsibility.[75] Many in the West perceive this move as a 'militarisation of the Arctic' and potentially part of Russian preparations for another Battle of the Atlantic. Certainly, the move merits concern from other Arctic players about Russia's intentions, and may force them to react with increased military activity of their own in the region. An arms race in the Arctic threatens to become another issue for European and international security. As will be shown later in this section, it is in the Arctic, surprisingly, that Moscow has responded to the NATO decision to deploy four battalions to reassure its Eastern allies vis-à-vis Russia.

Russian military reinforcement in the Arctic is mostly focused on naval, Air-Space Force and early-warning assets and is beyond the scope of this paper. However, to fulfil the hypothetical wartime needs of the new OSC North and to provide the necessary operational flexibility, land force formations have also been established for Arctic operations. The land forces which would come under an activated OSC North have been subordinated under the 14th Army Corps. The 200th Motor-Rifle Brigade in Pechenga (Kola Peninsula) is currently receiving specialist Arctic training (the 99th Tactical Group on Novosibirsk Islands has achieved full operational capability), while the 80th Motor-Rifle Brigade is being

---

[71] Vladimir Mukhin, 'Rossiya gotovit voennye bazy dlya zaschity Arktiki [Russia Prepares Military Bases to Defend the Arctic]', *Nezavisimaya Gazeta* [*Independent Gazette*], 17 October 2013, <http://www.ng.ru/armies/2013-10-17/1_arctica.html>, accessed 25 October 2016.

[72] *Ibid.*

[73] Aleksandr Emeljyanenkov, 'Minoborony sozdaet strategicheskoe komandovanie "Sever" [Ministry of Defence Establishes Strategic Command in the "North"]', *Rossiyskaya Gazeta* [*Russian Gazette*], 10 September 2014, <https://rg.ru/2014/09/10/sever-site.html>, accessed 24 October 2016.

[74] Murmansk and Arkhangelsk provinces, Nenets Autonomous province, Karelia, and Komi. The Northern Fleet is the peacetime structure that will be raised to OSC status in the event of hostility.

[75] Russian Ministry of Defence, 'Military District', <eng.mil.ru/en/index.htm>, accessed 24 October 2016.

established nearby in Allakurti with the exclusive task of defending Russia's interests along the Arctic coast.[76] The goal to have the 80th Brigade fully operational and one more Arctic infantry brigade (perhaps an 82nd Motor-Rifle (Arctic) Brigade) established on the Yamal Peninsula in Siberia by the Central MD by the end of 2016 has not been achieved, but remains a work in progress.[77]

Unlike their Western equivalents, which are de facto light infantry units making use of Arctic-capable transportation means, the Russian Arctic brigades will be fully fledged motor-rifle formations with the full corresponding range of heavy equipment (except MBTs). This is being achieved by installing standard combat modules that are typical for vehicles used by Russian motor-rifle units on the chassis of Russia's Arctic-capable DT family of vehicles. The result is vehicles ranging from armoured personnel carriers (like the DT-BTR) and infantry fighting vehicles to medium-range air-defence systems (Tor-M2DT and Pantsir-SA air-defence variants have been produced on Vityaz DT-30-series specialised arctic all-terrain vehicle chassis, and plans exist for a similar SA-17 Grizzly arctic conversion) and heavy artillery systems, including the powerful Uragan 220-mm MLR system. No doubt the ability to operate such a range of heavy weapons systems in the Arctic would give the Russian brigades a significant qualitative advantage over potential opponents.

Arctic garrisons designed to support autonomous operations by groups of 150 men for eighteen months at a time are under construction in five Russian Arctic locations[78] – Cape Schmidt, Wrangel Island, Franz Josef Land (Aleksandra Land), Kotelny Island and Novaya Zemlya. The first three of these were handed to the military at the end of 2014;[79] operations at Kotelny Island started in 2015. The original plans called for

[76] Ivan Petrov, 'Kurs na Arktiku [Heading for the Arctic]', *Rossiyskaya Gazeta* [*Russian Gazette*], 26 November 2014, <http://www.rg.ru/2014/11/26/flot-site.html>, accessed 12 January 2016.

[77] TASS, 'Dlya arkticheskoy gruppirovki voysk RF sformiruyut dve motostrelkovye brigady [Two Motor-Rifle Brigades Will be Established for the Russian Troops' Arctic Grouping]', 1 October 2014, <http://tass.ru/armiya-i-opk/1478121>, accessed 12 January 2016.

[78] *Pravda-TV*, 'Arkticheskiy trilistnik ili chto stroyat rossiyskie voennye v Arktike [Arctic Trefoil or What the Russian Military Are Building in the Arctic]', 3 May 2015, <http://www.pravda-tv.ru/2016/05/03/227282/arkticheskij-trilistnik-ili-chto-stroyat-rossijskie-voennye-v-arktike>, accessed 25 October 2016.

[79] *Ibid.*; TASS, 'Spetsstroy sdal v ekspluatatsiyu v Arktike tretiy voennyy gorodok [Special Construction Trust has Delivered the Third Arctic Military City]', 3 December 2014, <http://tass.ru/spb-news/1620782>, accessed 25 October 2016.

the construction of six camps,[80] with these autonomous installations augmenting the more traditional military camps under construction in the same and additional other locations. There are plans to establish at least one more reconnaissance brigade for Arctic operations.[81] This information was revealed by the Commander-in-Chief of Russian Ground Troops, Colonel General Oleg Salyukov, who announced changes to the Ground Troops reconnaissance cadets' training programme at the Novosibirsk High Military Command School.[82] The paramilitary Search and Rescue Centres of the Russian Ministry of Emergencies might provide some assistance to the new military command structures, with eleven such centres being established along the SMP.

It is noteworthy that, according to some reports, the 200th Brigade will receive one airborne battalion as an integral element to improve mobility and drastically reduce reaction time in the event of an emergency in the remote areas of the Russian Arctic. This structure (a mix of infantry and paratroopers within one formation) is unique for Russian combined arms brigades, and might be replicated in the two other Arctic brigades. One battalion of the 98th Guards Airborne Division at Ivanovo, in central Russia, has received specialist Arctic training and successfully carried out a landing operation at Novosibirsk Islands on 14 March 2014, suggesting that it has probably been tasked with supporting prospective Arctic operations too.[83] All Russian airborne and air-assault formations are to go through Arctic training in the near future. One battalion from each of the 76th Guards Air-Assault and the 106th Guards Airborne Divisions have undergone training and have taken part in Arctic exercises, including a parachute drop to the North Pole.

The establishment of a coastal defence division on the Chukotka Peninsula was announced in July 2016,[84] probably the re-established 99th Motor-Rifle Division, reorganised for the new role. The purpose of this new Arctic division is noteworthy. It was stated several weeks before news of its

---

[80] *Lenta.ru [Tape.ru]*, 'Rossiyskie voennye poluchili gorodok v 900 kilometrakh ot Severnogo polyusa [Russian Military has Received Town 900 Kilometres from North Pole]', 3 December 2014, <http://lenta.ru/news/2014/12/03/polar/>, accessed 12 August 2016.

[81] *TASS*, 'Dlya arkticheskoy gruppirovki voysk RF sformiruyut dve motostrelkovye brigady [Two Motor-Rifle Brigades will be Established for the Russian Troops' Arctic Grouping]'.

[82] *Ibid.*

[83] *Argumenty i fakty [Arguments and Facts]*, 'Massovuyu vysadku desantnikov vpervye v istorii RF proveli v Arktike [Massive Paradrop in the Arctic Carried Out for the First Time in the Russian Federation's History]', 14 March 2014, <http://www.aif.ru/society/army/1124149>, accessed 12 January 2016.

[84] Aleksey Ramm, 'V Rossii sformiruyut chasti beregovoy oborony [Coastal Defence Units will be Established in Russia]', *Izvestiya*, 16 January 2017, <http://izvestia.ru/news/656353>, accessed 21 March 2017.

establishment that Russia needed to put the US and its territory in direct danger in order to encourage it to steer Ukrainian and East European governments in a direction favourable to Moscow.[85] The 99th Motor-Rifle Division, established in 1983 and disbanded in 1996, was the successor to the infamous 126th Mountain Infantry Corps, relocated by Joseph Stalin to the Chukotka Peninsula in 1946, and the 14th Combined Arms Army, deployed to Chukotka to defend against a hypothetical US invasion and to provide a Soviet capability to invade Alaska.[86] It is the re-establishment of the Arctic 99th Motor-Rifle Division, therefore, rather than the 20th Guards OA and 1st Guards TA, that is Moscow's most direct response to the deployment of four NATO battalions in the Baltic States and Poland.

Furthermore, one of the 80th or 200th Arctic Brigades deployed on the Kola Peninsula, as well as (probably) the 82nd Arctic Brigade, all of which are currently being trained for Arctic operations, will subsequently be expanded to full-scale coastal defence divisions.[87] It is worth noting specifically that if the 200th Arctic Brigade is chosen for expansion to divisional scale, its position near the Norwegian border will mark it out as a direct response to NATO-enhanced forward presence in the country.

Other units will probably be assigned to support Russian Arctic operations on the easternmost end of Russian territory if it is operationally necessary. One battalion of the Russian Pacific Fleet's 40th Detached Marines Brigade on the Kamchatka Peninsula, alongside one battalion of the Pacific Fleet's 155th Marines Brigade from Vladivostok and a battalion of the 83rd Detached Guards Air-Assault Brigade (Ussuriysk) could be assigned to provide reinforcements to the OSC North grouping on the Novosibirsk Islands, as they did during exercises in 2014 (see Figure 8).

The establishment of new Arctic-trained brigades and battalions – comparatively inexpensive in relation to the Russian defence budget as a whole – will probably be fulfilled. The maintenance costs for the Ministry of Defence's four Arctic camps discussed above is RUB 3.28 billion for 2016–17.[88] The overall cost of Russia's Arctic programmes over

[85] Dmitriy Evstafjev, '"Kamchatskaya lodzhiya" ostanovit NATO ["Kamchatka Loggia" Will Stop NATO]', *Izvestiya*, 11 July 2016, <http://izvestia.ru/news/621607>, accessed 25 October 2016.
[86] Aleksey Volynets, 'Atomnaya bomba dlya Chukotki [Atomic Bomb for Chukotka]', *DV.land*, 31 July 2016, <http://dv.land/history/atomnaya-bomba-dlya-chukotki>, accessed 25 October 2016.
[87] Ramm, 'V Rossii sformiruyut chasti beregovoy oborony [Coastal Defence Units will be Established in Russia]'.
[88] Electronic tender for contract to maintain four Ministry of Defence camps in the Arctic zone (Kotelny Island, Aleksandra Land, Wrangel Island, Cape Shmidt) in 2016–17, <http://zakupki.gov.ru/epz/order/notice/printForm/view.html?regNumber=0173100004516001879>, accessed 25 October 2016.

Figure 8: Operational-Strategic Command 'North' Deployments and Possible Reinforcements.

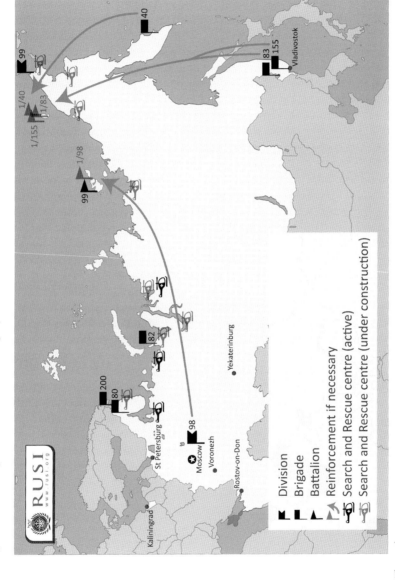

Source: The authors.

the next five years is RUB 222 billion, of which military-related expenses are just part.[89] However, the operational capabilities of these Russian Arctic units remain unclear in view of the lack of air mobility assets, which are vitally important for any successful operation in the Arctic. This deficiency will limit the ability to claim absolute control over even the Russian sector of the Arctic. Without the vital elements of air mobility and dedicated naval assets, Russian land forces will remain landlocked in the vast Russian Arctic territories without any prospect of carrying out serious operations beyond the immediate vicinity of their camps – even with the control of the Arctic airspace provided by dedicated fast jet assets. Russian industry has developed and flight-tested the Mi-8AMTSh-VA Arctic-certified variant of the Mi-8 (Hip) transport helicopter, which sits somewhere between the Super Puma and Merlin helicopters in terms of its capabilities. However, the prospect of the Russian Arctic forces getting in the near future delivery of the proper number of Mi-8AMTSh-VAs (probably no fewer than three regiments, 198 aircraft, to serve three geographically separated operational areas of the 80th/200th and 82nd Brigades, and the 99th Division) seems unclear in light of constraints imposed by the financial crisis and the diminished access to Ukrainian-produced helicopter engines.

It is just as obvious, however, that Russian Arctic deployments, as currently envisaged, reflect a mainly defensive mindset. For example, the 99th Tactical Group deployed at the Novosibirsk Islands has a battery of anti-ship missiles (AShMs). This is an inappropriate weapons system for the context, where polar bears are encountered much more frequently than ships. However, this deployment to the Novosibirsk Islands, with the prospect of replicating it at Wrangel Island and Cape Schmidt further to the east along the SMP, reflects a deep concern among the political-military leadership in Moscow about unauthorised activities carried out along the SMP route by Chinese ships on several occasions. Russia's insecurity about its northern possessions is probably the main driving force behind its military preparations in the Arctic.

The Russian land forces in the Arctic will include the following units in the near future:

The Northern Fleet – OSC North

- The 200th Detached Motor-Rifle Brigade (Pechenga, Murmansk province).

---

[89] *Kasparov.ru*, 'Rogozin: programmy v Arktike v blizhayshie 5 let potrebuyut 222 milliarda rubley [Rogozin: The Arctic Programmes Require 222 Billion Roubles for the Next 5 Years]', 14 April 2015, <http://www.kasparov.ru/material.php?id= 552D043153298>, accessed 25 October 2016.

- The 80th Detached Arctic Motor-Rifle Brigade (Allakurti, Murmansk province).
- The 61st Red Banner Marines Brigade (Sputnik, Murmansk province).
- The 420th Naval Reconnaissance Point (Zverosovkhoz, Murmansk province).
- The 536th Coastal Defence Missile Artillery Brigade (Olenya Guba, Murmansk province).
- The 186th Detached EW Centre (Severomorsk, Murmansk province).
- The 180th Naval Engineers Battalion (Severomorsk, Murmansk province).
- The 99th Tactical Group (Kotelny Island, Novosibirsk Islands archipelago).
- A tactical group (designated number unknown at time of writing) (Rogachevo, Novaya Zemlya archipelago).
- A tactical group (designated number unknown at time of writing) (Alexandra Land, Franz Josef Land archipelago).
- A tactical group (designated number unknown at time of writing) (Sredniy Island, Severnaya Zemlya archipelago).
- Other support and reserve units.

In addition, there are troops of the 45th Air and Air Defence Army (including the 1st Air Defence Division):

The Central MD

- A detached Arctic Motor-Rifle brigade to be established in 2017 (most likely destined to become the previously discussed 82nd Arctic Brigade) (Yamalo-Nenets Autonomous District).

The Eastern MD

- The 99th Coastal Defence Division, expected to be established in 2018 (Chukotka Peninsula, reportedly Provideniya Bay and Anadyr).
- A tactical group (designated number unknown at time of writing) (Cape Schmidt, Chukotka Peninsula).
- A tactical group (designated number unknown at time of writing) (Wrangel Island).

CONCLUSIONS

The Kremlin is aggressively investing in its military capabilities. Russia's military expenditure as a proportion of national GDP has increased by 50–66 per cent since the military reforms began in October 2008, and reached an estimated record of 5.81 per cent of GDP in 2016. This allows Russia to rapidly build new capabilities which contribute greatly to the overall potential of its land forces in defensive and, importantly, offensive roles. The Russian military is not as capable as it appears at first glance, however, with its public veneer masking many unresolved problems. Despite Russian leaders' aspirations, the establishment of widely hailed and capable new units is being delayed and delivery of many new weapons systems has been postponed. Political bravado about Russia's supposed successes in import substitution fails to conceal domestic technological inferiority in many critical areas. Nonetheless, the Russian military is evidently better equipped and trained now than eight years ago, when the current round of military reforms was initiated after its poor performance in the 2008 war with Georgia.

Moscow skilfully combines structural, material and doctrinal changes in its military with a more assertive foreign policy, propaganda and diplomacy, compensating for Russia's comparative weakness in relation to the West through assertiveness and improved military capabilities. Put simply, Moscow believes that in order to achieve its foreign policy goals, it is necessary to intimidate its fundamentally stronger opponents in order to forestall any challenge to Russian policies and aggressive actions. Consequently, state-level intimidation, brinkmanship and blackmail have become an integral part of Russia's grand strategy in what Moscow sees as its legitimate sphere of influence. Such behaviour is likely to continue.

At the same time, the Kremlin has demonstrated an impressive ability to understand where Western 'red lines' lie and to tailor its actions to remain just below that threshold, thus achieving its goals while minimising punitive reactions. Emboldened by its recent successes in confrontations with the West, and mesmerised by its new offensive capabilities (however relatively modest improvements in that area might be in reality), the

Kremlin displays an ever-increasing appetite for assertive action – which increases the risk of an inadvertent miscalculation or escalation. However, such a policy is the only option if Moscow is to capitalise on the funding that the Putin regime has sunk into defence, and for that reason alone the continued use of military power in Russian foreign policy should be expected.[1] The West, with its traditional preference for compromise over confrontation, and a desire to keep military expenditure to a minimum, is clearly uncomfortable and unprepared to adequately oppose these confrontational Russian tactics.

It is probably safe to say that NATO is at a crossroads once again. When the dissolution of the Warsaw Pact, followed by that of the Soviet Union itself, removed the immediate threat to members of the Western alliance, NATO struggled to find its new raison d'être. However, times have since changed: European borders are being redrawn by force, and Russian diplomats openly threaten the use of nuclear weapons against a small European nation that decided to improve its naval radar capabilities and fulfil its obligations to the Alliance.[2] However, despite Russia's threatening statements, there are still doubts being expressed by some NATO members over the need to restore European defence capabilities even to a state comparable to that of previous post-Cold War periods, when rhetoric from Moscow was far less aggressive.

The most recent edition of the Russian Federation's National Security Strategy, adopted on 31 December 2015, names 'the US and its allies' as the main obstacle to the promotion of Russian national interests and, therefore, as official enemies of the country.[3] Furthermore, the new strategy states that all out-of-area operations by NATO, if not authorised by the UN Security Council, where Moscow can veto them, are unacceptable to Russia, and represent a threat to its national security[4]– which the Russian government is determined to counter by any means, including military power. The strategic messaging contained in the Russian strategy is crystal clear: any

---

[1] The conclusion on sunk costs and their influence on the future course of Russia's policy was proposed by Dumitru Minzarari in conversation with Igor Sutyagin at the Aleksanteri Conference at Helsinki University on 22 October 2015.
[2] Teis Jensen and Adrian Croft, 'Russia Threatens to Aim Nuclear Missiles at Denmark Ships if it Joins NATO Shield', *Reuters*, 22 March 2015.
[3] *Rossiyskaya Gazeta* [*Russian Gazette*], 'Ukaz Prezidenta Rossiyskoy Federatsii ot 31 dekabrya 2015 goda No. 683 "O Strategii natsionalnoy bezopasnosti Rossiyskoy Federatsii" [The President of the Russian Federation's Decree of 31 December 2015 No. 683 "On the National Security Strategy of the Russian Federation"]', para. 12 of the 'Strategiya natsionalnoy bezopasnosti Rossiyskoy Federatsii [National Security Strategy of the Russian Federation]', 31 December 2015, <www.rg.ru/2015/12/31/nac-bezopasnost-site-dok.html>, accessed 25 October 2016.
[4] *Ibid.*, paras 15, 106–07.

state that wishes to be secure in relation to Russia needs to distance itself from the US and its security guarantees. Those that do not are viewed as legitimate targets for Russian coercion, intimidation and other hostile actions. NATO's out-of-area operations, aimed for example at resolving non-military crises concerning the southern allies, must also be stopped if not endorsed by Moscow, or Russia reserves the right to resort to the use of military power.[5]

There is, of course, no promise that secession from the NATO security mechanism will grant a state immunity from pressure by Moscow. The opposite is more likely, as the Kremlin has already shown on numerous occasions that it operates on the principle that it is always safer to hurt the small and weak than the strong and resolute. The annexation of Crimea illustrates this: Russian troops were extremely cautious during the first couple of days of the Crimean crisis, as symbolised by an incident – footage of which appeared briefly on social media – when a Ukrainian traffic police officer single-handedly stopped a company of Russian marines on their way to seize a Ukrainian military site and ordered them back to their barracks (the marines complied). Compare this to how explicitly aggressive Russia's actions rapidly became once the Ukrainians' reluctance to use force in self-defence became obvious.

European countries that question the threat assessment by East European NATO member states should, therefore, keep in mind that by remaining allied with Washington (that is, enjoying US and NATO security guarantees), they place themselves in the crosshairs of a Russian military machine that is now officially and overtly aimed at them. At the same time, any obvious NATO reluctance to take action to defend member states, including those further in the east of the bloc, is clear evidence of a Ukrainian-style lack of political will to fight and an invitation for further action from Russia. Issuing an invitation to attack one's interests, while at the same time being neither willing nor ready to fight to defend them, is perhaps a less-than-ideal security strategy.

Demonstrating such political incoherence on issues of defence under such circumstances sends Moscow the message, rightly or wrongly, that NATO security guarantees are open to question and should not be taken for granted. US President Donald Trump, who has repeatedly questioned the unconditional nature of America's obligation to defend European NATO member states, is simply reinforcing that assumption. From such a perspective, Moscow may believe it is worth trying to challenge NATO, especially if certain preparatory conditions are met. As this Whitehall Paper has shown, the Kremlin is making extensive preparations in terms

---

[5] *Ibid.*, para. 29.

of building up military forces capable of rapid and powerful offensive actions in areas bordering Russia. The Kremlin is also trying to gather all the anti-European forces in Europe under its banner and to water down the political unity of the West on issues such as the meaning of Western values, and what precisely NATO should defend. It would be an act of self-deception for any NATO member to argue that Russia's actions pose no threat to them.

Other powers around the world are watching the progress of this current confrontation between Russia and the West with great interest, in particular those that resent the 'unfair' model of relations imposed on them by Europe and the US during the Cold War era and the unipolar post-Cold War years, and that wish to change it. Such powers, and their anti-Western leaders, are learning the lessons being taught by Putin on effective tactics to challenge, weaken and divide the West in order to extract concessions. If the tactics currently being exercised by Moscow are allowed to provide enduring success, the West should expect repeated attempts to replicate them from other parts of the globe. The only way to prevent such a destabilising outcome is to adopt strategies to successfully deter and punish Moscow's adventurism, and thus prove to the world that the tactics of blackmail and intimidation cannot end in success. NATO's reluctance to challenge Putin's aggression since 2014 sends precisely the opposite message. It also suggests that NATO and its members are particularly vulnerable to such tactics because, in reality, they are deeply divided and lack the will to fight for their values and their allegedly united interests.

Concerted efforts to deter Moscow and prove its tactics ineffective is necessary to prevent an irreversible degradation of NATO's credibility in collective defence and of NATO's unity in upholding the international rules-based order, but action must not be left until too late. After all, as Carl von Clausewitz wrote in *On War*:

> A conqueror is always a lover of peace (as Bonaparte always asserted of himself); he would like to make his entry into our state unopposed; in order to prevent this, we must choose war, and therefore also make preparations, that is in other words, it is just the weak, or that side which must defend itself, which should be always armed in order not to be taken by surprise; so it is willed by the art of war.[6]

While the Russian military is not nearly as impressive as the Kremlin would like the world to believe, and certainly has its (sometimes very serious)

---

[6] Carl von Clausewitz, *On War*, Book 6, Chapter 5 (London: N Trübner, 1873), <https://www.clausewitz.com/readings/OnWar1873/BK6ch05.html#a>, accessed 25 October 2016.

shortcomings, as this paper shows, it is vitally important for the West to wake up and do precisely what Putin expects of it – to take Russia seriously. That does not mean surrendering to the Kremlin's blackmail – the specific outcome Moscow expects as a result of its policy – or overestimating Russia's considerable military capabilities. Rather, it requires abandoning deceptive self-assurances that everything will get better on its own and that Russia will quietly return to its post-Cold War place in the far corner of the room. War is a contest of wills: 'War, therefore, is an act of violence to compel our opponent to fulfil our will'.[7] It would be unforgivable to lose the challenge that Russia has laid down to the West due to a failure to recognise that war really can be won or lost before the first shot is fired. Remember the saying '*Si vis pacem – para bellum*', 'If you want peace – be ready for war'. However, as Russia's recent actions demonstrate to those willing to examine them, a misquoted version of the same saying is of equal value: 'If you want peace *too much* – you will inevitably get war'. We would all be wise to remember this.

---

[7] *Ibid.*, Book 1, Chapter 1.

APPENDIX I. ESTIMATED STRENGTH OF RUSSIAN GROUND TROOPS

The following assessment of the Russian Ground Troops' manpower and dynamics is based on the best open source information available, but is by its nature an estimate.[1] First, the planned total Ground Troops manpower is defined as 300,000 personnel.[2] The Commander-in-Chief of the Russian Ground Troops, Colonel General Oleg Salyukov, said 220,200 professionals in Other Ranks (OR)[3] would represent 81 per cent of manpower by 2021 (when the reforms are to be completed and the Ground Troops should reach their planned capacity).[4] Straightforward calculation reveals that the overall number of OR (professionals plus conscripts) is, therefore, planned to be approximately 272,000. That leaves approximately 28,000 billets to be filled by commissioned and non-commissioned officers.

Data published in late 2016 indicate that the Russian armed forces had reached a planned manning level of 93 per cent of planned strength across

---

[1] A direct comparison of forces has not been included here given the subjective nature of determining which of NATO's members count as Russia's 'neighbours' due to the structure of the Alliance and rotational deployments. Furthermore, while paramilitary forces in, for example, France and Italy, as well as Russia, are mostly irrelevant to such a comparison, Russian paramilitary forces in its exclaves would need to be accounted for, rendering any simplistic numerical comparison misleading.

[2] *TASS*, 'Den' Sukhoputnykh voysk Rossii. Dosje [Russia's Ground Troops' Day. Dossier]', 1 September 2015, <http://tass.ru/info/2303642>, accessed 9 December 2016.

[3] In the British Army other ranks (OR) refers to all ranks from private to sergeant, also known as 'enlisted men' in the US Army.

[4] Russian Ministry of Defence, 'Intervjyu glavnokomanduyuschego Sukhoputnymi voyskami general-polkovnika Olega Salyukova ko Dnyu Sukhoputnykh voysk [Interview with Commander-in-Chief of the Russian Ground Troops, Colonel General Oleg Salyukov for the Ground Troops' Day]', <http://structure.mil.ru/structure/forces/ground/day.htm>, accessed 19 October 2016.

all services[5] (it was 92 per cent one year earlier[6]). Under the assumption that manning in the Ground Troops' officer corps is at the same average level as in the armed forces in general, the officer corps had an approximate actual strength at the end of 2015 of approximately 26,000 officers. Salyukov also disclosed the actual number of Ground Troops OR (with an important clarification by *TASS*), at 183,400 in September 2015, including 88,200 professional soldiers.[7] That allows an estimate of the Ground Troops' manpower of approximately 210,000 at the end of 2015.

Estimates of the Ground Troops' manpower in 2014 are complicated by the lack of reliable sources of detailed information. However, it was officially admitted in September 2013 that the Russian armed forces were manned at 80.6 per cent of their planned level at that time.[8] The manning level increased to 90 per cent by mid-December 2014,[9] and reached 92 per cent by the end of 2015.[10] That allows a loose assumption to be made that the manning level of the Ground Troops in mid-2014, in the wake of Russia's involvement in Ukraine, was proportionally lower than that observed – and announced – in 2015 by Russian military officials. In this case, assuming the steady increase of the manning level from 80.6 to 90 per cent over the year, the Ground Troops' manpower might be estimated

---

[5] President of Russia, 'Rasshirennoe zasedanie kollegii Ministerstva oborony Rossiyskoy Federatsii [Extended Meeting of the Russian Federation Ministry of Defence's Collegium]', 22 December 2016.

[6] Aleksey Nikolskiy, 'Rossiyskaya armiya ukomplektovana na rekordnye 92 protsenta [Russian Army Manned at a Record 92 Per Cent]', *Vedomosti* [*Statements*], 15 December 2015, <http://www.vedomosti.ru/politics/articles/2015/12/14/620756-rossiiskaya-armiya-ukomplektovana-rekordnie-92>, accessed 14 October 2016.

[7] Viktor Khudoleev, 'Voyska s velikoy istoriey [Troops with a Great History]', *Krasnaya zvezda* [*Red Star*], 29 September 2015, <http://www.redstar.ru/index.php/component/k2/item/25942-vojska-s-velikoj-istoriej>, accessed 13 October 2016. *TASS* news agency has added the necessary clarification that the number 183,200 refers to privates and sergeants, not to the full strength of the Ground Troops. *TASS*, 'Den' Sukhoputnykh voysk Rossii. Dosje [Russia's Ground Troops' Day. Dossier]'.

[8] Flot – XXI Vek [Fleet – XXI Century], 'VS Rossii: v Moskve sostoyalos zasedanie Kollegii Minoborony Rossii [Russian Armed Forces: Collegium of the Russian Ministry of Defence Met in Moscow]', 17 September 2013, <http://blackseafleet-21.com/news/17-09-2013_vs-rossii-v-moskve-sostojalos-zasedanie-kollegii-minoborony-rossii>, accessed 13 December 2016.

[9] *TASS*, 'Nachalnik Genshtaba: armiya planiruet pokupat do 100 samoletov i bolee 120 vertoletov v god [Chief of the General Staff: Army Plans to Buy Up to 100 Aircraft and More than 120 Helicopters Per Year]', 10 December 2014, <http://tass.ru/armiya-i-opk/1637620>, accessed 13 December 2016.

[10] Nikolskiy, 'Rossiyskaya armiya ukomplektovana na rekordnye 92 protsenta [Russian Army Manned at a Record 92 Per Cent]'.

Table 7: Manpower Size of the Russian Ground Troops

	Officers	Other ranks			Ground Troops overall size	Percentage of professionals in all ranks
		Overall number	Professionals	Conscripts		
2014	–	–	–	–	199,000–205,000	–
2015	26,000	183,400	88,200	95,200	210,000	54.3
2016	26,000	217,500	109,000	108,500	243,500	55.4

as somewhere between approximately 199,000 and 205,000 in July–August 2014.[11]

It was planned in 2015 that 112,900 professionals would represent 51 per cent of OR by 1 January 2016,[12] making the planned number of conscripts 108,500, but the actual number of professional OR reached just 109,000 by October 2016.[13] Assuming that the number of conscripts remained in 2016 at the level envisaged for the beginning of that year, the overall OR strength would reach 217,500. Maintaining the assumption that the officer corps' manning equals the average manning level of the armed forces in general (which reached 93 per cent at the end of 2016, from 92 per cent at the end of 2015), one can conclude a 1 percentage point increase in the number of Ground Troops officers, which leaves their overall number effectively unchanged, at approximately 26,000. This makes the Ground Troops' strength in 2016 approximately 243,500 men, or 19 per cent undermanned (Table 7). It also means an incremental increase in the proportion of professionals (both OR and commissioned officers).

---

[11] The calculations presented in this appendix are based on official Russian statements which round up to the nearest 1,000 since a greater level of accuracy is not practical. Therefore, the authors' estimates and calculations which use these reported figures contain this inherent limitation in terms of potential for precise accuracy.

[12] *TASS*, 'Den' Sukhoputnykh voysk Rossii. Dosje [Russia's Ground Troops' Day. Dossier]'.

[13] Russian Ministry of Defence, 'Intervjyu glavnokomanduyuschego Sukhoputnymi voyskami general-polkovnika Olega Salyukova ko Dnyu Sukhoputnykh voysk [Interview with Commander-in-Chief of the Russian Ground Troops, Colonel General Oleg Salyukov for the Ground Troops' Day]'.

APPENDIX II. ESTIMATED STRENGTH OF RUSSIAN LAND FORCES IN 2014

As described in the Introduction, this paper considers Russian land forces as consisting of all Russia's conventional armed forces tasked to operate in the land domain – Ground Troops, Airborne Troops, coastal defence troops, and special operations forces.

Available information allows a rough estimate of the strength of Russia's land forces in 2014. Airborne Troops' strength was 36,000[1] and the marines numbered 12,500.[2] The Russian Navy's coastal troops included 10,500 men (including the coastal missile regiment) in the Kaliningrad region[3] and approximately 2,500 men subordinated to the Northern Fleet (the 200th Motor-Rifle Brigade[4]), with around 2,000 men serving in coastal missiles and artillery units in Russia's regions, except Kaliningrad. Special operations forces included around 15,000 troops in Spetsnaz brigades,[5] approximately 1,000 men in Special Operations

---

[1] *TVTs* (TV Channel), 'Sostav VDV Rossii uvelichitsya v dva raza [Number of Russian Airborne Troops to be Doubled]', 6 August 2014, <http://www.tvc.ru/news/show/id/46801>, accessed 13 December 2016.

[2] *Voennoe obozrenie [Military Review]*, '27 noyabrya - den morskoy pekhoty Rossii [27 November – Russia's Marines Day]', 27 November 2011, <https://topwar.ru/8798-morskie-soldaty-vchera-i-segodnya.html>, accessed 13 December 2016.

[3] Yuri Bogdanov and Ekaterina Neroznikova, 'Pribaltika ne zamechaet rezkogo sokrascheniya rossiyskikh voysk v Kaliningrade [Baltic States Do Not See Sharp Reduction in Russian troops in Kaliningrad]', *Vzglyad [Look]*, 10 June 2016, <http://vz.ru/world/2016/6/10/815489.html>, accessed 12 December 2016.

[4] Trude Pettersen, 'Na Severnom flote uvelichat chislennost morskoy pekhoty [Number of Northern Fleet's Marines to be Increased]', *BarentsObserver*, 28 November 2014, <http://barentsobserver.com/ru/bezopasnost/2014/11/na-severnom-flote-uvelichat-chislennost-morskoy-pehoty-28-11>, accessed 13 December 2016.

[5] Dmitri Savitskiy, 'Sily spetsialnykh operatsiy/Spetsnaz VS RF [Special Operations Forces/Russian Armed Forces' Spetsnaz]', *Kont*, 1 March 2016, <https://cont.ws/post/213495>, accessed 13 December 2016.

Forces Command (KSSO) units, and 1,300 men in naval Spetsnaz elements.[6] In total this provides an estimate of around 81,000 non-Ground Troops land forces in 2014.

On the base of assumptions explained in Appendix I, the strength of Russia's Ground Troops is estimated here as approximately 199,000–205,000 for mid- to end-2014. The overall strength of the Russian land forces for that period can therefore be estimated as between 280,000 and 286,000 personnel.

---

[6] *Ibid.*

About Whitehall Papers

The Whitehall Paper series provides in-depth studies of specific developments, issues or themes in the field of national and international defence and security. Three Whitehall Papers are published each year. They reflect the highest standards of original research and analysis, and are invaluable background material for specialists and policymakers alike.

About RUSI

The Royal United Services Institute (RUSI) is the world's oldest and the UK's leading defence and security think tank. Its mission is to inform, influence and enhance public debate on a safer and more stable world. RUSI is a research-led institute, producing independent, practical and innovative analysis to address today's complex challenges.

Since its foundation in 1831, RUSI has relied on its members to support its activities. Together with revenue from research, publications and conferences, RUSI has sustained its political independence for more than 185 years.

London | Brussels | Nairobi | Doha | Tokyo | Washington, DC